Understanding Foreign Policy Decisions

UNDERSTANDING FOREIGN POLICY DECISIONS

The Chinese Case

DAVIS B. BOBROW
STEVE CHAN
JOHN A. KRINGEN

THE FREE PRESS

A Division of Macmillan Publishing Co., Inc.

NEW YORK

Collier Macmillan Publishers

LONDON

Copyright © 1979 by THE FREE PRESS
A Division of Macmillan Publishing Co., Inc.

THE FREE PRESS
A Division of Macmillan Publishing Co., Inc.
866 Third Avenue, New York, N.Y. 10022

Collier Macmillan Canada, Ltd.

Library of Congress Catalog Card Number: 78-24667

Printed in the United States of America

printing number

1 2 3 4 5 6 7 8 9 10

Library of Congress Cataloging in Publication Data

Bobrow, Davis B
    Understanding foreign policy decisions.

    Bibliography: p.
    1.   United States—Foreign relations—China.
2.   China—Foreign relations—United States.   3.   International relations—Research.   I.   Chan, Steve, joint
author.   II.   Kringen, John A., joint author.
III.   Title.
JX1428.C6B6   327.73'051   78-24667
    ISBN 0-02-904410-3

To Gail, Pancy, and Kim

CONTENTS

LIST OF ILLUSTRATIONS

Figures

Tables

viii

PREFACE

It is increasingly apparent that the study of political behavior poses intellectual problems as complex as those offered in any area of the natural sciences. With recognition of this complexity, research is more frequently being conducted along the collaborative lines that have long been prominent in the natural sciences. This book partakes of this new "tradition" and is a collaborative effort in several ways. In terms of the actual research and writing, all three authors participated substantially in all phases of the research and writing process. Although each of us obviously worked in some areas more than others, the final product is truly a joint effort. What is presented here is the outcome of numerous successive drafts; it would be erroneous at this point to try to identify the individual source for particular ideas or phraseology.

Beyond the immediate participants, the research presented here is also collaborative in that it has benefited from the advice and support of numerous individuals and institutions. Several individuals generously provided us with data that have been incorporated into our analyses: Phillip Katz (the PAMIS data), Charles Hermann (the CREON data), and Daniel Tretiak (the NFFAP documents analyzed in appendix A). In analyzing these and the other data that are reported in the following pages, we were aided considerably by the research assistance of Gary Gaines and Janson Chang. Mary Bailey deserves special commendation for her Stakhanov-like efforts to type the several drafts of the manuscript. Patricia Joyce provided painstaking editorial help. Charles Smith and Colin Jones of the Free Press have been generous with their time and encouragement.

In terms of institutional assistance, the research reported here stems from a project funded by the Defense Advanced Research Projects Agency of the Department of Defense and was monitored by the Office of Naval Research under Contract N000 14-75-C-0846. In this regard, Robert Young and Stephen Andriole deserve mention for their support for what may at times have seemed to them to be a quixotic effort. The gathering of the semantic data at the Universities Service Centre in Hong Kong by John Kringen was supported by the University of Minnesota Graduate School. Finally, the computer time for this project was supported in part by the Computer Science Center of the University of Maryland.

Because intellectual endeavors rarely develop in a vacuum, the authors, either singly or collectively, are also indebted to numerous individuals for their help in refining their ideas. Particularly significant were James Bennett, John Lu, Oliver Selfridge, Lorand Szalay, Daniel Tretiak, and John Turner.

Obviously, none of the above individuals or institutions is responsible for any errors we may have made. We particularly emphasize that the views and conclusions presented are those of the authors and should not be interpreted as representing the official policies, expressed or implied, of the Defense Advanced Research Projects Agency, of the U.S. Government, or of the agencies and institutions with which the authors became affiliated after their work at the University of Maryland.

Understanding Foreign Policy Decisions

CHAPTER 1

PERSPECTIVE AND INTENTIONS

Foreign policy analysts in many countries frequently comment about the inconsistency, unpredictability, dubious rationality, and murky origins of the foreign policy actions of other nations. These comments often lead to judgments that others are deceptive, hostile, incompetent, or unstable in either a policy or personal sense. Foreign regimes acquire images ranging from naiveté to Machiavellianism and become viewed as at worst plain "bloody-minded" and at best "unresponsive" and "unreliable." Instances when they behave as one desires are remembered as the consequences of either the overwhelming "rightness" of one's own national position, or of dependency and overriding power, or as having been directed by exceptionally enlightened leaders. In our view, this style of interpretation is intellectually unfortunate and has the seeds of social disaster.

Intellectually, it leads to several unappealing conclusions. First, it implies that the foreign policy actions of others are in large measure incomprehensible and unpredictable. Accordingly, the possibilities for coordinated action are slim. Second, it suggests some highly uneven distribution of wisdom and morality among governments. Thus, a highly favorable distribution of leverage and power seems necessary to avoid international anarchy. Third, it implies that the exceptional instances where coordinated action occurs rest primarily on the vagaries of national leadership personalities. To the extent that foreign affairs experts accept these conclusions, they are likely to give overwhelming priority to unilateral positions of strength and dogmatic assertiveness, and to reconcile themselves to ad hoc, fragmented decisions.

What are the consequences of such a posture? If the problems that produce war and misery are susceptible to unilateral supremacy and ad hoc actions, the consequences are not necessarily disastrous. Optimism or pessimism would then depend on judgments about the values and competence of dominant regimes. Contemporary history does not generate confidence that the militarily and economically most powerful governments have especially benign values and competent policy systems. In any event, it seems clear that the international affairs of the present and foreseeable future do not allow for meaningful unilateral supremacy, and that the problems that generate war and misery will not yield to ad hoc actions. Accordingly, in the absence of the knowledge and will to engage in coordinated action, the nations of the world

1

will drift from crisis to crisis, reacting to rather than shaping the distribution of violence and wealth.

In part, this emerging state of interdependency follows from the entwined nature of security, economic, and environmental problems. In part, it follows from the dispersion of modern military weaponry and from the increasing mutual vulnerability and costs of military intervention. It also stems from tensions in the international system associated with economic interdependence and with the links of advanced transportation and communication. In sum, the effects make the opportunity costs of the inability to understand the foreign policy actions of others very substantial, and the consequences of misunderstanding and error in such judgments become grave indeed.

Our goal in the work reported here is to demonstrate that an alternative pattern of interpretation of the foreign policy action of others can be attained under reasonably demanding intellectual standards. If we are successful, the possibilities available for foreign policy planning and coordination become substantially enlarged. Our position is not that problems between nations are simply matters of communication. Rather, we believe that poor comprehension of others' foreign policy decision processes provides a tenuous foundation for foreign policy choice and interpretation.

It is clear that different regimes time and again interpret the same literal action, statement, or situation in different ways (Jervis 1976). As a result, they often pass each other in the night when they try to engage in clear communication and signaling. Some of these occurrences involve inevitable human error and bureaucratic slippage (for example, messages do get lost, and circulating them takes time). Others can be attributed to inherent ambiguity and noise, or even to deception. However, many of these occurrences cannot be dismissed so easily; they reflect fundamental differences between regimes in the treatment of international affairs issues. If knowledge of such differences in treatment can be captured in verifiable ways, the benefits for the conduct of foreign policy are obvious and substantial.

Like attribution theorists (Hastorf et al. 1970: 61–90), we assume that foreign policy elites try to predict social behavior (and avoid suprise), as do most human beings. In their efforts to do so, they search for causality and order, ignoring randomness interpretations. Further, foreign policy participants, like most social scientists, realize that particular isolated acts may signal many alternative combinations of actor intention and capability. Accordingly, foreign policy decision makers tend to rely on previous attributions of intent and capability, disregarding occasional behavior that contradicts those attributions unless the behavior in question is extremely deviant from the pattern of expectations.

If one accepts these assumptions, two conclusions follow. First, the interpretations that foreign policy elites make regarding the international environment, the behavior of foreign regimes and movements, and the past and probable future behavior of other institutions and individuals in their own national foreign policy process are patterned and, thus, are predictable in principle. Second, if we are to realize these predictive possibilities in actual analysis, we must capture the already established structures of causal interpretation and expectation held by decision makers, inasmuch as foreign policy decision making involves processing new situations and courses of action through these structures. Therefore, in order to understand decision processes, we need to identify the historically established categories and decision rules that will be brought to bear, the sorts of behavior that will or will not seem extremely deviant, the central points for revision in existing decision structures, and the consequences of such revision. Since there is little reason to expect that foreign policy decision makers with grossly different experiences have developed the same set of interpretations and expectations, it is reasonable to begin with the notion that the pertinent structures vary across foreign policy decision systems.

More specifically, we seek to demonstrate that it is feasible to capture structures of foreign policy interpretation and expectation for regimes whose participants and processes are not accessible in any direct sense. These structures will predict changes in behavior and provide explanations for them across a variety of substantively interesting foreign policy situations. And they will not be static formulations, nor will they be limited to a particular foreign policy issue area or decision problem. This objective of a dynamic, wide-ranging modeling of foreign policy interpretive and anticipatory structures is necessary if we are to have any confidence in the durability of our formulations and in a payoff from their development. That is, we need to meet this objective for our strategy to produce findings that are of more than historical interest. Success in meeting this objective will necessarily involve demonstrating the merits of the systematic application of a number of individually weak methods to fragmentary data.

Further, we wish to demonstrate that it is possible to develop explicit models of foreign policy decision making and to derive falsifiable predictions from them without having to make the unwarranted assumptions that foreign policy decision makers are simpleminded, homogeneous across political cultures, unopinionated about the biases and proclivities of their information and implementation institutions, or lacking in a sense of history. Our discovery and modeling approaches must not impose simplicity by relying from the outset on relatively simple theories drawn from psychology or organizational behavior. We need to allow for lengthy chains of contingent analysis and evaluation of likely and actual policy consequences in our modeling of policy choice. We seek to develop structures that discriminate foreign policy situations that decison makers can process relatively easily in their cognitive terms from ones that are to them ambiguous and confusing. In other words, we hope to identify those foreign affairs problems for which the structures of interpretation and expectation have clear implications and those for which they do not.

Because we believe that foreign policy decision processes involve cognitions about a policy system as well as about an external environment, the cybernetic conception of communication and control is particularly attractive. Decision processes involve a number of attempts to affect and cope with an environment, in our case an international environment, through cycles of information assessment, decision choice, and policy implementation (Steinbruner 1974; Thorson 1974; Bailey and Holt 1971; Simon 1969; Deutsch 1966). A simple representation of this system can be seen in figure 1-1.

FIGURE 1-1
FOREIGN POLICY DECISION-MAKING SYSTEM

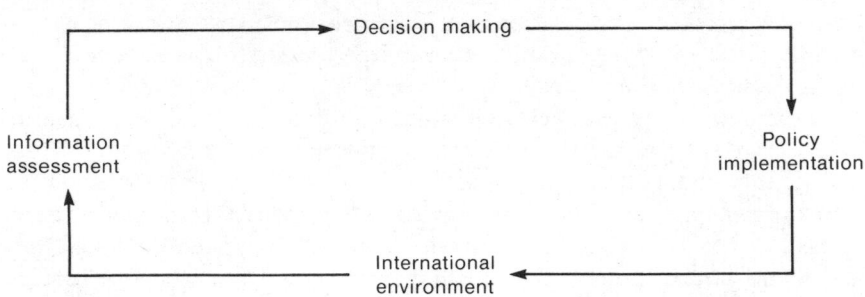

Our task, then, is to deal with beliefs pertinent to all four elements in this representation. Foreign policy actions are the joint product of these several sets of cognition and not of any single one. In line with our view that decision makers are not devoid of a sense of history, the structures we seek should contain beliefs about sound and unsound decision practices drawn from what are thought by the groups under study to be cases of notable success and failure. And the structures of interpretation and expectation we discover should include some process rules as well as beliefs about the characteristics of domestic and foreign individuals, groups, and institutions.

In searching for such structures of interpretation and expectation, we seek to learn the answers to two general questions for other national cultures. First, what is for them a sound description, explanation, or prediction of how other nations act in foreign affairs? Second, what is for them a compelling prescription to induce other nations to act in particular ways?

Our contention is that we will gain some knowledge by working at the national culture level that we would otherwise lack. Structures of interpretation and expectation that operate at this level determine in important ways how the phenomena emphasized by those who work with broader units (for example, the international system) will be treated for policy making and international bargaining purposes. They also set boundaries and issue agendas in terms of which the more limited units of analysis (for example, those featured in bureaucratic politics perspectives) will have to operate. The structures at the national culture level set an acceptable range for policy dialogue and mandate that certain issues be dealt with. They provide conventions that individuals and organizations are under great pressure to conform to if they wish to be treated as "serious" and "responsible." Whether or not these conventions yield falsifiable predictions about foreign policy behavior is an empirical question. We believe that they do and that they vary across national decision systems, with important substantive implications for foreign policy outcomes. The issue, then, is not that foreign policy participants in any given nation are homogeneous in a strict sense, because, of course, they are not. It is whether they are sufficiently like each other, compared with other national decision-system participants, for the similarities to matter.[1]

We pursue our general perspective through the study of a particular national foreign affairs decision system, that of the People's Republic of China. We focus on a particular national "case" to apply our approach in sufficient detail to establish the extent to which it illuminates a variety of foreign affairs choices across a number of events and issues, and to clarify our ability to arrive at conclusions that have some analytic value of relatively lasting interest. This act of choice also puts us in the position of providing the reader with a particular way of judging our success: do our analyses enhance understanding of Chinese foreign policy?

We choose China for several reasons. First, it is likely to play an important role in international affairs over the next few decades. Second, it offers a set of system characteristics different from that of the United States, the nation from which most of our knowledge about foreign policy decision processes derives. The Chinese case seems particularly apposite to our concern with differences rather than similarities in decision processes. If Chinese decision processes are significantly different from those of the United States, our general perspective seems to warrant broader application. If they are not, our basic position becomes suspect. Third, while analysis of Chinese decision processes presents analytic problems perhaps more difficult than for many other nations, the differences are of degree rather than kind. Even modestly improved understanding of Chinese decision processes should bolster our expectations for the analysis of more accessible decision systems. Finally, the Chinese emphasize the development of a coherent rationale for political action and the widespread presentation of that rationale in public media. Such public display offers a starting point to construct a decision-process model at the national culture level.

Our cognitive approach assumes that there are indeed decision rules in foreign policy choice and that these decision rules can be discovered. These assumptions are shared by other major approaches to the study of foreign policy making. In this respect, rational-choice and bureaucratic-politics

1. Obviously, data-access problems have extremely gloomy implications for the analysis of foreign affairs decision making should our position on the "levels of analysis" issue prove untenable.

decision models differ primarily in their assumptions about information assessment and the types of values employed in reaching decisions. In fact, the very concept of decision making implies the application of decision rules to specific cases. While questions have often been raised about the possibility of discovering foreign policy decision rules given the inevitable data constraints, few challenges have been made to the proposition that foreign policy making is essentially decisional (e.g., Schilling 1961).

There is another alternative. Research on organizations indicates that policy making cannot always be represented in terms of decison making. Policy frequently is less the product of conscious choice than the consequence of ad hoc adaptations to little-understood problems and opportunities. And to the extent that these adaptations are truly ad hoc, decision rules as such do not exist. Because the study of foreign policy making has focused on case studies of the handling of major conflict events, it is possible that the decisional nature of the foreign policy process has been overstated. That is, by focusing on events known to be critical by the participants at the time, we have a rather biased sample from which to generalize about foreign policy making in general. For example, decision makers' propensity to employ commonly shared historical analogies as the bases for handling current conflicts (e.g., Jervis 1976; George and Smoke 1974; May 1973) may be limited to only critical policy problems. It is reasonable to suspect that the policy process operates differently in terms of everyday matters of competition and cooperation.

Cohen et al. (1972) offer a model of organizational choice that provides an interesting contrast to the usual decision-making models. This framework, which they describe as a "garbage can" model, is proposed for policy situations with three conditions. First, policy preferences are ill defined and inconsistent. The policy-making process is to a substantial degree one of defining problems and discovering preferences. Second, the technologies for producing favorable outcomes are ill understood. Learning occurs on a simple trial-and-error basis. Third, there is fluid participation in policy choice. Different individuals participate to different degrees at different times. As a consequence, policy choice is determined by the interplay between streams of opportunities, problems, solutions, and participants. Timing, in the sense of the matching or mismatching of these streams, is particularly critical. Solutions may be put forth long after the applicable problems have been solved; participants may come and go as opportunities are lost. While Cohen et al. do allow for the introduction of organizational procedures and more sophisticated learning strategies into their model, the emphasis on timing gives their model of policy making a stochastic character.

In terms of the potential relevance of this model, foreign policy choice is often characterized by problematic preferences and unclear technology. The characteristic of fluid participation seems less applicable to foreign policy making, given the usual continuity of substantial national-security and foreign policy bureaucracies. However, the policies of rotation evident in these bureaucracies as well as the substantial pressures on top decision makers to deal with many problems at one time can introduce a considerable degree of variation in participation. For example, Olsen (1972: 61) observes that not even the Cuban missile crisis could attract the full attention of the President and the Director of Central Intelligence.

The contrast between "garbage can" and decision-rule models of foreign policy choice is particularly evident where regimes emphasize public presentation of presumably consistent rationales for policy. The People's Republic of China is a notable extreme case. To the extent that publicly stated rationales do indeed underlie policy choice, patterns in the treatment of actors and events should conform to publicly stated logics. If there is little congruence between treatments and stated decision rules, two possibilities exist: (1) there are decision rules, but they are different from those publicly stated, and (2) there are in fact no consistently applied decision rules. In the second alternative, the "garbage can" prevails. Case studies of particular issues over time or of several incidents at one precise point in time are unable to distinguish between our three alternative possibilities. If we are to do so, we must deal with a sufficient time span and variety of problems to minimize the illusory order that particular individuals or epiphenomenal stimuli may provide, and examine a sufficiently large sample to allow unexpected patterns to become discernible.

Although details of our methods will be introduced later as appropriate, it is helpful to summarize here the tools we use and our general strategy of inference. We opt for an ensemble of methods rather than relying on any single one, because we believe that the tools at hand to inform us about inaccessible decision processes are, in essence, "weak." Evidence about the validity and reliability of these methods in informing us about foreign policy decision processes is sparse. Consequently, we stress the necessity for systematic assessment of areas of convergence and divergence in findings produced by diverse research techniques (Campbell and Fiske 1959). Further, emphasis needs to be placed on developing and testing falsifiable propositions regarding decision processes. Our strategy of inquiry seeks to test substantive propositions about structures of interpretation and expectation, and to assess alternate methods and data sources.

The logic of the choice and application of these methods is a simple one. The foundation of the strategy is a qualitative content analysis of a wide variety of Chinese documents, conducted in an operational-code fashion. Content analysis of this sort has a long history in research on the foreign policy beliefs of inaccessible decision makers (e.g., George 1959). Although an imperfect tool, it has been underutilized in comparative foreign policy research (Horelick et al. 1975: 58). The aim of our effort is to identify systematically the officially stated Chinese views regarding the international environment, the roles and attributes of particular sets of nation actors, and the appropriate analytic procedures and policy instruments for coping with foreign policy problems. The yield of this effort is an extensive set of propositions regarding the foreign policy beliefs of Chinese decision makers. In two senses, this set of propositions can be described as partially ordered. Comparison of these propositions across different documentary sources and over time allows some assessment of whether or not these propositions actually constitute elements of the Chinese foreign policy belief system. In other words, some partial ordering of confidence estimates is possible. The set of propositions is also partially ordered in that the cognitive structure linking the various belief elements (identified in our propositions) into a coherent whole is only partially specified. While in some areas these linkages can at least be crudely specified, in other areas both the linkages and some of the elements are missing. After we have exhausted the potential of content-analytic procedures of this sort, the application of alternate methods becomes necessary to validate specific propositions regarding Chinese foreign policy beliefs and to specify more completely the structure in which they exist.

To do this, we employ several different research methods. Since a crucial question in any content-analytic effort is that of whether or not the views identified in documents represent the views of pertinent individuals in decision-making contexts, we have engaged in an analysis of Chinese perceptions of major political symbols. For obvious reasons, this analysis is restricted to a nonelite group of former residents of the People's Republic of China. However, since the nonelite population is similar to the decision-making elite in terms of language, culture, and political socialization experiences, it can provide a partial check on our content-analytic inferences. The analysis involves comparing the responses of Mainland and Hong Kong Chinese in verbal-association tests, the particular technique being known as Associative Group Analysis (Szalay and Maday 1973; Szalay and Brent 1967).

Moving beyond research simply at the perceptual level, we engage in three sorts of analyses that explore the relationship between our propositions regarding Chinese foreign policy beliefs and patterns of Chinese foreign policy behavior. Since military conflict constitutes a prime area of concern in the foreign policy agenda of any elite, we compare Chinese behavior in a number of historical conflict situations in order to identify patterns in their conflict behavior. The stable patterns of action revealed in this analysis provide a crude baseline for comparison with some of our major inferences regarding Chinese beliefs. To assess the extent to which existing event-data sets are reflective of Chinese perceptions and historical experience and can be used to track Chinese foreign policy behavior, we conduct analyses of alternative event-data sources and event lists. Finally, we test propositions about the linkages between Chinese beliefs and Chinese policy behavior in two ways. One involves a quasi-experimental analysis of Chinese responses to a set of foreign policy events. The other consists of a multivariate analysis of Chinese treatment of international actors. Because our knowledge of the Chinese use of official media as a policy instrument is well developed, we can derive specific hypotheses about how Peking will respond in the official media to different types of international events and actors and test them against quantitative content-analytic data from P.R.C. media.

In sum, our strategy does not seek bold theoretical or methodological breakthroughs. Instead, it involves the incremental reduction of uncertainty about the foreign policy decision-making process of a national culture through a series of steps to clarify and test Chinese foreign affairs decision logics at different times, for different historical cases, and with diverse data and analytic procedures.

In considering the chapters that follow, our success can be judged by the extent to which our findings about China answer the following four questions in positive ways:

1. Do different regimes use generically different decision logics and information-processing rules for foreign policy decision making?
2. Are propositions about those logics and rules confirmed by the use of several diverse data sources and methods?
3. Do those rules and logics have significant implications for foreign policy actions and yield predictions that can be disconfirmed?
4. Can we identify at least a partial structuring of decision logics and information-processing rules?

We organize the material to answer these questions in the following way. Part I provides the intellectual context for our findings with respect to Western research on international conflict and foreign policy decision making and the study of China. It provides some basis for relating our work to that of several scholarly communities. Part II concentrates on critical international incidents often labeled as crises. We select this element of international affairs for special emphasis for several reasons. First, the turning point and potentially escalatory nature of such incidents give understanding about their treatment by governments particular significance. Second, by focusing on international crises we can examine in depth the differences between American and Chinese foreign policy cognitions. Third, we can clarify the degree to which decision logics and information rules for dealing with critical international incidents can be understood apart from more general beliefs related to foreign policy decision making. For the Chinese such a separation seems unwarranted; part III accordingly proceeds to present the general analytics that the Chinese apply to foreign affairs decision processes. Part IV presents several amplifications on the themes developed previously. Here some of our qualitative inferences are subjected to quantitative tests and we explore the limits of our previous analyses. Finally, part V synthesizes what we have learned about Chinese foreign policy decision processes, and in the light of those results returns to the general themes raised in the previous pages. The appendixes present supporting technical detail and methodological material.

PART I

Intellectual Context

CHAPTER 2

FOREIGN POLICY DECISION MAKING IN WESTERN CONFLICT RESEARCH

The research strategy we have chosen emphasizes the cognitive aspects of foreign policy decision making, contending that there are significant differences between national cultures in this respect. We also adopt an incremental and largely inductive approach to formulate sets of candidate explanations, and pursue a quantitative strategy to test falsifiable predictions deduced from our understanding of Chinese decision processes. These emphases are not widely shared among students of foreign affairs. Accordingly, a brief review of opposing and supporting approaches is useful in clarifying the reasoning that underlies our position. Lengthy responses to some of the major criticisms of cognitive research have been ably provided by others (Holsti 1977: 1–34; Jervis 1976: 13–31), so we will content ourselves with a very summary treatment of major alternative positions. Support for our approach can be found in the literatures on artificial intelligence and operational code; we shall relate our approach to them.

Alternative Approaches

One major alternative approach assumes that environmental conditions substantially determine policy responses. The logic is similar to that of the stimulus-response model in behavioral psychology, contending that the decision processes that occur between environmental conditions and policy responses do not have significantly different implications. These processes can be placed in a "black box" and ignored in predicting and explaining policy responses. This stance is shared by studies at the level of global and regional systems (e.g., Choucri and North 1975; Forrester 1971; Kaplan 1957) and by pattern analyses of national attributes and interactions (e.g., Rummel 1969a, 1969b, 1965; Banks and Textor 1963).

We find this position unattractive for our purposes. Even though their findings are often statistically significant, strategies that rely on attribute data, unmediated stimulus-response mechanisms, or structural models of economic and territorial imperatives leave much foreign policy activity unexplained even in a "variance accounted for" sense. Few clues result from these studies to discriminate the situations they handle poorly from those they handle well. Even when black-box strategies do relatively well with regard to gross activity dimensions over long-time periods, they have not been particularly helpful for understanding particular policy choices that are likely to change more quickly. For example, such strategies are better at dealing with total arms budgets than with their components. They are more useful in handling changes in formal alliance membership than fluctuations in the degree of joint action by alliance members in the face of particular problems. Because decision processes are excluded and the environmental characteristics used have relatively long-time constants, black-box strategies do not illuminate the impact of alternative short-term actions on policy responses. International politics will then, in Karl Deutsch's felicitous phrase, have a very "long turning radius" indeed.

Another major approach distinct from ours does deal with decision processes and indeed emphasizes their importance and diversity. It tends, however, to exclude cognitive elements. This approach stresses bureaucratic considerations and their massive effects on the information, decision, and implementation elements in the cybernetic representation introduced earlier (Halperin and Kanter 1973; Allison 1971; Ellsberg 1971; Neustadt 1960). The standard operating procedures and imperatives of roles in large bureaucracies are offered as the key predictors of foreign policy actions. We have no quarrel with the pertinence of these considerations, only with their sufficiency for explanation. Governments do in fact face unexperienced foreign affairs problems and act in unprecedented ways. The views and policy positions of individual leaders often diverge significantly from their organizational roles, and the political coalitions between individuals and bureaus do not always coincide neatly with inferences about institutional incentives and perspectives. We need not assume that decision makers are predominantly simpleminded, parochial in their outlook, or perverted in their political priorities.

If we are to gain a sound understanding of the import of bureaucratic considerations in foreign policy decision making, it seems wise to place organizational leaders in a context of beliefs and perceptions shared by the national elite. Cognitive context can help in two ways. First, it can identify areas where the elite's views are ambiguous, ambivalent, or simply under-developed. These areas are more susceptible to the disturbance of events, more likely to produce policy disagreements, and less likely to be assigned or delegated to routinized organizational processes. Second, as noted in chapter 1, shared beliefs and perceptions among a national elite set the boundaries and agenda in terms of which organizational leaders function. They stipulate the range of acceptable policy dialogue, mandate that certain issues be addressed, and provide conventions that individuals and organizations are under great pressure to conform to if they wish to be effective bureaucratic players.

Even when we turn to approaches that grant importance to cognitive elements, we still find substantial bodies of work whose assumptions we do not share. Most fundamentally, we disagree with the universality assumption, which tends to underlie many applications of situational, rational-actor, and psychological approaches. Each of these strands of work on foreign policy decision making merits brief mention.

The situational approach is perhaps best illustrated by the study of international crises as decision makers' responses to perceptions of high threat, great surprise, and short response time (Hermann 1969). These properties of the definition of the situation are treated as givens, from which analysis proceeds. In our view, prior steps are necessary to capture the definition that different national elites will attach to situations of particular kinds. There simply is no strong basis for assuming that decision makers with grossly different experiences and beliefs will have the same expectations about international relations occurrences, make the same interpretations about the intentions and capabilities of adversaries, and use the same time perspective for choosing and evaluating policy alternatives (Handel 1977; Neustadt 1970; Russett 1969). We cannot realize the potential of the situational approach in the absence of more certain knowledge of how decision makers will view alternative policy developments and external events. We have no basis to assume that the definition of any particular situation will be similar across national elites.

By rational-actor analysis, we have in mind the application of rather formal deductive logics to build elegant and parsimonious models for predicting and prescribing policy responses (e.g., Schelling 1960). This approach may have great value for problems when the issue domain is quite closed (for example, strategic deterrence), the parties have rather complete information, and the major values involved are shared by the major participants. Unfortunately, many foreign policy problems are too messy and too little understood for these conditions to hold. Most of the time foreign policy analysts are not justified in starting out as if they already knew the goals being pursued by government leaders, their interpretation of the available information, or their perception of the available policy courses. In fact, these are precisely the "bread and butter" questions of applied foreign policy analysis. Unwarranted stipulation of issues, diagnostic logics, and utility schedules can result in models that produce more misinformation than enlightenment. Obviously, a reversion to more classical forms of rational-actor analysis, as exemplified by national interest formulations, results in a loss of analytical elegance. Research propositions are often vague and only become specific with after-the-fact interpretation (Morgenthau 1948).

A third approach, which emphasizes cognitions but discounts national differences, takes the form of applying what are asserted to be general theories drawn from psychology. Cognitive-consistency approaches are often cited as a case in point (Jervis 1976; Bonham et al. 1976; Abelson et al. 1968; Newcomb 1953). Our reservations about the cognitive-consistency perspective will illustrate our reservations about "general theories" that contend universal applicability. Most fundamentally, one must have substantial knowledge about the content and organization of the beliefs of a population before one can sensibly apply cognitive-consistency theory (Holsti 1967: 35). The theory does not deal with the action consequences of alternative belief packages or of information as it affects those packages. It allows for numerous forms of cognitive adjustment to information, and, depending on which adjustment occurs, different foreign policy action choices are likely. There are, in addition, good reasons from theory and experience to be skeptical about the appropriateness of consistency-theory inferences across cultures and institutional settings. Reservations are especially warranted about cross-cultural commonalities in the tolerance for inconsistency (Hiniker 1969). The existing research sheds little light on whether or not information that would be discordant for analysts reared on syllogisms and central-tendency reasoning has the same properties for analysts reared on the dialectics of Marxist or Maoist thought. To generalize these points, the elegance of available theories is not matched by their pertinence to foreign policy behavior. Further, whatever applicability and validity they have for foreign policy decision processes remain moot until after the sort of work we propose has been completed. Obviously, these reservations lose importance if one's intent is simply to provide a post hoc explanation for known behavior and to show that any sort of found behavior can be made plausible.

Supporting Approaches

Substantial bodies of work demonstrate that knowledge about elite beliefs and perceptions can improve explanations and predictions of foreign policy behavior, and that this knowledge is attainable (at least by the standards we apply to other forms of knowlege about international relations).

Basic research on the nature and consequences of "misperception" supports our view about the importance of elite beliefs and perceptions for explaining and predicting policy responses (e.g., Jervis 1976, 1969; Holsti 1969; Holsti et al. 1969; Pool and Kessler 1969; de Rivera 1968). It indicates that analytical results are more robust when we include data on decision makers' assessments of the environment. Likewise, analyses of problems of strategic warning attribute past failures not so much to inadequate information about enemy actions as to inappropriate interpretation of enemy intentions (e.g., Handel 1977; Ben-Zvi 1976; Whaley 1973; DeWeerd 1962; Wohlstetter 1962; Wasserman 1960). Failures in warning stem largely from the inability to grasp the foreign policy analyses and prescriptions of the decision makers in adversary governments, and from the tendency to attribute to them one's own utilities, beliefs, and logics. Beyond failures of warning, a weak understanding of the concerns and calculations of other governments results frequently in a breakdown in international communication, thus contributing to the occurrence of crises (e.g., Brandon 1973; Hoffmann 1972; Tuchman 1962).

While recognizing the importance of cognitive elements in determining policy behavior, one may still shun work of this kind on the grounds that we are technically unable to do more than provide descriptions and anecdotes of a cautionary nature. This argument should have been laid to rest long ago given the operational code, symbol usage, propaganda analysis, and "culture at a distance" studies done during and shortly after World War II (George 1959; Leites 1953; Mead and Metraux 1953; Lasswell et al. 1949). In any event, it surely seems uncompelling given work in the last decade on cognitive mapping and computer simulation of belief systems, content-analytic approaches to crisis decision making, and man–machine decision gaming and simulation (Axelrod 1976; Bonham et al. 1976; Schank and Colby 1973; Holsti et al. 1968; Pool and Kessler 1969; Guetzkow et al. 1963).

Our optimism rests less on the contributions from the decision-making approach (Paige 1968; Snyder et al. 1962) than on recent progress in the operational-code and artificial-intelligence approaches to foreign policy analysis. While they are no better, and perhaps less good, at the persuasive reconstruction of particular decision cases, recent operational-code and artificial-intelligence efforts have made notable progress on three counts. The first is to constrain the set of plausible outcomes of particular situations; the second, to generate falsifiable predictions; and the third, to identify key decision points for selecting one rather than another foreign policy action. Knowledge on these counts obviously improves our ability to forecast what will not happen as well as what will happen, increases confidence in the reasoning we use, clarifies which aspects of foreign policy cognitions merit particular attention, and informs efforts to assess alternatives for signaling to and communicating with foreign elites.

Artificial-intelligence research attempts to capture the structure of interpretation and expectation of a decision system in a dynamic fashion through a model that allows for learning and adaptation. Such a model has obvious potential for exploring alternative "what if" scenarios and for establishing the conditions conducive to alternative pasts and futures. However, we do not find ourselves attracted to that part of the artificial-intelligence literature marked by: (1) an extremely narrow focus (for example, citizen votes on one issue or statements by a candidate on a narrow band of concerns); (2) a very closed domain for interpretation (for example, as in automata for repairing mechanical systems); or (3) extensive access to representative members of the population whose decision process is being modeled (for example, medical diagnosticians, analysts of international terrorism). Our substantive problem simply does not meet some of the crucial conditions embodied in these requirements (Bobrow and Collins 1975; Schank and Colby 1973). Rather, we are drawn to the work of Alker, Bennett, and Christensen, which models decision processes of governments in interaction with other governments and incorporates "explicit feedback via learning or trial and error problem-solving from success or failure" (Alker and Christensen 1972: 191). In studying UN peacekeeping decision making, this model emphasizes the role of "logics, rules (or hypotheses) by which action predisposing precedents are determined" (Alker and Christensen 1972: 195), and the modification of these logics and rules in the light of success and failure. Obviously, such an enterprise hinges in important ways on the precedents included in the memory bank, the rules for matching them to fresh decision situations, and the procedures for adding, deleting, and redefining precedents.

Bennett and Alker (1977) enrich the UN peacekeeping study in numerous ways, using South America in the late nineteenth century as a case. Particularly pertinent to us are their treatment of differences in the goal sets and priorities among actors, and the modification of these sets in the light of developments. Actors have to make decisions about how to decompose problems, avoid uncertainty, search efficiently, and benefit from experience (Cyert and March 1963). Understanding why a government behaves as it does thus requires an understanding of how it (1) transforms values into goals, (2) concludes that it has particular problems, (3) factors these problems for policy treatment, (4) interprets precedents as alternative strategies for dealing with problems, (5) modifies precedent lists, and (6) searches precedents and allocates search priorities. In the analysis of Bennett and Alker, actors are allowed to vary in a number of these respects. They may find themselves without clear precedents, or behaving unwisely in the sense of pursuing infeasible strategies. While they are given rules to categorize other participants in the foreign affairs of the region, they are allowed to have different role perceptions.

A number of simulations of alternative histories led Bennett and Alker to a conclusion of direct and encouraging relevance to the work we report in this book. The nature of the precedents available to decision makers and the rules they use to search among and select from them have greater influence on differences in policy responses than do goals and their adjustment. These factors are also more important than bureaucratic politics within national units. "The significance for outcomes of whether the actor seeks to equalize status ranks, avoid vulnerabilities in its security structure, or realize successive increases of status is less than the significance of the set of historical precedents from which the actor must seek solutions to its self-defined problems" (Bennett and Alker 1977: 294). And in turn, "accurate, reliable coding of precedents requires detailed knowledge of how the responsible statesmen evaluated contextual possibilities and constraints, and how they built the many 'lists' of abstract relations such as 'friends,' 'dependents,' and 'similarly economically situated' " (Bennett and Alker 1977: 295).

We agree with their conclusion and suggest that our analyses and findings are the sort required for meeting the needs they emphasize. Modeling of foreign policy decision-making processes in the artificial-intelligence tradition requires a rather well-structured understanding of the perceived precedents. Thus, the strategies held by relevant national elites and the rules they use to relate these strategies to evolving situations are important matters for empirical analysis. Parts II and III of this book seek to provide such a foundation for our illustrative case of the People's Republic of China. They show that the Chinese decision logics are sufficiently durable so as to make our analysis of more than historical interest. It seems clear that precedent construction, filing, search, and application involve treatments of both actors and situations. We will subject some of our inferences about how the Chinese will treat particular events to empirical tests in part IV.

We can now turn to the second body of recent work whose premises and conclusions in large measure support our approach. It concerns the operational-code approach to the analysis of belief systems (George 1969).[1] While our emphasis is on the national elite as the unit of analysis and that of the recent operational-code literature is on individual statesmen (e.g., Holsti 1977; Walker 1977), many of the same issues arise. As in our case, the operational-code literature has been characterized by an increasing tendency to view political elites as "naive scientists" engaged in information processing in which they are less than perfect (e.g., Ross 1977). Like us, it is concerned with issues of evidence and inference, and with lessening the "private" nature of analysts' judgments about the cognitions of others. And also similar to us, they recognize that the presence of ambiguity in the rules and logics of a particular foreign policy maker's belief system is not an illusion but indicates instead realistic complexities. This awareness alerts us to the need to view policy choice not simply as the product of an operational code but also as a result of the situational information that has been processed through a code.

The linkage between the code and policy actions obviously depends on what analysts choose to include in the cognitive elements we style as an operational code. If they include only matters of basic beliefs about the nature of politics and expectations about the future and its controllability, the linkage will be tenuous at best. To return to the cybernetic framework introduced in chapter 1, we would only be considering beliefs about the decision-making and international environment elements. If analysts add beliefs about information and implementation (the other two elements in our earlier framework), the linkage may well improve. Instrumental beliefs about strategy and about institutional linkages between government policy organizations and the external world are crucial for precise inferences about the implications of cognitions for policy action in particular situations. Although couched in somewhat different language, this need has been recognized in recent operational-code work, and some instruments have been developed to meet it in a reliable manner (Holsti 1977).

Elaboration of code elements related to all four parts of our cybernetic framework clearly will increase the extent to which one can posit a process that links external events and actors to the eventual policy actions by the decision system under analysis. We formulate and structure the international envi-

1. Our thinking on these points has benefited from exposure to a number of working papers by Alexander George in addition to the works we cite in this chapter.

ronment, decision-making, and information-assessment elements in part III of this volume. Particular aspects of the policy-implementation element are developed in parts II and IV. Nevertheless, without direct access, confirmatory tracking of that process is not possible. One can impute a process and, given a sufficient variety of events with responses, see if observable policy actions differ from events of one kind to those of another kind as one would expect. Similar checking strategies can be followed with regard to observable treatments of different parties to international affairs. The logic of analysis is quasi-experimental and has the strengths and weaknesses inherent in that method. We will engage in this analysis in part IV. As the "test" situations and nations we use vary greatly and are spread over time, we gain some measure of confidence in the extent to which policy actions compatible with our expectations are not in fact caused by factors other than code cognitions. Given our concern with national elites rather than particular statesmen, it is reasonable to assume that factors associated with differences in organizational position and individual leverage average out across events and do not introduce systematic error. In sum, we suggest that it may be easier to establish by customary if limited scientific criteria the explanatory power of an "operational code" for a national elite over situations and years than for a given individual with a narrow class of stimuli such as international crises.

CHAPTER 3

APPROACHES TO THE STUDY OF CHINESE FOREIGN POLICY

Our research strategy bears some surface resemblance to much of Western research on Chinese foreign policy. An emphasis on elite decision patterns, a reliance on content analysis of public Chinese documents, and a restriction to the national level of analysis are notable features in common. And like most of the China literature, our approach tends to deemphasize the role played by constraints and opportunities provided by the international environment. The purpose of this chapter is to indicate briefly the particular areas of continuity between our work and the approaches of others. Equally important, we will indicate our concerns with what we hold to be major limitations in much of the literature, limitations we hope to escape at least in part. In evaluating this book, success in this regard should receive careful scrutiny.

Explaining Foreign Policy Decision Making

Most explanations of Chinese foreign policy decisions have emphasized the imperatives of national interest, cultural tradition, or ideology. In doing so, each of these sources has been treated in what Robert Boardman (1974) has usefully called a *teleological* manner. Policy behavior results from the goals and motives of individual leaders in Peking or of the elite as a whole. Explanations then take the form that China does X because Mao or Peking wants Y. Chinese decision making supposedly follows from the application of clear and immutable goals to situations on the basis of careful calculation about the progress different alternatives will yield. Before turning to the analysis of these differing categories, two general corollaries of the teleological stance should be confronted.

First, the Chinese are rarely seen to have the difficulties in the conduct of foreign policy that harass other regimes with respect to goal conflict, uncertainty, uncoordinated implementation, inadvertence, and blunder. There are exceptions to this competence assessment (e.g., Whiting 1975b), but by and large such factors play little role in explanations of Chinese foreign policy. This stance, which operates as if foreign policy decision making were almost uniquely simple and easy for Chinese officials, is highly dubious.

Second, the sources of policy stressed in the literature (national interest, cultural tradition, and ideology) all lead to explaining Chinese policy as resulting from highly fixed, internalized rules. Consequently, China is often treated as a ship on automatic pilot, "plowing its way single-mindedly through the oceans of international affairs, relatively uninfluenced by the waves and storms around it" (Harding 1976: 1). To the extent that the actions of others affect Chinese foreign policy, they do so only by providing obstacles that slow the ship down. The international environment is almost de facto precluded from the role of presenting Peking with stimuli that induce the Chinese to engage in foreign policy decision making. For example, the alliance systems in Asia created by the United States and the Soviet Union to "contain" China gain importance solely because of their deterrent value against potential Chinese aggression. Analyses seldom consider them as possible major threats against which Peking feels compelled to react in its foreign policy. Boardman (1974: 11) provides another illustration, showing the tendency to treat China's international environment as primarily a constraint on its policy. U.S. analysts and government officials have tended to perceive cautious and restrained Chinese foreign policy behavior in potential military-conflict situations primarily as an indication of the effectiveness of U.S. containment policy rather than as a sign that the attribution of aggressive goals to the Chinese merits reassessment.

We question this assumption of fixed, internalized rules for several reasons. First, it assumes a degree of prescience about the nature of the international environment rarely found in human affairs. Second, it has some suspiciously self-serving properties, including the placement of responsibility for improved relations primarily on China. Third, it bolsters the credentials of those who argue that explaining Chinese foreign policy calls primarily for Sinological credentials and not particularly for international affairs knowledge.

With respect to the specific policy sources usually advanced, it is important to note the limitations in their application. National-interest explanations have not been more successful for the study of China than for other political systems. One reason is that almost any activity can be rationalized after the fact. For example, one "interest" often attributed to the Chinese is that of destabilizing the international system. Belligerent Chinese statements supporting national liberation movements are thus "explained." Unfortunately, the national-interest explanation is also offered when the Chinese refrain from supporting interventions, suggesting that this restraint is designed to embarrass the United States and erode its support in the Third World. It is hardly surprising that, faced with attributions of such cleverness and guile, Kuo Mo-jo commented, "We Chinese just cannot live up to Mr. Nixon's aspirations for us" (Chalfont 1972).

The use of culture and tradition as the source of Chinese foreign policy decision making is more complex but not obviously more satisfactory. One school of *reductive* analysis holds that Chinese tradition makes itself felt through the personalities of individual Chinese (e.g., Solomon 1971; Pye 1968, 1967). The personality characteristics attributed to individual members of the Chinese culture give rise to a national character, which in turn is extrapolated from the realm of domestic social relations to that of foreign affairs. The difficulties involved in inferences of this sort are well known and formidable (Terhune 1970). Yet the literature pays little attention to the difficulties in inferring political behavior from cultural products, to the distribution of cultural traits within a population, and to the development of composition rules that link different levels of social organization. More generally, explanations of contemporary Chinese foreign policy draw on the Chinese tradition in an arbitrarily partial and selective fashion. For example, the Confucian injunction of hierarchical social relations allegedly generates Peking's preoccupation with dominance and subjugation in international affairs. Yet there is little pressure to explain Peking's apparent emphasis on the importance of military force, given the Confucian rejection of the efficacy of physical coercion. There are, of course, major exceptions, which attempt to apply systematically a relatively coherent and isolated body of tradition to the analysis of China's foreign relations. In particular, the impact of the Chinese strategic tradition, particularly in the game of *wei-ch'i*, on current Chinese political-military doctrine and practice has been usefully explored (Boorman 1972, 1969). Nonetheless, a rich cultural tradition such as that of China contains precedents for the post hoc explanation of almost any conceivable line of foreign policy.

In view of the prominence that the Chinese give to public justification of their policy in terms of the writings of Marx, Lenin, and Mao, ideology seems a reasonable source of explanations for foreign policy actions. However, even in the context of teleological approaches, which stress the importance of goals, ideology is often treated as detrimental to decision making. At best, ideology is held to signify a lack of realism and utopian illusion; at worst, it results in messianism and irrationality. Thus, Chinese policy failures are explained as the results of dominance by ideologues, and successes as the achievement of pragmatists (Hiniker 1977). Similarly, Chinese policy rationales, such as Mao's views on nuclear weapons, are usually seen as irrational (that is, as contradictory to Western beliefs) without taking into account the Chinese context. The Chinese leadership, as a whole, is seen as isolated, ignorant, inflexible, and prone to succumb to fits of irrationality, as illustrated by the Great Leap Forward, the Cultural Revolution, and the intervention in the Korean war. When the Chinese leadership is defined as pragmatic, as with the current post-Mao leadership, ideology is assumed to have no significance and these leaders are presumed to be "pragmatic" in the same sense as Western decision makers. The view that Chinese ideology represents a meaningful, pedagogical codification of historical experience and a set of guidelines for the sophisticated and pragmatic treatment of policy problems receives less attention. Of course, if the reliance on tradition limits our ability to explain Chinese foreign policy decision making because it is unique, a dependence on irrational ideology has the same weakening effect because it makes Chinese behavior appear random and thus unpredictable and inexplicable.

Inadequacies in the analysis of each of these factors are compounded by the usual treatment of the relationships between them. Past research has tended to treat national interest, tradition, and ideology as mutually exclusive sources of decision. Sometimes they are seen to be competitive (for example, is the Peking leadership "Chinese" or "Communist"?). Or like simple arithmetic, the Chinese decision calculus simply sums national interest, tradition, and ideology. Acknowledgment that these elements might be closely intertwined is rare (e.g., Boyd 1972; Van Ness 1970). Equally rare are analyses of the relationships between these factors, such as the question of the manner in which the Maoist ideology constrains Chinese interpretations of national interest. In sum, most previous research on Chinese decision making slights the known complexity of decision-relevant perceptions (e.g., Axelrod 1976).

As a consequence, there exist significantly divergent assumptions and conclusions about the conduct of Chinese foreign policy. As a field of inquiry, Sinology has adapted with ease to highly varied images of China—as an aggressive, expansionist Communist monolith, as a fragmented polity characterized by rampant leadership conflict, and as an insecure, pragmatic middle power. The periodic shifts in this image have resulted less from major scholarly discoveries than from changes in the official positions of the U.S. Government or developments concerning China that analysts did not anticipate (for example, the Sino-Soviet dispute, the Cultural Revolution, Nixon's visit to China).

Efforts to narrow the range of conflicting assumptions and conclusions about Chinese foreign policy and to move beyond an essentially reactive scholarly posture have been hampered by the general absence of research that systematically uses elite perceptions to distinguish probable from improbable policy actions. The dominant mode of analysis in Chinese foreign policy has been the examination of *case histories,* particularly those involving actual or potential conflict with the United States. Given the well-known limitations of the case-study approach, more effort goes to generating than to eliminating alternate plausible explanations. The case-specific emphasis discourages cumulative research (even simple comparative analysis across cases is infrequent), and it tends to promote anecdotal description rather than testing, refining, and generalizing observations.

In addition to case studies, research on Chinese decision making has stressed the chronological survey of major domestic and foreign events, relying on *"juxtapository linkages"* (Harding 1976: 14). Explanations of this sort involve relying on the post hoc reconstruction of particular episodes in Chinese foreign relations history by juxtaposing concurrent events. The results often suffer in two respects. First, while a linkage between different events is posited, its exact nature is rarely explicated. Second, such propositions are usually based on ad hoc observations, making empirical falsification of their validity almost impossible. For instance, J. D. Simmonds (1970) explains the Bandung period in Chinese foreign relations in terms of Peking's need for a peaceful international environment to pursue its First Five-Year Plan (Harding 1976: 15). At the same time, he explains the Quemoy crisis in terms of Peking's need for a foreign enemy in order to mobilize the domestic populace for the Great Leap. Thus, the domestic-foreign linkage posited by Simmonds apparently does not preclude very different foreign relations postures by Peking in its pursuit of domestic industrialization.

In contrast to these predominant research orientations, the few efforts that have specified the linkage between perceptions and behavior do provide a clear, relevant, and defensible set of inferences. In particular, the analysis by Van Ness (1970) of Peking's support for revolutionary movements demonstrates that even modest efforts to measure and test policy behavior can provide significant results.

Beyond the Unitary-Actor Assumption

While most research on Chinese foreign policy has tended to treat foreign policy decisions as the product of a unitary actor (that is, Mao or a unified elite), there have been a number of attempts to examine policy in terms of the interplay of individuals and institutions deriving from two traditions. The first is one of *environmental determinism*. The second is that of *Kremlinology*, familiar to all students of Communist political systems.

The environmental deterministic approach uses biographical information to identify possible conflicts among the Chinese leadership (e.g., Lambert 1974; Klein 1968, 1962; Teiwes 1967). The logic of inference runs as follows: (1) gross socioeconomic variables (for example, age, family, class, level of education) correctly classify and capture the socialization experiences of the leaders (Searing 1969); (2) these socialization experiences shape the leaders' views on issues and, ipso facto, their policy responses; and (3) divergent socialization experiences create different views on issues and, hence, elite conflict. Unfortunately, these relationships are usually assumed rather than empirically demonstrated for the Chinese case. The dependent variables of elite perceptions and behavior are rarely specified. Further, the theoretical possibility that heterogeneous socialization experiences can promote elite unity (Coser 1956) is never entertained.

Data on the elite's early childhood and adolescent socialization experiences are sometimes supplemented with career experience, institutional affiliation, and bureaucratic specialization (e.g., Sung 1975; Whitson 1969). The basic logic of inference is again deterministic. The leaders' appraisals of and recommendations for policies follow from their bureaucratic responsibilities and incentives. Analyses of Chinese foreign policy decision making from a bureaucratic-politics perspective often extrapolate decision makers' policy positions and motives from their organizational roles (Harding 1976: 20–26). Decision makers are treated as if they were creatures of the organizational milieu in which they operate. Yet we know of numerous instances in which Chinese leaders' views diverged significantly from the interests and perspectives of the organizations they presumably represented. For instance, Lin Piao and Lo Jui-ch'ing, both representatives of the military establishment, adopted very different policy positions on the Vietnam war and Sino-Soviet rapproachement in the leadership "debate" during the mid-1960s (Yahuda 1972; Ra'anan 1968; Zagoria 1967). Similarly, it is anomalous that Chou En-lai, a "moderate" in every China watcher's definition, supported the "radicals" led by Mao during the Cultural Revolution, instead of taking the side of his fellow government administrators, such as Liu Shao-ch'i and Teng Hsiao-p'ing. Thus, data on bureaucratic position and training are not fully indicative of policy views; where one stands does not necessarily depend on where one sits.

Inferences about tensions between the representatives of different institutional "interest groups" in China usually draw on a second approach—textual analysis of statements by Peking's leading cadres. Kremlinology has a long tradition in the study of both Chinese and Soviet politics, analyzing what has been called "esoteric communication" (Griffith 1967a). This kind of documentary analysis, heavily reliant on the expertise of the individual analyst and the intensive scrutiny of particular documents, has several important limitations. Since the usable data base is quite small, analysis sometimes requires rather heroic leaps of inference, particularly about the implications of the tone and setting of a document, the audience to which it is addressed, and the identity of unnamed adversaries. Because this type of research is often a matter of educated but nonetheless subjective interpretation, the same textual evidence can yield different conclusions by different analysts (e.g., Yahuda 1972; Ra'anan 1968; Zagoria 1967). Furthermore, inconsistencies in the policy rationales presented publicly by different leading spokesmen may not necessarily indicate disagreements between them. They may instead reflect needs to address multiple domestic and foreign audiences, placate the organizational constituencies of various leaders, deceive or confuse foreign adversaries, or preserve the regime's policy options and hedge its commitments. These problems affecting data interpretation are seldom taken up by those who engage in the analysis of "esoteric communication" and remain difficult to resolve.

In sum, while we are certain that the Chinese elite does not constitute a homogeneous group, the methodologies for identifying intraelite differences in a systematic and reliable fashion do not seem to exist. The environmental deterministic and Kremlinological approaches occasionally succeed in pointing out these differences. Unfortunately, they provide few criteria to distinguish between successes and failures, and few clues on how to improve the proportion of successes. Accordingly, we have no confidence that attempts to disaggregate the unitary character of the Chinese elite would produce more enlightenment than confusion about its foreign policy decision making.

Methodological Concerns

In the analysis of Chinese foreign policy, concerns about method have received little attention. When such issues are raised, often it is only to note that data sources are sufficient or inadequate. The question of standards for assessing sufficiency or inadequacy has received little attention. Few suggestions have been offered on how to cope with abundant or scarce data. Indeed, there has been little effort to explore alternative techniques or employ more innovative modes of analysis.

The study of Chinese foreign relations largely lacks systematic analyses that map policy situations, identify behavior patterns, or estimate the parameters of international interaction. There are few quantitative pattern analyses of the international or domestic ecology of Chinese foreign policy decision making (e.g., Liao 1976; Onate 1974; Rhee 1973; Bobrow 1969a), of Chinese attention to or assessment of international developments (Dillon et al. 1977; Liao and Whiting 1973; Tretiak 1971, 1969), and of Chinese behavior in international interactions or transactions (e.g., Duncan and Siverson 1975; Scott 1973; Field 1972; Sigler 1972a; Smoker 1969, 1964; McClelland 1969). In fact, the literature cited includes almost all the existing quantitative work on Chinese foreign relations, and many of these works are not addressed to substantive concerns about Chinese foreign policy.

The argument that data problems are responsible for the general absence of more systematic analyses of Chinese foreign policy decision making is somewhat misleading. Referring back to the cybernetic model described in chapter 1, there are three great unknowns about foreign policy decision making: (1) elite perceptions and policy responses; (2) participants in decision making and their interactions; and (3) the analytic-cognitive basis for decision making.

With regard to the first area, analysts of Chinese foreign relations are not more handicapped by the availability or quality of data than their colleagues studying many other countries. They are certainly not constrained by the lack of source material for engaging in such standard international relations research as content analysis of elite perceptions, event analysis of governmental policy responses, and voting analysis of coalition formation in the United Nations. While some data pertaining to such matters as economic productivity, defense spending, military deployment, and foreign aid programs may be less readily available and accurate for China, such problems are not fundamentally different from those for research on other "closed" political systems and, perhaps, some "open" political systems as well. Furthermore, the inferential problems in the use of media-based data are substantial whether these data are derived from "closed" or "open" political systems. For example,

similar problems exist in inferring elite perceptions from their public statements because of the problems of deception and multiple audiences. Similarly,
event data, whether derived from Chinese or Western media, provide only
partial and selective coverage of governmental policy behavior and reflect to
at least some degree the concerns and interpretations of the elite.

With regard to the second great unknown, that of decision participants and
their interactions, the problem of the inaccessibility of foreign policy decision
processes to direct observation is not fundamentally dissimilar for China and
most other countries. Even in the case of the United States, the nation whose
decision processes have been most studied, internal decision making has been
most frequently researched through post hoc case studies employing interviews and the memoirs of decision participants. Extrapolation of their findings
beyond the particular cases studied remains a difficult enterprise. Problems of
possible self-justifying distortion abound.

As for the final great unknown of decision makers' cognitive approach to
problem solution, it is likely that, if anything, analysts of Chinese foreign
relations enjoy a relative advantage in this regard. China provides a relatively
promising case for studying elite belief systems because Chinese leaders
emphasize the development and propagation of explicit policy rationales. The
regime's public injunctions about the proper diagnosis and treatment of policy
problems are therefore useful for illuminating the cognitive-analytic basis of
its decision processes. While documentary analysis of these injunctions
provided in various publicly available political and cultural materials is by
itself insufficient for specifying the nature of Chinese decision making in
particular case histories or by particular leaders, it does enable us to (1) identify
general tendencies in the Chinese belief system, and (2) assess their relative
durability over time and in relation to different contexts and issues.
Hypotheses derived from this material about the national culture can in turn
be tested by different methods and data, as we report later.

The availability of a large volume of public media statements to be used in
developing a model of Chinese cognitive processes does not mean that the
translation from officially stated views to actual policy beliefs is either simple
or easy. With regard to the analysis of Chinese policy beliefs, past efforts of this
sort have been deficient in several respects.

At the most mundane level, research using official media sources has paid
insufficient attention to the comparison of public statements over time and
across documentary sources. Such analyses are necessary, however, to assess
the degree to which policy rationales are durable and constant across actors
and institutions. As will be indicated in subsequent chapters, these are complex
issues. Our own research has demonstrated that while there is considerable
consistency over time and across sources in the general policy logics that the
Chinese publicly present, this does not mean that the public treatment of
particular nations is constant across media sources. Our comparative analysis

of alternate media sources, presented in appendix A, indicates substantial differences across sources, with the sources intended primarily for external consumption (for instance, *Peking Review*) being particularly deviant in their thematic content.

Second, to the extent that officially stated views have been used to infer Chinese policy beliefs, most analyses have focused on single belief elements (e.g., Dillon et al. 1977). Yet, since policy beliefs do not exist in isolation, the linkages between individual beliefs need to be explored to discern the chains of contingent reasoning that represent actual decision processes. In a similar vein, individual belief elements have not been systematically examined in terms of the degree to which they have unambiguous decisional implications. As we shall show in chapter 10, official Chinese policy logics can be linked together into chains of reasoning. Further, their policy statements vary considerably in decision import, a fact with significant methodological and substantive implications.

Last, few attempts have been made to determine the degree to which officially stated views conform to the logics actually used by Chinese decision makers. And those few attempts (e.g., Schwarz 1966; Lewis 1964) have relied on the comparison of views stated in public and restricted-access documentary sources. The absence of research demonstrating a linkage between the logics and symbolism embodied in official statements and the perceptions of individual Chinese is crucial not only in terms of standard validity concerns but also in terms of the need for greater understanding of the filters employed by the Chinese in communication. Even if the actual views of individual Chinese correspond in some fashion to those presented in public forums, it cannot be assumed that they correspond in all respects. Because media content analysis alone, however sophisticated, cannot resolve this issue, a greater understanding of the relationship between official views and actual beliefs and of the Chinese communications filters requires some systematic, direct research on actual perceptions. While our ability to garner such perceptions unfiltered by media institutions and policies is seriously limited, some steps are possible, and we report them in part III of this volume as cross checks on inferences drawn primarily from our content analysis of public Chinese media.

Conclusions

Our review of Western research on Chinese foreign policy leads to the conclusion that notable progress is needed and possible with respect to explanation and method. It also leads us to conclude that it is reasonable and still productive to work at the national level of analysis. Although the amount of research on Chinese foreign policy is substantial (Dial 1973), it often lacks systematic treatment and methodological sensitivity. Of course, the absence of a set of cumulative findings about foreign policy decision making is not unique to the study of China (e.g., Horelick et al. 1975). However, this is hardly reason for a sense of intellectual satisfaction.

While the procedures and data used in the following chapters are not without their limitations, self-consciousness on these scores, we hope, will improve the attempts at systematic diagnosis and explanation to which we now turn.

PART II

Critical International Incidents

We now turn to the substance of our own work. The next three chapters examine Chinese decision making with regard to violent or potentially violent events and compare it with U.S. decision logics for treating similar kinds of incidents. We focus on this part of international affairs because of its obvious policy importance and because U.S. scholarship and political practice have treated it extensively. Additionally, such critical incidents and flares of international violence lend themselves to highlighting differences between U.S. and Chinese foreign policy cognitions. We want to find out whether two of our basic assumptions are sound. The first is that there are important differences in foreign affairs decision processes between national elites. The second is that our approach provides worthwhile knowledge about the past and probable future behavior of the People's Republic of China.

It will quickly become apparent that the critical international incidents discussed at length by U.S. and Chinese sources are different in obvious respects. While the U.S. materials emphasize short-term incidents, the Chinese emphasize rather extended wars and conflicts. Of course, it is possible that each elite also gives great attention to what the other talks about but does so in a highly discreet manner. Nevertheless, since open statements do reveal policy views and sanctioned history that are important for decision making, it is reasonable for our purposes to treat those aspects of international affairs viewed as critical in public discussion as important. Accordingly, what we seek to clarify in the following chapters is not how different elites treat the same situations, but rather how their memories, conceptions, and decision logics differ about critical situations in international affairs.

Because of the emphasis we and others have placed on the role of precedents, chapter 4 deals with the problems of developing an appropriate precedent set for Chinese decision makers. This discussion is particularly apposite given the importance attached to historical experience in the Chinese operational code, to be discussed in part III. As we shall see, errors in developing a precedent set can distort severely the referents and interpretations used by other regimes to understand, anticipate, and influence what the Chinese will do in crises. Chapter 5 presents in a summary form the maxims and logics that American analysts and decision makers tend to apply to the diagnosis and management of critical incidents. Chapter 6 presents a comparable analysis for the Chinese and relates it to how the Chinese have actually behaved in past critical situations.

CHAPTER 4

ALTERNATIVE HISTORIES

To varying degrees, we are all captives of history. Foreign policy decision makers are no exception in this regard. Generals often plan for the last war; diplomats, for the last peace (May 1973; Tuchman 1962). Thus, foreign policy decision making in a large measure reflects remembered experiences of oneself as well as those of significant others. "Lessons" derived from these experiences exemplify particularly successful or unsuccessful policies and are used to validate one's own policies and anticipate those of others. Successful policies are often treated as positive examples to be repeated and generalized as sound policy, while unsuccessful policies are isolated as negative examples to be avoided. Even when history provides mere analogies rather than explicit guidelines, it influences decisions indirectly by shaping decision makers' receptivity to and interpretation of current information (e.g., George and Smoke 1974; Holsti 1969; Jervis 1969; Paige 1968).

Of course, we need not be concerned with the effects of history on foreign policy decision making if national elites draw on a common history and compile it in a basically uniform way. Research on human cognition and psychology (e.g., Tversky and Kahneman 1975; Jervis 1969; de Rivera 1968) as well as some of the case studies cited above suggest that neither of these assumptions is warranted. Accordingly, we need to identify the similarities and differences in the historical precedents that are particularly salient to national elites. We also need to determine the interpretation given by elites to these precedents and the policy implications they draw from them to guide current policy judgments and anticipations. Naturally, questions such as these have a significance far beyond the illustrative treatment of the Chinese "memory" we present below. They are of fundamental importance to any attempt to build empirical models of foreign policy decision processes on the basis of what are to the revelant decision makers sound indicators of others' foreign policy behavior and wise maxims for choosing their own behavior.

In pursuing the implications of historical precedents for foreign policy decision making, we address three questions. Are there substantial similarities or differences between the Chinese stock of remembered historical events and those of other nations? Basic similarity on this score alone is, however, insufficient to infer cross-national homogeneity in remembered experiences. We also need to determine whether the remembered events have the same content for different elites. In other words, are there substantial similarities or differences in the Chinese and non-Chinese perceptions of the same objective events? Yet even agreement about the interpretation of basic historical "facts" does not guarantee agreement about their policy implications. Do common remembrances lead elites to draw similar or different historical lessons for current policy problems? As we shall see, the Chinese and Soviet elites draw very different policy conclusions from similar precedents.

Our analysis necessarily relies primarily on open-source materials, some of which were sponsored directly by governments. To that extent, we are hostage to the sources and the interpretations of the regimes we choose to examine. It is foolish to argue for the integrity of these sources and interpretations in any strict sense. We have little confidence that they mirror exactly the cognizance, interpretation, or application of historical lessons by the relevant foreign policy elites. We use our source materials instead as imperfect approximations useful for illuminating the questions we have posed. If these open-source materials do not support our argument of cross-national heterogeneity, then it becomes rather suspect. Conversely, substantial differences in national treatment of historical precedents based on such materials, although insufficient in themselves for validating our argument, do suggest that it has sufficient merit to warrant further investigation. Finally, we concentrate on the relative differences between various national "memories," and only discuss particular "remembered" incidents as they represent general patterns of interpreting and treating historical precedents.

Event Inventory

We begin with the degree of overlap between the events that the Chinese treat as significant past military conflicts and those "remembered" by others. We initially restrict our attention to conflicts during 1959–1968 as provided by three compilations: (1) a Chinese chronology of "imperialist wars" (Writing Team 1974); (2) an inventory of "local wars" presented by an East European social scientist (Kende 1971); and (3) a list of international crises that generally reflects the views of U.S. officials and analysts (Phillips and Moore 1975). Obviously, the authors used different criteria to define conflict events and to decide on their inclusion or exclusion in developing these inventories. However, this is not crucial for our purposes, since we are only interested in identifying a candidate set of occurrences for Chinese precedents involving actual or threatened military conflict, and in assessing the *relative* differences between the Chinese precedents and those of others.

Even a cursory review of the events presented in table 4-1 shows some interesting discrepancies between the three event inventories. For instance, the East European list does not mention three "big" events from the U.S. perspective: the Cuban missile crisis, the *Pueblo* incident, and the Soviet bloc invasion of Czechoslovakia. Similarly, the U.S. list does not include the

TABLE 4-1

CROSS-NATIONAL COVERAGE OF INTERNATIONAL CONFLICTS, 1959–1968

Chinese List	East European List*	U.S. List
Laos, May 1959	Nyasaland, 1959	Haiti–Cuba, 1959
Nicaragua, May 1959	Laos, 1959–1962	Dominican Republic–Cuba, 1959
Sino-India, August 1959	Congo-Kinshasa, 1960–1964	Panama–Cuba, 1959
Dominican Republic, 1959	Angola, 1961–	China–Nepal, 1960
Congo, 1960	Cuba, 1961	Congo, 1960–1961
Nicaragua, 1960	Tunisia, 1961	Kuwait–Iraq, 1961
Guatemala, 1960	India–Goa, 1961	Bay of Pigs, 1961
Dominican Republic, May 1960	Indonesia–West Irian, 1962	Goa, 1961
Guatemala, February 1960–1962	Guatemala, 1962	Berlin Wall, 1961
South Vietnam, 1961	Colombia, 1962	Cuban missile crisis, 1962
Angola, March 1961	Yemen, 1963–1969	India–China, 1962
Bay of Pigs, April 1961	India–China, 1962	Taiwan Straits, 1962
Tunisia, July 1961	Brunei–N. Borneo, 1962	Haiti–Dominican Republic, 1963
Cuban missile crisis, 1962	Guinea-Bisseau, 1962–	Kenya–Somali Republic, 1963
Laos, May 1962	Malaysia, 1963–1966	Berlin Autobahn, 1963
Yemen, 1962–1970	Algeria-Morocco, 1963	Algeria-Morocco, 1963
Guinea, January 1963	Somalia-Ethiopia, 1963–1964	Malaysia, 1963
Cambodia, 1963	Congo-Kinshasa, 1963–1969	Cyprus, 1963–1964
Haiti, 1963	Cyprus, 1963–1964	Yemen, 1963
Gulf of Tonkin, August 1964	Kenya-Somalia, 1963–1967	Malaysia, 1964

(continued on following page)

TABLE 4-1 (continued)

CROSS-NATIONAL COVERAGE OF INTERNATIONAL CONFLICTS, 1959-1968

Chinese List	East European List*	U.S. List
Mozambique, September 1964	South Yemen, 1964–1967	Ethiopia-Somalia, 1964
Congo, November 1964	Laos, 1964–	Gulf of Tonkin, 1964
Cyprus, 1964	Colombia, 1964–1969	China-India, 1965
South Vietnam, March 1965	North Vietnam, 1964–1968	Kashmir, 1965
Dominican Republic, May 1965	Mozambique, 1954–	Jordan-Syria, 1966
Rhodesia, April 1966	Dominica, 1965	Rhodesia blockade, 1966
Arab-Israel, June 1967	Bolivia, 1965–1967	Sino-Soviet, 1967
Czechoslovakia, August 1968	Peru, 1965	Arab-Israel, 1967
	India-Pakistan, 1965	Cyprus, 1967
	Thailand, 1965–	Hong Kong, 1967
	Israel-Arab, 1967	Israel-Jordan, 1968
	Congo-Kinshasa, 1967	Pueblo incident, 1968
	Zimbabwe-Rhodesia, 1967–	Czechoslovakia, 1968
	South Yemen, 1968	
	Chad, 1968	

* Adjusted to exclude wars not described by Kende as involving international conflict.
Sources: Chinese list (Writing Team 1974); East European list (Kende 1971); U.S. list (Phillips and Moore 1975).

Dominican conflict in 1962, which is mentioned in both the East European and Chinese lists. The Chinese chronology is unique in its failure to mention the 1962 Sino-Indian and 1965 Indian-Pakistani wars. Also, unlike the U.S. inventory, it does not mention the Sino-Soviet dispute, the *Pueblo* incident, the Indonesian-Malaysian confrontation, and the disturbances in Hong Kong in 1967. These omissions by the Chinese all refer to events involving themselves or their close allies. And with the exception of the Hong Kong incident, they all involved the threat of significant military escalation.

TABLE 4 - 2
REGIONAL DISTRIBUTION OF CONFLICTS, 1946–1969

	Chinese List	East European List*	U.S. List
Europe	3 (7%)†	2 (3%)	10 (15%)
Asia	13 (30)	17 (29)	24 (36)
Middle East	9 (20)	17 (29)	17 (26)
Africa	7 (16)	12 (20)	4 (6)
Latin America	12 (27)	11 (19)	11 (17)
	N = 44	59	66

* Adjusted to exclude wars described by Kende as not involving outside participation.
† The figures within parentheses are percentages.

Table 4-2 provides an assessment of chronic tension areas of the world as revealed by our three sources. It shows that for the period of 1946–1969, differences among these sources reflect systematic patterns of emphasis or deemphasis of particular geographical regions. The Chinese and East European lists pay far greater attention to African conflicts than the U.S. list. They devote, respectively, 16 and 20 percent of their coverage to Africa, compared with only 6 percent for the U.S. list. Conversely, the U.S. list gives greater emphasis to European conflicts (15 percent) than do the Chinese (7 percent) and the East European (3 percent) lists. Conflict events relating to Latin American countries receive more coverage in the Chinese list (27 percent) than in the East European (19 percent) and U.S. (17 percent) lists. Such differences in the presentation of the regional distribution of violent events have obvious implications in terms of an elite's allocation of its policy attention to monitor, store, and retrieve such events.

Discrepancies in national "memories" such as those presented so far may be dismissed as being obvious. Yet it is vitally important to attend to these discrepancies in empirical research to explain and predict foreign policy behavior. In this regard, we need to be particularly aware of the potential distortions in the available data sets used in such research. To illustrate our point, we examine the extent to which one disciplined academic effort, avowedly seeking to avoid any particular national bias, relates to the three lists with different national origins. Table 4-3 shows the data coverage of the

TABLE 4 - 3
CONFLICT COVERAGE, 1959–1968

CREON Event N	Chinese	East European	U.S. Policy Community
0	20 (71.4%)*	19 (41.3%)	11 (32.4%)
1–5	2 (7.1)	6 (13.0)	5 (14.7)
6–10	1 (3.6)	2 (4.3)	3 (8.8)
11–20		3 (6.5)	3 (8.8)
21–30		2 (4.3)	
31–50		4 (8.7)	4 (11.8)
51–75	1 (3.6)	2 (4.3)	2 (5.9)
76–100	2 (7.1)	2 (4.3)	1 (2.9)
101–150		2 (4.3)	1 (2.9)
151–200		1 (2.2)	2 (5.9)
201–250			
251–300		1 (2.2)	
301–350	1 (3.6)		
351–400			
401–450			
451–500			
501–600	1 (3.6)	1 (2.2)	
601–700			
701–800			1 (2.9)
801–900		1 (2.2)	1 (2.9)
	$N = 28$	46	34

* The figures within parentheses are percentages.

incidents in these lists by the Comparative Research on the Events of Nations (CREON) project (Hermann et al. 1973). The figures indicate the number of incidents in these lists receiving particular levels of CREON event coverage, and the percentage of these incidents receiving these levels of CREON coverage.

Two aspects of these figures merit attention. First, because of the sampling procedure used by the CREON developers with regard to actors and time, substantial percentages of the incidents in all the lists receive no or very little coverage. Second, this sampling procedure does not have a random effect on the lists. The quality of coverage for incidents included in the Chinese list is particularly poor; 71 percent of these incidents are not covered. In contrast, this omission is much less serious for the U.S. compilation, amounting to only 32 percent of its incidents.

Nor is it the case that our two "foreign" sources are in agreement on all important matters, even though the two precedent sets come from outside the capitalist West. To establish this point, we looked at the period common to both the East European and the Chinese lists (1945–1969). Also, in the interest of comparability we eliminated from the East European list those military conflicts that the author claims did not involve outside participation. Of the events on the Chinese list, over one-fourth do not appear on the East European list. Of the events on the East European list, half are absent from the Chinese compilation (see appendix B). As another example, the role of imperialist intervener is an obviously germane way to store and search precedents. Compared with the East European list, the Chinese list has precedents for imperialist intervention by many more nations (ten as contrasted with four), including interventions by the Soviet Union and three non-European nations, (Israel, Rhodesia, and India). Moreover, the Chinese list gives substantially less importance to the one-time colonial powers of Western Europe and instead sees imperialist intervention as widely distributed.

These findings support the conclusions of most other analyses of cross-source differences in event data (Burrowes 1974; Hoggard 1974; Doran et al. 1973; Azar et al. 1972; Sigler 1972b; McClelland and Young 1970; McClelland and Hoggard 1969; Smith 1969). They indicate that it is highly unwarranted to use such data as "objective" records of international affairs history and to extrapolate from them the perceptions of national elites other than the one from whose sources they are derived. More generally, our findings suggest that simply increasing the number and variety of sources used will not increase the accuracy of the precedent set attributed to the memories of others. Instead, the challenge is to increase our confidence in the appropriateness of the sources we use to identify what are for particular national elites part of the pertinent past.

Event Perceptions

Precedents in our usage consist of events and associated patterns of activity that are at the heart of strategy. We have illustrated that the precedent set may be rather different for different regimes. We will show now that even when an event is included in the precedent sets of different regimes, the associated activities may be substantially different. In other words, the same objective event may be perceived differently.

To illustrate, we use the Vietnam war, which was included in the Chinese, East European, and U.S. conflict inventories presented earlier. Table 4-4 shows the characterization of U.S. behavior toward North Vietnam (D.R.V.) and China (P.R.C.) as presented by two sources, the *Deadline Data on World Affairs*, used by the CREON developers, and the *People's Daily* of China.

The U.S. behavior reported in these sources is significantly divergent, even after allowing for possible differences in coding judgments. While the CREON data drawn from the *Deadline Data* show that 51.7 percent of the U.S. actions directed at North Vietnam belong to the category of verbal hostility, the *People's Daily* portrays the primary type of U.S. action as military coercion (88.2 percent). Similarly, while the CREON data did not record any overt acts of U.S. military coercion against China, the Chinese source included twelve such instances.

TABLE 4 - 4

ACTION EMPHASES: EXAMPLES FROM THE VIETNAM WAR

Actions	USA-DRV		USA-PRC	
	Deadline Data (CREON)	People's Daily	Deadline Data (CREON)	People's Daily
1. Yield, grant, decrease military capability, consult, carry out agreement, reward, improve relationship	0	0	0	0
2. Agree, promise, offer, positive intention	5 (8.6%)*	1 (0.4%)	0	0
3. Positive request, positive proposal, negotiate	0	0	0	1 (0.2)
4. Positive comment, approve	8 (13.8)	0	0	8 (2.0)
5. Negative comment, accuse, deny	30 (51.7)	15 (6.6)	7 (46.7)	256 (63.8)
6. Demand, protest, negative proposal, negative request	1 (1.7)	5 (2.2)	1 (6.7)	59 (14.7)
7. Threaten, warn, reject, negative intention	6 (10.3)	6 (2.6)	7 (46.7)	65 (16.2)
8. Force, demonstrate, increase military capability, aid opponent, reduce relationship, seize, expel, subvert	8 (13.8)	202 (88.2)	0	12 (3.0)
	N = 58	229	15	401

* The figures without parentheses are the event frequencies for the following months: April 1963, May 1963, June 1963, July 1964, August 1964, September 1964, January 1965, February 1965, and March 1965. The figures within parentheses are percentages.
Source: Bobrow et al. 1977.

Some reasons for these discrepancies are easy to identify. Sampling differences, as in the example of regional attention presented earlier, constitute one such factor. Also, coding differences due to the divergent political perspectives of the sources may have an important effect. For example, an action of U.S. military assistance to the Republic of Vietnam (R.V.N.) might well be coded as a friendly U.S. action toward South Vietnam by U.S. coders. Yet the same analysts might well code Chinese military aid to the National Liberation Front as hostile action toward South Vietnam. If Chinese analysts were doing the coding, we may expect exactly a reversed interpretation in terms of friendliness or hostility toward the R.V.N. and N.L.F. Such discrepancies are acceptable as long as we use the data to identify U.S. or Chinese interpretations of the actions taken by themselves or an adversary. If, on the other hand, we assume that the action patterns presented are in some common-sense usage "objective" and shared by all parties, we clearly are introducing a major element of distortion and bias. We are not justified in assuming that data sources from politically diverse systems will provide the same patterns of previous action and interaction.

Nor should we dismiss too quickly discrepancies such as those in table 4-4 as solely a function of "ideology." We have already shown in table 4-1 that there are substantial differences in the "remembered" critical incidents by sources outside the capitalist West. Thus, factors unrelated to ideology may also be responsible for different interpretations of history. An example from the polemics of the Sino-Soviet dispute shows different perceptions of national experience. In one of the Chinese open letters to the Communist Party of the Soviet Union (C.P.S.U.), Peking charged that the "leaders of the CPSU have raised a hue and cry about the 'Yellow Peril' and the 'imminent menace of Genghis Khan,'" and proceeded to lecture Moscow about history (The Editorial Department of *People's Daily* and *Red Flag* quoted in Griffith 1964: 477):

> Lu Hsun, the well-known Chinese writer, has a paragraph about Genghis Khan in an article he wrote in 1934. We include it here for your reference as it may be useful to you.
>
> He wrote that, as a young man of twenty, "I had been told that 'our' Genghis Khan had conquered Europe and ushered in the most splendid period in 'our' history. Not until I was twenty-five did I discover that this so-called most splendid period of 'our' history was actually the time when the Mongolians conquered China and we became slaves. And not until last August, when browsing through three books on Mongolian history, looking for history stories, did I find out that the conquest of 'Russia' by the Mongolians and their invasion of Hungary and Austria actually preceded their conquest of China, and that the Genghis Khan of that time was not yet our Khan. The Russians were enslaved before we were, and presumably it is they who ought to be able to say 'When our Genghis Kahn conquered China, he ushered in the most splendid period of our history'" [Lu Hsun, *Collected Works,* Chinese ed., vol. 6, p. 109].

Strategic Ends and Means

In addition to events and associated patterns of actions, precedents provide strategies in terms of injunctions of "oughts" and "ought nots." They impact on an elite's decision processes in several ways. First, instances of past policy success are used as supporting evidence for one's basic world views or current policies. For example, the Chinese cited the victory of the Khmer Rouge as a validation of the Maoist dictum that "weak countries can defeat strong countries, small countries can defeat large countries" (Yeh 1975: 15).

Similarly, past difficulties are recalled to vindicate optimism in eventual Communist success. Thus, in discussing the opposition of "American imperialism and its running dog, the Chiang Kai-shek reactionary clique," Mao commented after the Communist victory in 1949: "They have left us some difficulties, such as blockade, unemployment, disaster, inflation, and the high prices of commodities, etc. These are real difficulties, but comparing them with what we had during the past three years, we see that we can now have a breathing spell. We have rushed through the past three years. Is it not possible for us to overcome the little difficulties we have now?" (Mao quoted in Cheng 1966: 152).

Optimism about eventual success is further bolstered by recalling important historical occurrences that ostensibly indicate favorable long-term trends. Thus, Lin Piao argued in 1965:

> U.S. imperialism is preparing a world war. But can this save it from its doom? World War I was followed by the birth of the socialist Soviet Union. World War II was followed by the emergence of a series of socialist countries and many nationally independent countries. If the U.S. imperialists should insist on launching a third world war, it can be stated categorically that many more hundreds of millions of people will turn to socialism; the imperialists will then have little room left on the globe; and it is possible that the whole structure of imperialism will collapse [Lin quoted in Griffith 1967b: 442].

Given that the historical experiences of oneself and others are seen to validate the elite's world views and policies, they provide positive examples to be replicated in other contexts. Lin Piao's famous article on people's war from which the above quotation is extracted provides such an example. Successful Chinese strategies in the Anti-Japanese war and the subsequent civil war were generalized to the global level. The struggle against imperialism was to be carried out by national liberation movements in the "rural" areas of the world (that is, Asia, Africa, and Latin America), leading to the encirclement and defeat of the "urban" areas (that is, Europe and North America).

Historical precedents can influence decision processes in yet another way. Perceived policy failures by oneself or others are used as negative examples that merit attention and avoidance. For instance, internal P.L.A. documents argued as follows:

With regard to the disarmament problem, if some agreement should be made in the morning, it may be broken in the evening. We Chinese people have to fall back on our own experience. During the period of the Peiyang warlords anybody participating in that government simply entered a pigpen. Under Chiang Kai-shek's dictatorship, whoever participated in his government at most was given a position as Minister of Agriculture and Forestry, or Minister of Economic Affairs or Minister of Health. What use was that? [Cheng 1966: 480].

The failures of those who are like oneself serve as important warnings to potential dangers that must be coped with, lest they develop into real catastrophes. In this regard, the Hungarian uprising in 1956 appeared to be of special significance to the Chinese leaders, and Mao repeatedly referred to its lessons in top-level cadre meetings (e.g., Mao 1969: 66–67, 74, 87, 96, 255), warning that "it was a case of reactionaries inside a socialist country, in league with the imperialists, attempting to achieve their conspiratorial aims by taking advantage of contradictions among the people to foment dissension and stir up disorder" (Mao quoted in Schram 1967: 31).

Another way in which perceived historical precedents can influence decision processes is through their use for anticipating others' behavior. In accord with our later discussion of Chinese emphasis on military vigilance, internal army documents enjoined military officers to guard against surprise attack by enemies: "The time in which they usually launched an attack has always been set for Saturday midnight. During World War II there were many surprise attacks, such as Hitler's attack on Poland, Norway, Denmark and Russia and Japan's attack on Pearl Harbor. They were all carried out on Sunday mornings. Future sudden attacks will also be, possibly, made under the same conditions" (Cheng 1966: 544). Anticipation of others' future behavior can also be based on one's understanding of their perception of significant experiences. In this context, Edgar Snow (1971: 180–81) commented that "the Chinese believed that the lesson of Vietnam, and no mere change of Presidents, was what made it possible for Mao in 1970 to speak differently about Nixon. 'Experience' had made Nixon relatively 'good.' "

Even though historical precedents may not under certain contexts provide explicit guidelines for policy imitation or avoidance, they can influence decision making by providing illuminating analogies. Thus, Chinese military cadres were told that "at the present some parts of Africa are going through experiences similar to what we experienced in China 60 years ago in the Boxer uprising. Some of the events were like those which occurred during the Hsin-hai of Revolution [1911], while others resembled what happened around the 'May 4th' [movement, 1919]. We had not yet begun the period of the Northern Expedition and that of the War of Resistance against Japan, and we were still far from the events of 1949 in China" (Cheng 1966: 484).

The use of historical precedents for policy planning and analysis is, of course, not unique to the Chinese. Yet even when there is a general agreement about particular historical "lessons," different national elites are likely to draw different conclusions from them in concrete policy applications. To illustrate these differences, we will examine briefly Chinese views on the feasibility and desirability of compromises with an enemy, and contrast these views with those of the Soviet elite, an elite whose operational code bears a significant resemblance to that of the Chinese (Leites 1953).

Similar to the U.S. and Soviet elites, the Chinese elite views the lesson of Munich as a particularly salient reminder of the danger of appeasement. Thus, according to Lo Jui-ch'ing, the Chief of Staff of the People's Liberation Army, "the Munich policy of Chamberlain and Daladier, which inflicted harm on themselves as well as on others, will live in history as a byword of infamy. Today [1965], whoever plots another Munich in the face of the war blackmail of the U.S. imperialists will, like Chamberlain and Daladier, begin by doing harm to others and end by injuring himself" (Lo quoted in Zagoria 1967: 170). Lo also argued that "whoever pins his hopes for preventing war on treaties and agreements will certainly be badly fooled" (Lo quoted in Zagoria 1967: 170), and pointed out that once imperialists

> think they can swallow you up, when they consider the situation to be in their favour, and when they have sharpened their knives, they will immediately drop this mask [of "peace" and "friendship"] and tear all the sacred treaties, solemn agreements and inviolable pledges to shreds. Modern history provides countless instances of this sort. A case in point was the undeclared *blitzkrieg* which Hitler launched against the Soviet Union less than two years after he had concluded a non-aggression treaty with it [Lo quoted in Zagoria 1967: 169].

According to the above views, the only realistic line for Communists to pursue is a policy of "standing firm" against imperialist aggression. Appeasement policies are both futile and dangerous because Communist compromises would be misperceived by the imperialists as signs of weakness and thus further increase their aggressive appetite ("yield an inch, they will ask for a yard"), because they are "mad men" inherently prone to risk war ("the class interests of monopoly capitalists impel them to embark on mad war adventures in the quest for profit"), and because they are inherently irrational in the calculation of costs and benefits ("they invariably underestimate the strength of the people and overestimate their own, and so again and again they fight 'the wrong war, at the wrong place, at the wrong time, and with the wrong enemy' ").

Yet paradoxically, Chinese decision makers are enjoined by Mao to "make use of contradictions, win over the many, oppose the few, and crush our enemies one by one" (Hung 1973: 12). To carry out this injunction, they are reminded of Lenin's statement that "there are compromises and compromises," suggesting that under certain circumstances a policy of appeasement is warranted. According to the Chinese, "an outstanding example was the Brest-Litovsk Treaty concluded by the Soviet Republic led by Lenin with German imperialism in 1918. . . . Thanks to the conclusion of the

Brest-Litovsk Treaty, the Bolshevik Party won the time to consolidate the Soviet regime, build the workers' and peasants' Red Army and rally the revolutionary forces, thereby laying the groundwork for victory in the civil war that was to break out" (Hung 1973: 12).

Significantly, this exhortation of "flexibility in revolutionary tactics" appeared in the aftermath of Nixon's Peking visit. Nevertheless, such exhortation was not without precedent. Thus, the same Lo Jui-ch'ing who was cited earlier for arguing a "hard-line" policy against U.S. aggression in Vietnam indicated that

> imperialism always uses the counter-revolutionary dual tactics of armed aggression and fraudulent peace, sometimes alternately, sometimes simultaneously, against the revolutionary people of any country. The people in their turn must make skillful use of revolutionary dual tactics in struggling against imperialism. The signing of the Soviet-German nonaggression treaty on the eve of the Anti-Fascist War and the conclusion of the Korean armistice agreement and of the two Geneva agreements after the War all show that so long as the basic interests of the people are not violated, it is perfectly permissible and even necessary to conduct negotiations with the imperialists and reach certain agreements with them on appropriate occasions [Lo quoted in Zagoria 1967: 192].

There is no basic disagreement between the Chinese views identified above and those of the Soviet elite about the interpretation of the lessons contained in the Munich and Brest-Litovsk episodes (Leites 1953). Yet application of these lessons to actual decision making is quite a different matter. The Sino-Soviet polemics regarding the Cuban missile crisis provide a revealing example in this regard. The Chinese basically charged Khrushchev "with having staged 'another Munich' at the cost of Cuban independence and the international Communist and revolutionary movement" (Griffith 1964: 61), and asserted that "the attempt to play the Munich scheme against the Cuban people . . . is doomed to complete failure" (*People's Daily*, quoted in Griffith 1964: 61). Moreover, they indicted the Kremlin leadership for having committed simultaneously the cardinal errors of both "adventurism" and "capitulationism." Thus, in an open letter to the Soviet government in 1963, the Chinese argued that

> in recklessly introducing the rockets into Cuba and then humiliatingly withdrawing them, the Soviet leaders moved from adventurism to capitulationism, and brought disgrace to the Soviet people, the Cuban people, the people of the countries in the socialist camp and the people of the whole world. They have inflicted unprecedented shame and humiliation on the international proletariat. All this has been unalterably written into history. No matter how the Soviet leaders lie or what sleight-of-hand they perform, they can never wash away their shame [*Peking Review*, quoted in Griffith 1964: 384–85].

To this Chinese charge, Khrushchev countercharged that "critics of Soviet Cuban policy . . . were now making the same error as Trotsky at Brest-Litovsk in 1917" (Krushchev quoted in Griffith 1964: 90). Thus, even though they shared similar interpretations of the lessons of Munich and Brest-Litovsk, the two Communist elites used them in significantly divergent ways to draw policy conclusions. This phenomenon suggests one major difficulty in the use of historical precedents alone to explain and predict policy behavior: history allows sufficient latitude so that different precedents are available to justify divergent policy selections.

Conclusions

We have provided several empirical illustrations to support our contention that the recognition, interpretation, and application of historical precedents tend to differ substantially across national elites. These illustrations show that it can be seriously misleading to project one's own notions about events, actions, and strategy onto others. Indeed, we argue on this score that even rigorous academic work that seeks to be politically and culturally neutral can seriously distort the precedent set of foreign elites.

To avoid misunderstanding, we do not contend that reliance on official public sources, especially those of "closed" political systems, ensures that we have a valid grasp of the precedents known to or used by a national elite. These sources may convey intentional manipulations for propaganda purposes or post hoc rationalizations to adjust views and beliefs in accord with decisions or actions already taken by the elite. National security considerations may also suppress discussion of issues of real concern to the elite in public media sources. Nor should we assume homogeneity of elite views or control of press organs by those in charge of foreign policies. The Chinese experience is again informative in this regard. Mao had to go to Shanghai and rely on that city's press (*Wen Hui Pao*) to launch the Cultural Revolution because governmental institutions in Peking, including *People's Daily*, were controlled by his opponents. Similarly, there are sometimes substantial intraelite differences in the use of historical precedents for formulating Chinese foreign policies, such as during the Vietnam war (e.g., Ra'anan 1968; Zagoria 1967). We have no confidence that public media treatment will invariably display these intraelite differences or reflect the views of those actually responsible for the conduct of Chinese foreign policy.

Nevertheless, we do contend that in trying to establish precedents for an inaccessible foreign affairs elite, it is more sensible to rely on sources whose editors and writers are particularly likely to share its perceptual frame of reference. It seems only reasonable to expect that indigenous and official sources are more likely to reveal the views and concerns of the decision makers we seek to understand than are foreign or unofficial sources. In addition to their mass audiences, junior officials and cadres acquire historical precedent sets and learn to apply them to decision making from such official media. Consequently, information from these sources provides a more accurate picture of the definition of past situations by other national elites.

CHAPTER 5

WESTERN PERSPECTIVES AND TENDENCIES

In the preceding chapter, we suggested that national elites differ in their recognition, interpretation, and application of precedents as historical lessons. In this and the following chapter, we move beyond the empirical demonstration of differences in precedent specifics to compare generalized perspectives about the nature of critical international incidents. Under situations of potentially great change in important matters, it is reasonable to expect national elites to supplement specific historical analogies (Kilpatrick 1969) with broad interpretive principles (Holsti and George 1975; Janis 1972). This chapter presents some Western maxims drawn from both the social science literature and the more descriptive, historical literature on international crises. Chapter 6 draws out equally pervasive perspectives from Chinese writings and examines Chinese behavior to determine if expectations generated by the basic perspectives are supported in practice.

The Western literature is voluminous and varied in terms of theory and method. Our intent here is not to provide a complete summary of this literature, assess it from a scientific point of view (for recent reviews and assessments, see Hopple and Rossa 1978; Tanter 1978), or divine signs of change in the basic conceptions in current research (e.g., Tanter 1978; McClelland 1977). Instead, our concern is with identifying widely shared notions that have broad implications for the recognition, diagnosis, and treatment of international incidents. While the two basic perspectives, that of situational decision making (Brecher 1977, 1974; Hermann 1972, 1969, 1963; Robinson 1972, 1962) and that of interaction between political units across nation-state lines (Young 1968; McClelland 1961), differ in numerous respects, they rest on some shared perspectives. And there is some evidence that these fundamental views are also held by at least some pertinent U.S. officials (Lentner 1972). These shared perspectives are identified and their implications discussed below.

1. *International crises are "unusual" situations that trigger exceptional coping mechanisms by political institutions and individual decision makers.* Accordingly, "crisis" foreign relations are treated as different from "normal" foreign relations. And in policy terms, "crises" are seen to require different patterns of information search and policy choice. Yet, paradoxically, quan-

titative analyses frequently use the same indices for crisis and noncrisis periods (for example, quantity of event interaction, number of policy alternatives considered) and measure only differences of degree (e.g., Andriole and Young 1977; Andriole 1976).

2. *International crises are occasions that create stress for the units under analysis, be they the international system, alliances, policy bureaucracies, or individual officials.* Consequently, analysis often focuses on pathologies in decision making, by identifying such correlates of stress as information overload (Holsti and George 1975; Holsti 1972; Milburn 1972). With a few exceptions (e.g., Hermann 1969; Hopmann 1967; Coser 1956), little attention goes to the possibility that crises reduce stress on decision systems by, for example, promoting domestic political unity, inducing alliance cohesion, and focusing high-level attention on a single problem.

3. *Triggered by abrupt or acute changes in the behavior of some foreign nation(s) or external political movement(s), international crises present anomalous, irregular, deviant, low-probability problems for policy treatment.* One corollary is the assumption that the initiation of crises is characterized by, at best, substantial uncertainty and, at worst, surprise. Another is that a high degree of uncertainty operates during all phases of crisis decision making and not just on incident prediction (Young 1975; Hermann 1972, 1969; Nicholson 1972). The logical conclusion of these assumptions is that not only the onset but also the conduct and consequences of crisis cannot be predicted with confidence. In policy terms, the result is an emphasis on the maintenance of a general posture of preparedness and of equipping oneself with alternative capabilities, and a willingness to discard standard patterns of operation in decision making and implementation in favor of ad hoc extemporization.

4. *International crises portend the widespread disturbance of what would otherwise be an ongoing, stable set of international relationships.* This principle of potential, severe destabilization provides one reason not to ignore anomalous, hard-to-predict events. It lends them importance and tight connection with highly valued concerns. The contrary possibility that critical incidents are potentially effective actions to achieve stability in what would otherwise be a chronically unstable situation is almost ruled out prima facie. For example, few analysts have argued that the Soviet Union and China were acting to stabilize the existence of friendly regimes threatened with extinction in the Cuban and Korean crises respectively (Allison 1971; Whiting 1960). Equally little credence goes to arguments that foreign-backed attempts to overthrow weak regimes and divide up their territory may do more to enhance than to reduce order and stability. If crisis incidents have such severe ripple effects, the appropriate policy is to act immediately to reestablish the status quo ante in the region of the incident. The contrary view that international relations are inherently fluid and may easily reverse themselves to redound to one's advantage even without intervention is not given much weight. Similarly, the proposition that intervention will in and of itself increase the likelihood of

future destabilizing events is incompatible with this perspective. This in-compatibility is inevitable given that, as we shall now see, destabilization is often associated with narrower and more self-centered grounds for responding to an international incident.

5. *International crises involve threats posed to one's own interests by some foreign party.* The assumption is frequently made that in international crises, one is being challenged with deprival of something of value (Brecher 1977; McClelland 1977, 1974; Williams 1976). Several implications follow from this assumption. First, if one is not threatened by an international situation, a crisis per se does not exist. Second, others start crises with intentionally hostile aims; one is always the injured or potentially injured party reacting to the initiatives of others. Third, the threat in question is not one of long standing or simply a general property of the nature of contemporary foreign affairs. Instead, it is in some sense specific in focus and isolated in at least the temporal sense. All of these assumptions have important restrictive effects for crisis warning and management.

Thus, emphasis goes to the analysis of the conditions and stimuli external to the nation-state in trying to anticipate, avoid, or manage crises. For example, international crises resulting from insurgency movements (for example, Vietnam, Korea, Cuba, Angola, Bangladesh) are usually perceived as a result of foreign intervention and subversion, and not of the domestic sociopolitical conditions in the countries affected. The linkage between domestic and foreign conflict (e.g., Rummel 1971*a*, 1971*b*; Wilkenfeld 1969; Tanter 1966) is not emphasized in the explanation and prediction of international crises. Similarly, there is little consideration of the degree to which international crises may be precipitated by foreign governments' attempts to exploit the domestic vulnerability of their adversaries (for example, Turkey in the Cypriot crisis, India in the Bangladesh crisis), or initiated by policy elites in order to alleviate their internal economic problem (for example, Pearl Harbor for Japan, the Yom Kippur war for Egypt). The general Western tendency assumes that the foreign policy events initiated by most other governments and political movements are intended for the consumption of the United States and its allies, and not of their own domestic publics or indigenous and regional adversaries. Few analyses examine the domestic considerations involved in crisis recognition and treatment by the United States or by other countries (Bell 1971; Halper 1971). To the extent that domestic factors (for example, public opinion, Congressional sentiment, bureaucratic incentives) are considered (e.g., Steel 1973; Thomson 1973; Ellsberg 1971), they are usually treated as constraints on decision makers attempting to cope with crisis occurrences. The possibility that decision makers are pursuing domestic opportunities or struggling with domestic problems rather than reacting to foreign threats receives short shrift in the classification and interpretation of crisis events. Episodes such as the *Mayaguez, Pueblo*, Gulf of Tonkin, and Bay of Pigs incidents are included in the standard inventories of international crises experienced by the U.S. government, implying that these incidents involved major foreign military threats and U.S. efforts to cope with these threats. Nevertheless, it seems reasonable to suggest that the *Mayaguez* incident, for example, was more a domestic political than a foreign military threat issue for the U.S. decision makers, that the actions taken by the U.S. Government were directed more at the domestic audience than at the foreign audience, and that the Cambodian action presented more an opportunity than a threat to the administration, providing it with a convenient and timely occasion to demonstrate its "toughness" in view of the adverse political reactions to the Communist victory in South Vietnam in both foreign and domestic quarters (particularly among conservative Republicans for a President who had to face a stiff nomination fight in the upcoming election campaign).

The emphasis on threats of foreign origin also tends to induce the view that such threats can be interpreted in terms of the existing bloc organization of international politics. Threats ostensibly are from outside a bloc and directed at all of its members by another bloc. Accordingly, it is expected that these blocs will respond to threats en masse. While this may or may not have been justified with the Warsaw Pact and NATO alliances during the height of cold-war bipolarity (Tanter 1974; McClelland 1972), it can introduce expectations and reactions that may not be warranted for loosely affiliated sets of governments (for example, the Arab League). Concomitantly, it tends to focus planning attention away from crises within blocs ostensibly organized against external threats. And in spite of the destabilizing premise noted earlier, it leads to the slow recognition of the destabilizing consequences of such crises for existing alliances, as illustrated by the effects of the Suez and Cyprus incidents for the NATO countries and the Quemoy crisis of 1958 for the Communist states.

The emphasis on crises as a result of threats from some foreign party to the grouping to which one belongs obviously limits the focus of efforts to anticipate crises. Another sort of bounding follows from the conception of critical international incidents in terms of the geographic arena of action and the instruments of policy. Like incidents in daily life, the prevailing Western conception stipulates that these incidents involve an identifiable hostile initiator, a specific locale, and a particular mode of interaction (for example, cursing, punching). Planning then focuses on a response in the area of the triggering event, and views attempts to shift or add conflict arenas as somehow unwarranted and inappropriate (for example, Khrushchev's demand for the withdrawal of U.S. missiles from Turkey in the Cuban missile crisis, the putative Arab oil embargo against the United States in the context of the 1973 Arab-Israeli war). Also, shifts in the mode of interaction (for example, from military aid to economic sanction) are usually neither planned for nor viewed as the sensible responses of an intelligent adversary. Indeed, the whole Western perspective emphasizes containment and isolation of the incident to the point where jumping or broadening in locale or instrumentality suggests a failure in crisis management. The consequence is that U.S. crisis-management strategy tends to be limited to a narrowly reactive posture, which precludes imaginative efforts to shift either geographic location or policy instruments.[1]

This view of crises as incidents to be isolated from the broader context of global politics by an exercise of statecraft leads to a relative lack of interest in the spillover and contagion effects of particular incidents as they occur or for subsequent learning. There is little in the way of in-depth analysis of how one crisis can induce the occurrence of another (for example, the temporal coincidence of the Sino-Indian war and the Cuban missile crisis, the imitation effect of incidents and outcomes involving international terrorism and national liberation movements). In this sense, Western treatment of critical incidents differs markedly from the attention paid to similar questions for international wars (e.g., Davis et al. 1976; Singer and Small 1972) and military coups (e.g., Li and Thompson 1975; Midlarsky 1970; Putnam 1967).

6. *The earmarks of the onset and continuation of international crises are acts of conflict and violence in general and of military-political threats and activities in particular.* Accordingly, the recognition of approaching crises, the judgment of the consequences of the actions of one's own government and of other key parties, and the storage and recall of "historical lessons" all focus on the increased likelihood and severity of military combat (Hazlewood et al. 1977; Blechman and Kaplan 1975). Yet there are numerous conceivable instances where an increase in detente or cooperative arrangements between governments or the withdrawal from military confrontation may provide occasions for crisis at least from the perspective of some third parties. Examples include the Nixon visit to China for the Japanese, the Portuguese withdrawal from Angola for the Rhodesians and South Africans, the separate Israeli-Egyptian peace agreement for the Syrians and the Palestine Liberation Organization, and a Sino-Soviet rapprochement for the United States. Accordingly, a whole class of events with substantial destabilizing and threatening implications for participants in international politics are for practical purposes excluded from consideration in favor of often minor military episodes (for example, the *Liberty, Pueblo,* and *Mayaguez* incidents) in which U.S. military elements were involved.

Also, warning perspectives and systems tend to concentrate on conflict indicators, especially of imminent military action, and ignore signals of desire to avoid or minimize the criticality of international incidents. Steps such as negotiation proposals, temporary truces, appeals to third-party intermediaries, and restraint in military mobilization and engagement are not as salient as conflict measures, even though governments often engage in mixed sig-

1. Truman's order for the Seventh Fleet to intervene in the Taiwan Straits after the outbreak of the Korean war provides a possible exception. However, it may be reasonably argued that Truman was more concerned with the prevention of further Communist attacks in a different theater than the retaliation against the North Korean attack by damaging the interests of China qua sponsor.

naling as they try to sidestep and limit international incidents with escalatory potential.

The emphasis on military-political relations between governments is not surprising, given the preoccupation to contain incidents within one set of policy instruments and the experience of manifest threats to the United States prior to 1973. Other precipitants of international crises, such as resource competition (e.g., Choucri and North 1975), trade embargo (e.g., Sathre 1978; Russett 1969), and socioeconomic deprivation (e.g., Bobrow 1968), are thought to be secondary in importance. As a result, the policy measures and institutions for avoiding and managing crises are primarily ones of a military-political nature. To respond to actual or imminent international crises triggered by insurgency movements (for example, Vietnam, Laos, Cuba), local political disturbances (for example, Lebanon, the Dominican Republic), or secessionist activity (for example, Zaïre), the primary focus is on the use of force either for its direct physical effect or as the prime tool of coercive diplomacy (George et al. 1971). Such military measures are held to promise "quick fixes" in contrast to the cumbersome and slow instruments available to deal with the contributing socioeconomic issues. And as the observers of bureaucratic politics would suggest, reliance on military institutions and instruments tends to drive out or lower the probability of alternative conceptions. The military institutions become the prime focus for the analysis, anticipation, and response planning of critical international incidents, and tend to emphasize their own domain of expertise. And high officials faced with crises turn to those who supposedly are assigned and prepared to deal with them (Bobrow and Kudrle 1976).

7. *International crises are incidents that last for only a short length of time.* The short-lived nature of international crises obviously supports and is supported by the previous elements in our discussion. Incidents must be short-lived if they are really to be deviations from the flow of long-term processes in international political-economic affairs. If they are over quickly, military-political measures seem the only ones available, since other forms of policy cannot impact immediately. Perhaps most important, the fleeting nature of the decision situation lends itself to "now or never" formulations that stress the dangerous consequences of inaction or delayed action. All the opportunity cost lies with waiting, since the situation will not dissolve or become benign but may instead break through its boundaries. Given the emphasis on threats from others, urgency and time-sensitivity are usually addressed in terms of the need to react to possible new situations created by the actions of other governments before they can only be reversed with major war. Examples of such pressures to act quickly include the possibility that the North Korean attack could overrun the entire peninsula in the initial days of the Korean war, that Soviet missiles could become operational in the Cuban missile crisis, or that the Egyptian army would collapse in the 1973 Arab-Israeli war, resulting in Soviet intervention. In other words, time pressure tends to be treated only in terms of

its relevance for denying opportunities to the adversaries of the United States; it is almost never discussed in the context of seizing opportunities to launch policies that the United States was already predisposed to undertake (for example, the *Mayaguez* incident, the Gulf of Tonkin incident, the endorsement by the United Nations for the Korean intervention while the Soviet Union was boycotting its meetings). The latter possibility is, of course, quite incompatible with the conventional view of crisis decision making as reactions to cope with major and unanticipated foreign threats that destabilize the international status quo.

Conclusions

The views we have summarized are understandable for a national elite that prefers to think of itself, and the nation for which it is responsible, along the lines that have marked the American self-image during much of the time since World War II. The image is of a nation that prefers a tranquil international environment, which allows business as usual, and yet possesses the will and capacity to deal decisively with those who would prevent or interfere with the global access of its public or private sector (Huntington 1973). It is also a self-image of heroism as in some sense rising bravely to occasions rather than engaging in tedious planning and institutional readiness to anticipate them. If one views oneself as benign, then disruptions can only come because someone else is hostile, unless one accepts the possibility of inherent conflicts of interest. Obviously, the latter possibility eliminates the possibility that the United States is in some automatic sense "on the side of the gods." The emphasis on military instruments and events fits well with classic American "ideal" norms about the role of central government and the unfettered operation of the private sector, and can readily be interpreted in the defensive mode that occurs throughout the policy conception we presented. Obviously, an emphasis on military options also has attractions for the possessor of unquestioned military superiority and for a national elite that sees no apparent foreign economic threats.

Our presentation of these views deals with a cognitive frame of reference. It is not concerned with their historical accuracy as descriptions of what U.S. officials have thought or necessarily done. Nor are we making a judgment about the quality of the practical and moral consequences of these views. We do not assume that they have been instrumental in creating particular desirable or undesirable states of international affairs in the postwar period. However, we do believe that unawareness about their influence and unwarranted assumptions about their cross-national applicability can result in a serious lack of realism. We also believe that the visible and ongoing changes in the distribution of military capability in the world and the growth of economic interdependence deprive these views of much of whatever positive import for policy they may have once had.

CHAPTER 6

CHINESE PERSPECTIVES AND TENDENCIES

We now turn to Chinese perspectives on critical international incidents. The analysis we report in this chapter is inductive and largely qualitative. It does generate expectations—hypotheses, if you will—some of which are subjected to more rigorous tests in part IV of this volume. And as promised in chapter 1, we shall use several methods and forms of evidence. We first report a qualitative content analysis of a variety of Chinese documents, consisting of political, military, and cultural materials. While most are composed of what were originally public Chinese documents, we have also used a number of documents with restricted access in China (Chen 1969; Mao 1969; Cheng 1966). As a partial control for overrepresentation of the views of particular agencies, leading spokesmen, or policy epochs, we have made a conscious attempt to examine texts produced by different institutions and individuals during widely separated points in time. In order to provide partial confirmation of our inferences from qualitative textual analysis, we then report a semantic analysis of referents used by recent Mainland refugees and a Hong Kong Chinese control group, and conclude the chapter with an interpretive examination of Chinese behavior in some major cases of international tension.

Apparent Doctrine

To understand Chinese beliefs about critical international incidents in particular and foreign affairs in general, we must come to grips with the nature of the authorized belief system. While we defer extended discussion of the major elements of that system to subsequent chapters, we must face some of its basic properties now. Chinese doctrine emphasizes dialectical reasoning about all problems. El Guindi and Selby (1976) have addressed the nature of such thinking in other societies in ways applicable to the Chinese case. They stress the need to be able to adapt to novel situations and yet make decisions, calling the first requirement dialectical tension and the second, decidability. In the most simple formulation of a dialectical system, decidability is handled by dichotomy. A person simply has to choose whether an event falls into a defined category *(P)* or does not do so *($\sim P$)*. Other possibilities are excluded. The possibilities for making complex choices and having alternatives that enable flexible judgments suffer as a result of decidability. These can be provided only

54

by allowing individuals to move between the two supposedly exclusive categories or to refrain from committing to one or another categorical interpretation. If this sort of hedging and compromise becomes the rule rather than the exception, the categorical distinctions of simple dialectical reasoning fall into disuse, making decisions about events and actors increasingly difficult.

All belief systems need to provide both flexibility and rigidity in the sense of simple choices. They do so by containing open as well as closed concepts.

> [Closed concepts] . . . are "rigidly defined sets of logical (symbolic) statements about the relationships between coded aspects of the real and symbolic world. They are deterministic statements that do not allow contingency. They are algorithmic in nature; that is, they yield determined solutions for appropriate inputs" (El Guindi 1972: 81). When a concept is closed, it displays a high degree of decidability. Informants do not hesitate to classify an event if it can be assigned (in a given context) to a closed concept. In Zapotec, for example, an event is either "field" or it is "not field" in most contexts. "Closed concepts," El Guindi (1972: 55) goes on to suggest, "are associated with a complex ideology, relative inflexibility, and a high degree of sociological differentiation. Conversely . . . open concepts are associated with a less complex ideology, relative flexibility, and weak or neutral affective relations. *Closed concepts are mediated by open concepts.*"
>
> However much closed concepts provide fixity and ideological richness to the system, their rigidity and high level of definition have the disadvantage of discouraging two kinds of events: (1) handling novel inputs, and (2) permitting subjects to "move around" in their own belief system. Open concepts are important for both reasons. Because open concepts (in a given context) are comparatively ill defined, they "pose" great problems of decidability; at the same time, however, they can encode novel phenomena. The openness of concepts permits change and adaptability. . . .
>
> If all were decidable and fixed, the novel inputs could not be entertained. This, in turn, would render belief systems extremely fragile and undefended against infrastructural changes. However, it would certainly permit rapid, efficient assessments of states of affairs, and would therefore minimize . . . ambiguity. In the structural semantic sense the system would be a global paradigm: it would have clear distinctive features, easy access, rapid processing time, with the added feature of core memory requirements approximately the size of Nova Scotia. A hypothetical system in which all the concepts had the property of openness, on the other hand, would pose endless problems of decidability. A subject would never know the structural assignment of any event in the system, and the system would serve little or no interpretive function [El Guindi and Selby 1976: 183–85].

The Chinese belief system resembles others in that it provides both open and closed elements, and thus offers to its adherents some capacity for decidability and flexibility. The commitment to dialectical reasoning leads to a particular form for each type of element. The difference in the forms is not that they contain and assume the existence of opposites. Rules, maxims, and decision logics all employ terms from the poles of a continuum, whether they are closed or open in the terminology just used. Instead, the difference lies in the relationships between the poles on the continuum. For closed elements, the poles are mutually exclusive and cannot be applied simultaneously to an event, situation, or actor. Decidability benefits by the enjoinder to place an event, situation, or actor at one and only one point on some dimension of interpretation. For open elements, the poles, while representing opposites, are not mutually exclusive and can be applied simultaneously. They call on users of the belief system to combine rather than to choose some exclusive category (for example, be "both red and expert"). Open elements in the Chinese belief system often take the form of what we call bimodalities—that is, of rules and maxims whose key terms are opposites to be applied concurrently. The injunction to combine several opposed positions on a dimension of interpretation produces the dialectical tension discussed by El Guindi and Selby and offers a wide range of possibilities, thus providing flexibility. Yet it raises problems of decidability, since rather than simplifying choice it compounds the number and complexity of alternatives. As we shall now see, the Chinese conceptions of international conflicts and their management follow in a doctrinal sense both from some of the "closed" and some of the "open" bimodal elements in their belief system. (We will explore these elements at greater length and provide substantiation in part III.)

Some pertinent closed elements of the orthodox Chinese Communist world view are as follow:

1. The basic and universal trait of actor relationships is that of "contradiction"; in international relations, "nonantagonistic contradictions" (that is, cooperation) are relative, conditional, and temporary, while "antagonistic contradictions" (that is, conflict) are absolute, basic, and protracted.
2. The "resolution of antagonistic contradictions" (the outcome of competition among actors) is arrived at through "struggle" (coercion) among the relevant actors; however, this resolution is always temporary and unstable.
3. The "resolution of antagonistic contradictions" is determined by the relative capability of the actors ("political power grows out of the barrel of a gun").
4. The behavior of actors is influenced by their economic characteristics; for governments, their foreign policy is determined by their domestic economic and political conditions.
5. The nature of actor relationships is constantly changing; friendly relations can become hostile and strong actors can become weak.
6. "Quantitative changes" (incremental changes in actor attributes) can over time lead to "qualitative changes" (step-level leaps); the occurrence of a "qualitative change" indicates that a structural transformation in actor relationships has taken place.

7. So long as they can grasp correctly and act in accordance with the laws of social development as embodied in the writings of Marx, Engels, Lenin, Stalin, and Mao, Communist actors will be successful change agents.

Some open elements particularly relevant for dealing with situations that U.S. analysts may well consider international crises are as follow:

1. Decision makers should be both bold and cautious, attending to the opportunities as well as the threats presented by the situation.
2. They should be both resolute and flexible, and engage in the controlled use of confrontation as well as compromise tactics.
3. They should be both persistent and decisive, and pursue protracted struggle with the enemy as well as dealing swift blows when circumstances permit.
4. They should be both confident and vigilant, and ready to repulse surprise attacks as well as to anticipate them.

Obviously, these injunctions stress simultaneous attention to alternative policy stances. We call them "bimodal maxims" and will discuss them in more detail as they apply to international crises later in this chapter.

On the bases provided by these closed and open beliefs, it is hardly surprising that the Chinese doctrinal conception of critical international incidents differs substantially from the mainstream of Western discussion. We summarize the basic precepts for the Chinese in juxtaposition to the Western views introduced in the previous chapter in table 6-1.

Chinese doctrine presents the relations between nations as inherently unstable and crisis-prone. Parties have basically incompatible interests, and none voluntarily accommodates the interests of another. International relations consist of zero-sum competition temporarily masked by the use of conciliatory tactics pending an opportune moment to resume conflict. Cooperative arrangements between actors are temporary and conditional; differences in their interests are protracted and fundamental. Accordingly, international crises are seen merely as intensifications of the existing tension between actors, and not as aberrations from the norm of international relations. Rather, detente measures and friendly relations are departures from the routine. The U.S. notion of crises as inherently system-destabilizing events is not shared. Nor do the Chinese agree about the undesirability of such "disturbances" in international relations. In the words of Chou En-lai,

> the present international situation is one characterized by great disorder on the earth. . . . Such great disorder is a good thing for the people, not a bad thing. It throws the enemies into confusion and causes division among them, while it arouses and tempers the people, thus helping the international situation develop further in the direction favorable to the people and unfavorable to imperialism, modern revisionism, and all reaction [Chou 1973: 22].

TABLE 6-1
CRITICAL INTERNATIONAL INCIDENTS: DIVERSE BASIC BELIEFS

Standard Western Views	Standard Chinese Views
1. Trigger exceptional coping mechanisms by political institutions and individual decision makers.	1. Differ only in the level and intensity of actions and signals.
2. Create stress for the international system, alliances, policy bureaucracies, and individual officials.	2. Provide opportunities to advance one's interests as well as stresses and dangers.
3. Result from abrupt or acute changes in the behavior of some foreign nation or external political movement, and present anomalous, irregular, deviant, low-probability problems for policy treatment.	3. Result from long-term economic processes and predictably reflect the normally competitive and antagonistic nature of international relations.
4. Portend the widespread disturbance of what would otherwise be an ongoing, stable set of international relationships.	4. Characterize the inherently unstable, fragile, turbulent, and perpetually changing nature of international relations.
5. Involve threats posed to one's own interests by some foreign party.	5. Stem primarily from domestic, not foreign phenomena (at least in initial stage).
6. Consist of acts of conflict and violence and of military-political threats and actions in particular.	6. Entail the controlled use of confrontation and compromise, and centrally involve economic problems and solutions (military-political matters are only their concomitants or consequences).
7. Have a very short life.	7. Extend over a long time; dealing with such protracted phenomena requires persistent struggle, perseverance, and patience.

Crises are inevitable and recurrent, and therefore they can be anticipated and planned for. After all, international crises are consequences of long-term economic forces. Contrary to the U.S. emphasis on the isolated, short-term crises, such incidents are part of the flow of long-term processes. Crises do not lend themselves to immediate resolution; instead, conflict settlement requires "protracted struggle." Because crises are not resolved once and for all, it is imperative to maintain constant vigilance. Thus, Mao warned that

> the imperialists and domestic reactionaries will certainly not take their defeat lying down and they will struggle to the last ditch. After there is peace and order throughout the country, they will still engage in sabotage and create disturbances in various ways and will try every day and every minute to stage a comeback. This is inevitable and beyond all doubt, and under no circumstances must we relax our vigilance [Mao quoted in Schram 1967: 9].

The concept of crisis applies most consistently to economic phenomena (e.g., Political Education Section 1975; Ke 1975; Writing Team 1974; People's Publishing House Editorial Staff 1974). Political and military crises are consequences or concomitants of economic crises. Regardless of the nature of the political system, the occurrence of crisis is inevitable. Crises reflect the naturally existing "contradictions" in every political system; they are as possible in "progressive" systems as in "reactionary" systems. However, crises in "progressive" systems are only temporary "difficulties," while crises in "reactionary" systems are insoluble within the structures of these systems. Consequently, crises in "reactionary" systems are likely to increase in frequency and severity. For instance, one Chinese analyst commented:

> So-called "Keynesianism" is the product of the great capitalist crisis of the 1930's. After the Second World War, the monopoly capitalist class of every important capitalist nation, panicking in the face of frequently occurring crises, looked upon Keynesianism, especially inflationary policy, as a miracle drug to rescue capitalism. However, now the monopoly capitalist class is like the sorcerer who cannot control the evil spirit called out by the amulet he has used. This inflation is increasingly threatening every major capitalist nation. Especially going into the 1970's, inflation is like an unbridled mustang thrashing about. The quickness of its pace, the broadness of its scope, and the severity of conditions are all occurrences seldom seen in history [Ke 1975: 99].

Another analyst provided the same sort of appraisal:

> The sharp contradictions between the relations of production and the production forces have plunged capital-imperialism and social-imperialism into hopeless political and economic crises. The "dollar empire," as the United States once was called, is today shaken to its foundation with economic crises occurring frequently, financial crises growing ever more serious, balance of payments in the red year after year and the storms of dollar crisis erupting repeatedly. Different crises have intertwined to bedevil the U.S. economy, which finds no solutions in sight [Chang 1973: 6].

Economic crises, if not managed properly, can lead to political crises. The Chinese quote Engels to the effect that "crisis is a most powerful lever for political change" (Ke 1975: 102). In "progressive" systems, indications of a developing political crisis include an increase in "ideological problems," such as a deterioration of social discipline, an increased incidence of complaints against the regime, and a reduction in the organizational effectiveness of governmental institutions. In "reactionary" systems, political instability becomes manifest through increased opposition to the regime (for example, labor unrest, farmers' protests, political demonstrations). The "reactionary" regime responds by escalating its repressive measures (for example, press censorship, police brutality, martial law). Also it makes a greater effort to preserve the interests and positions of the capitalist elite (for example, through deficit spending, erecting import tariffs, expanding military-related industrial production). Although these efforts by the "reactionaries" may damp the critical incident in the short run, eventually they will only aggravate the crisis in the long term. For instance, increased military spending (for example, developing new weapons systems, waging foreign wars, stationing troops abroad) fuels domestic inflation and contributes to international tension (for example, competition for overseas markets, monetary instability, trade deficits, arms race). Thus, the writers of *International Knowledge* argue that "the results of the policies of war and aggression carried out by United States imperialism have been the creation of severe monetary, financial and economic crises" (People's Publishing House Editorial Staff 1972: 126).

Domestic economic and political crises can impact on foreign crises in two ways. First, domestic "difficulties" in "progressive" systems are interpreted by "reactionaries" as signs of weakness. Hence, they encourage belligerence on their part to exploit the perceived vulnerability. For example, Chinese Foreign Minister Chen Yi warned of a possible U.S.-backed Nationalist invasion of the Mainland in the early 1960s as a result of China's economic problems:

> The first possibility is [for the Americans] to create an incident in the Taiwan Straits. Thinking particularly that the Chinese economic situation is difficult they may attempt to have Chiang Kai-shek land on the mainland and start a civil war.... On the one hand we must overcome the economic difficulties due to the three years of natural calamities and, on the other provide against the provocations of Chiang Kai-shek supported by America. Also we must provide against incidents that may occur on other borders . . . [Chen quoted in Whiting 1975a: 63–64].

Second, in their attempts to ameliorate domestic crises, the "reactionaries" often initiate foreign expansion to find new markets for their products and new sources of raw materials for their industries. Foreign expansion leads to increased conflict between capitalist societies and between them and exploited societies. Such conflict in turn exacerbates domestic problems in capitalist societies, thus creating a spiraling feedback system of internal instability and external aggression (Fu 1973). Devoid of the wisdom acquired by the Chinese Communists (that is, Marxism-Leninism and the thought of Mao Tse-tung), the "reactionaries" cannot understand and manage such problems. Consequently, short of revolutionary changes, the "reactionary" systems will not escape from this cycle of domestic and foreign crises. The crises stem from the "contradictions" inherent in those systems. In the words of Mao: "There are difficulties confronting us and there are also difficulties confronting the reactionary forces. But the difficulties confronting the reactionary forces cannot be overcome, because they are nearing death and are without a future. Our difficulties can be overcome because we are a new force with a bright future" (Cheng 1966: 152).

Figure 6-1 shows the Chinese conception of the structure of crises in "reactionary" systems. Chinese views on the dynamics of international crises resemble in major ways those of Nazli Choucri and Robert North (1975, 1972). To oversimplify the Choucri-North argument, conditions internal to a nation-state (for example, population growth, technological development, natural-resource requirements) primarily determine its foreign policy. When changes in these domestic conditions cannot be coped with effectively by internal mechanisms, there will be "lateral pressure" for foreign expansion. In the long run, such expansion is likely to produce international conflict. Both the Choucri-North conception and Chinese doctrine attach only minor importance to the influence of individual decision makers or decision-making institutions in the occurrence and development of resultant international crises. "The national leader or policy-maker will remain seriously boxed in—caught in the interstices of the larger international system and its subsystems (including wide sectors within his own country)" (Choucri and North 1972: 113). Accordingly, the factors responsible for crises and their aftermath cannot be readily manipulated by decision makers, at least not through ad hoc

FIGURE 6-1
CHINESE VIEW OF CRISES IN REACTIONARY SYSTEMS

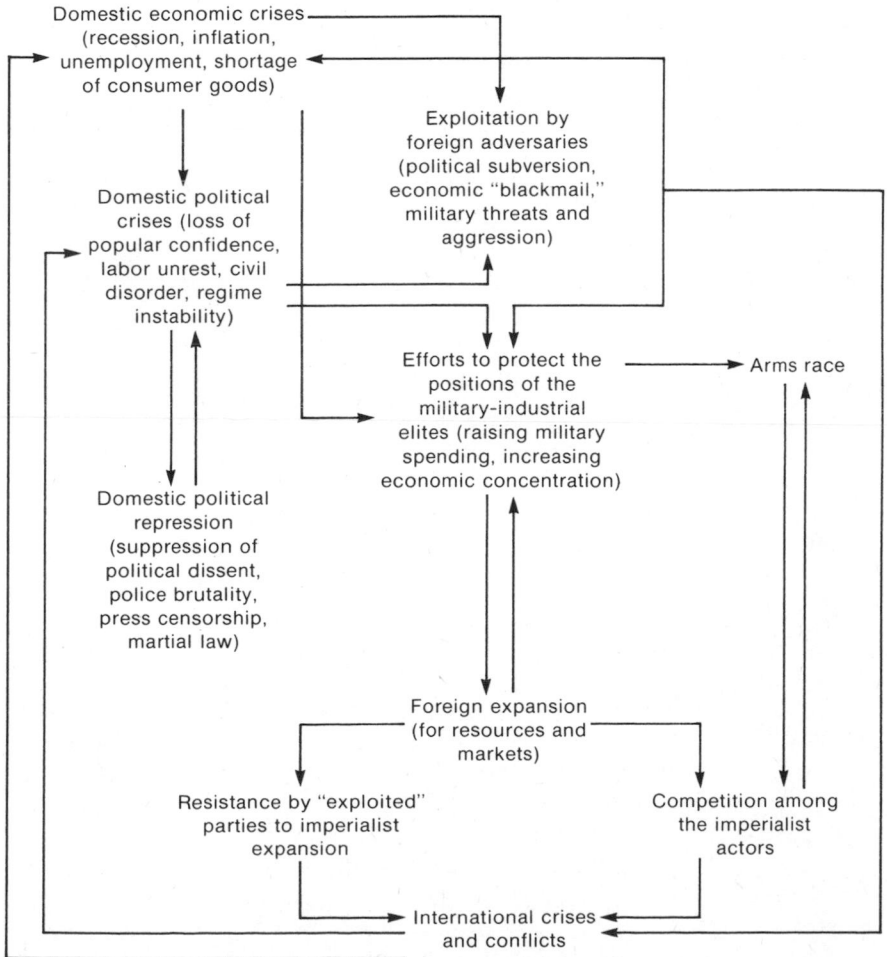

"quick fixes" to subdue crises after their occurrence. Actor capabilities are important considerations for Choucri and North, as are gaps between resource demand and supply. Competition for foreign raw materials, markets for finished products, and investment opportunities often lead to arms races between the expanding powers. This contest to develop and demonstrate military strength in turn increases the probability of military clashes.

Chinese doctrine also attaches importance to the relative capability of actors. Crises are more likely when the contestants achieve an approximate parity in their strength (that is, when the inferior party achieves a "qualitative leap" in capability). Under these circumstances, the superior party is likely to take extreme measures to avert any change in the favorable status quo, while the inferior party is likely to take greater risks to improve its position. Accordingly, parity in national power promotes rather than deters international conflict. Parenthetically, this maxim challenges the traditional view of the effects of balance-of-power systems in the U.S. literature (e.g., Kaplan 1957; Morgenthau 1948), and agrees with analysts (e.g., Claude 1962; Organski 1953) who have observed that, historically, wars are more likely when the capability gap between antagonistic nations becomes narrow than when one side has predominance.

Chinese rhetoric contends that domestic economic and political problems and relative military capabilities (in balance and imbalance terms) are the major predictors of critical international incidents. We infer that the Chinese will emphasize control or encapsulation of their own domestic crises (for example, the economic setback resulting from the Great Leap Forward Campaign, the recurrent elite conflict over leadership succession) to avoid their being exploited by China's foreign adversaries. We also expect them to monitor closely economic and political conditions in countries that are the "significant others" to them (for example, the United States, the Soviet Union, Japan). Domestic crises—whether in China or in the "reactionary" countries —make salient potential foreign threat. Thus, domestic crises in China entice imperialist aggressors to exploit China's vulnerability, while domestic crises in "reactionary" countries prompt their elites to undertake foreign "adventures" to alleviate internal tension.

Because domestic crises in "reactionary" systems indicate a decline in their power, the Chinese view them as opportunities. Domestic crises in opposed nations convey the possibility of revolutionary change. The Chinese are likely to respond with increased support for antiregime groups. Also, the Chinese expect that domestic pressures will induce "reactionaries" to intensify their foreign exploitation, thus alienating intermediate actors traditionally committed neither to the Chinese nor to their adversaries. Chinese efforts to mobilize broad-based coalitions with third-party states (for example, the Third World countries) to oppose the "reactionaries" will consequently benefit.

The Chinese assessment of a favorable shift in the balance of power has a bimodal quality. On the one hand, improvement in the capability of the "progressive" systems (for example, the East-Wind-Prevails-over-the-West-Wind debate) provides an opportunity to "get tough" with the "reactionaries." On the other hand, such changes imply potential "trouble," because the "reactionaries" will not tolerate them and will redouble their attempts—to the point of risking wars—to preserve their superior status. Consequently, decision making under these circumstances calls for both "caution" and "boldness."

Chinese documents (e.g., Cheng 1966) also suggest some general principles for crisis management. We will summarize them briefly and then turn to the "open," heuristic beliefs that govern how they are applied to situations that pose problems of threat, short decision time, and possible surprise.

1. Prepare for crises in advance through developed contingency plans. "All comrades of our Party should fully estimate and be prepared to use an invincible will to overcome all difficulties by following a well-mapped-out plan" (Mao quoted in Cheng 1966: 152).
2. Face openly the existence of crises when they occur and their possible and actual negative implication. Concealment only impedes effective crisis management. Thus, "difficulties are facts and we have to admit as many as there are, and we cannot adopt the 'doctrine of non-recognition.' We must admit difficulties, analyze difficulties, and struggle against difficulties" (Mao quoted in Cheng 1966: 151).
3. Mount vigorous "educational" campaigns to deal with the increased incidence of "ideological problems" in one's own population, policy institutions, and military.
4. Modify one's own posture to adapt to the crisis and limit its negative consequences through resource reallocation, organizational restructuring, and personnel changes.
5. Devote special attention to economic factors, which ultimately determine the capacity to deal with crises.
6. Increase the activity and effectiveness of coercive institutions—the military and the public security forces—to cope with attempts by internal and external "reactionaries" to exploit China's difficulties.

In sum, the management precepts stress mental readiness for the occurrence of crises as inevitable, specific plans for particular possible incidents, and the strengthening of the domestic economic and political fabric to cope with unwanted situations and shape their consequences.

Obviously, these maxims are open to numerous interpretations and leave many decisions unclear. They become transformed into practical, concrete steps through the use of heuristics to cope with particular situations. The heuristics provided by the Chinese belief system as presented in doctrinal materials emphasize the bimodal maxims to which we referred earlier. The importance and rich implications of these maxims for dealing with serious situations suggest that we now explore them at greater length.

Four bimodal attitude pairs are particularly pertinent to Chinese decision making about critical international incidents, and about how they deal with situations Western analysts would characterize in terms of high threat, short decision time, and significant surprise (Bobrow 1969*b*).

1. *Optimism-Pessimism.*   Communists should be completely confident about their eventual success and the correctness of their ideological axioms, but they should be completely skeptical about immediate success and their ability to apply these axioms.
2. *Boldness-Caution.*   Communists should be unafraid of taking on all opponents in terms of their ultimate goals, but they should be extremely cautious in specific encounters with the enemy.
3. *Rigidity-Flexibility.*   Communists should be completely uncompromising about their principles and ultimate goals, but they should be completely flexible in specific situations.
4. *Emotional Arousal–Analytic Distance.*   Communists should be emotionally aroused about long-term goals and the righteousness of their cause, but they should be completely objective in analyzing specific problems.

These bimodal maxims help decision makers to cope with the stress and uncertainties resulting from the short response time, high threat perception, and inadequate mental preparation in a crisis situation. One member of each pair operates against tendencies for decision makers to become more pessimistic about their ability to control events, more willing to take risks, more inclined to hold on to rigid policy positions, and more affected by personal emotions in crisis situations.

Among these attitude pairs, the optimism-pessimism bimodality serves as the most important device for coping with these "pathologies." The optimism component stresses the inevitable vindication of the Communist cause, and consequently reduces psychological stress resulting from the inherent uncertainties of the situation. First, confidence rests on the unique wisdom of Marxism-Leninism and the thought of Mao Tse-tung, and the tenet that history works inexorably in favor of the Communist cause. Decision makers are helped then to interpret current foreign threats and policy setbacks as temporary difficulties. The expectation of Communist victory in the long run reduces time pressure. Crisis occasions are less likely to be perceived as "now or never" situations, since the opportunity costs of inaction or delayed action affect only the time schedule and not the outcome of eventual Communist success. Also, the relatively extended time horizon the Chinese leaders use in evaluating policy problems mitigates against hasty actions designed for immediate policy gratification. It leads instead to an emphasis on "protracted struggle."

Second, as we will see in more detail in chapter 9, the Chinese logics for information assessment and policy choice stress that every phenomenon has good and bad aspects. Situations are never all good or all bad. Threat and opportunity are not mutually exclusive categories for evaluating crises. The Chinese perceive that international crises among "reactionary" systems indicate not only the danger of foreign aggression but also the fundamental weakness and instability of these systems. Furthermore, even if the results of a crisis are totally negative from China's perspective, it can serve as a negative example or lesson. Given the Chinese view of perpetual changes in actor relationships and capabilities, negative consequences are never irreversible. If they correctly apply their ideological axioms, Communists are assured of eventual success in overcoming temporary inferiority.

Third, the danger attributed to current internal and external threats is limited by comparing past difficulties with present difficulties. Positive thinking takes this syllogistic form: (1) we have faced formidable difficulties in the past and have overcome these difficulties; (2) current difficulties are less severe than past difficulties; and (3) therefore, we can overcome the current difficulties. The revolutionary experience of the Chinese Communist Party is frequently cited to damp "panic" and "defeatism." In addition to controlling threat perception, this syllogistic reasoning supports a positive assessment of bold options. Western astonishment at seemingly "irrational" Chinese gambles (for example, the intervention in the Korean war, the Cultural Revolution) may in part be a result of the failure to grasp the Chinese frame of reference, especially with regard to the tremendous odds that they feel they have successfully overcome in their domestic revolutionary experience (for example, the Long March).

Confidence in eventual Communist victory is balanced by pessimism about immediate success. The pessimism component of the optimism-pessimism bimodality stresses the inevitability of setbacks and mental preparation for them. This component is based on the belief that the "reactionary" actors are inherently aggressive and will not give up their struggle easily. It also reflects awareness of China's military vulnerability. Accordingly, the elite repeatedly urges the Chinese people to prepare for adversities. They urge mental preparation for surprise enemy attacks. Constant vigilance must be maintained against "reactionaries," who are inherently aggressive and basically irrational in chronically underestimating China's capabilities. The image of "reactionaries" as "madmen" prone to risk wars leads to visible planning for "worst case" contingencies, such as nuclear war. Thus, Mao argued that "one must hope for peace in the world, but must prepare for the worst, for the most disastrous events; we came from Yenan, and we must be prepared to return to Yenan" (Mao 1969: 74). However, alarmist warnings are not accurate reflections of elite views about the desirability or inevitability of events; they do indicate efforts to prepare the nation psychologically for possible "setbacks" (Bobrow 1969*b*). Stress on the inevitability of "setbacks" on the road to eventual Communist victory provides the rationale for "protracted struggle." Communists should never expect easy and quick successes and should instead wage persistent struggle against the enemy over an extended period of time. Accordingly, Chinese cadres are told that "we must be prepared to walk along a winding road and we should not expect to pick up something cheap" (Cheng 1966: 151–52). Peking's mass-persuasion strategy attempts to convey that (1) the threat of imperialist aggression is formidable, but not so formidable as to make efforts to resist it hopeless; (2) the danger of imperialist aggression is ever present but can be deterred by effective preparation; and (3) the defeat of imperialists is inevitable but it can only be achieved through arduous struggle. In order to generate the necessary mass commitment and sacrifice, Peking stresses emotional arousal in its propaganda.

Emotional arousal does not, however, negate the need for analytic distance. Here the pessimism component again comes into play. Pessimism operates against "blind optimism" by enjoining analysts to be highly skeptical about their ability to apply the Communist axioms correctly. By promoting objectivity and humility, it encourages analysts to reckon realistically with policy constraints. It also reinforces the cautionary aspect of the boldness-caution bimodality (despise the enemy strategically, but respect him tactically). Further, pessimism about the chances of immediate Communist victory legitimates the pursuit of temporary compromises with secondary enemies ("unite all those who can be united to oppose the main enemy"), thus reinforcing the flexibility aspect of the rigidity-flexibility bimodality. And, as a result of their pessimism about avoiding crises, Chinese leaders place a high premium on contingency planning. Advance planning facilitates swift responses to enemy actions and reduces the time pressure on decision makers. As we will argue later, Peking's behavior in past military conflicts tends to suggest the existence of carefully mapped-out contingency plans. To the extent that this characterization is valid, short response time applies only to the Chinese search for information regarding enemy actions and tactical intentions on the basis of which preplanned responses will be activated; it does not apply to the Chinese search for policy alternatives.

The boldness component of the boldness-caution maxim also helps to deal with stress from perceived threat. Communists should be willing to take on all opponents—"be afraid of nothing" (as manifested in bellicose statements). The extended isolation experienced by the Chinese Communist Party both before and after its domestic victory reinforces this attitude. Coupled with the optimism orientation discussed earlier, an emphasis results on "self-reliance" in domestic as well as foreign policies. Boldness also helps to meet the need for quick decisions. As we shall see in chapter 8, Chinese descriptions of an ideal Communist actor include the attribute of decisiveness.

Bold decision making does not, however, obviate the need for caution in particular circumstances. Chinese decision makers are enjoined to avoid "recklessness" (for example, fighting with two fists in two directions simultaneously") and to pursue "united front" tactics in order to isolate the enemy. The cautionary element leads to an emphasis on engaging in military confrontations with superior adversaries only under carefully controlled conditions, and on choosing the "incidental" aspects of these confrontations (for example, time, place, target, and nature of the confrontations) to enhance Peking's ability to control the evolution of the conflict (Bobrow 1965).

Finally, the rigidity-flexibility maxim provides yet another device for coping with external threat. The rigidity element supports "standing firm" against imperialist threats; compromises with imperialists will only increase their appetite and encourage further aggression on their part. Inferior parties (including China) cannot hope to advance their cause except through resolute struggle against the superior parties. As a result, the rigidity element indicates the need for defiance and perseverance even under extremely adverse conditions. On the other hand, the flexibility element supports eclectic opportunism in the choice of tactical maneuvers for specific encounters with the enemy. It legitimates the use of various detente measures for controlling and avoiding conflict escalation, including measures of "temporary truce" and "partial agreement" to reduce the immediate threats of imperialist aggression.

We shall turn later in this chapter to historical instances of Chinese behavior to clarify the implications of the doctrinal precepts just discussed. For now, several broader implications should be kept in mind. The bimodal maxims are appropriate to rather complex and diverse patterns of behavior. For example, they are conducive to belligerent statements supporting national liberation movements (the boldness element) and simultaneously limited physical involvement in Chinese support to these movements (the caution element). The first element in each maxim has particular import for broad, long-run Chinese foreign policy "strategies"; the second, for "tactical" decisions about immediate actions in specific situations. As heuristics, the maxims enjoin decision makers to blend the two sets of considerations to meet the particular realities confronting them. The second element in each maxim also serves to lessen the fragility of the belief system in that it encompasses and provides a way of dealing with policy failures and visible disparities between hopes and realities. Because these incongruities can be accommodated by the belief system, their occurrence does not argue for a basic structural change in the belief system. Finally, the paradoxes inherent in these maxims mean that they do not provide automatic answers to Chinese decision-making problems raised by international crises. They are guides to decision makers that can be used to illuminate consideration of situations and policy alternatives. They leave open questions such as the proper mix of values, the position of actions on the continuum reflected in each maxim, and the most appropriate measure for dealing with particular anticipated or actual critical incidents. They thus allow for and indeed are conducive to elite policy debates centered on different views about the relative emphasis on the polar elements in each maxim.

Semantic Evidence

The Chinese doctrine we infer from their documents presents a conception of the sources, likelihood, and management of international crises substantially different from mainstream Western views. We now introduce some semantic evidence that buttresses our confidence in the validity of our inferences about Chinese views (Kringen 1978). Are the beliefs and logics manifest in officially authorized texts held in fact by individual Chinese?

Having no access to Chinese leaders, we have to pursue the question on the basis of responses provided by a nonelite population. As a result of the Peking government's intense political socialization efforts, we view recent political refugees from the Mainland as useful informants about the cognitive—as opposed to the affective—content of elite beliefs. Since these refugees represent a rather biased sample of the Mainland population (as indicated by the very fact that they chose to leave the Mainland), correspondence between their views and those views indicated in the official media will lend greater credibility to our documentary inferences. In this regard, the political "deviancy" of the refugees provides a relatively strong rather than weak test of the official Chinese conception of crises presented earlier.

Language and environment, as well as socialization, shape people's beliefs. For this reason, we compare responses of Mainland refugees with those of Hong Kong Chinese. Since these two groups of subjects share the same language and living environment, the differences in their perception of political-military symbols are more likely to be a result of their different socialization experiences. On the other hand, similarities in their response patterns may be indicative of a basic cultural norm shared by all Chinese, regardless of their "liberal" or "Communist" upbringing.

The semantic data were gathered through a technique called Associative Group Analysis (Kringen 1978; Szalay and Brent 1967). Details of the research design and execution are presented in appendix C. Briefly, subjects respond to specific political-military symbols with as many written responses as they can in a period of one minute. Because the order in which responses are recorded is indicative of differing levels of salience in those responses, the associations are weighted according to the order in which they are given. The exact weighting scheme used has been determined in a test-retest comparison for a group of Hong Kong students. These weights are: first response, 5; second response, 4; third through fifth responses, 3; and sixth response and beyond, 2. The weighted responses to each stimulus are then summarized in a list of "shared" responses (those given by two or more persons) and are combined into major themes by two coders. These themes in the Mainland and Hong Kong group responses to the stimulus "crisis" *(wei-ji)* are summarized graphically in figure 6-2 and described in table 6-2 (see pages 70 and 71).

In line with our documentary analysis, the largest response component for the Mainland group is *economy, economic* (component 1). The Mainland group's emphasis on this component is considerably greater than that of the Hong Kong group (28 percent to 17 percent). Further, in the *livelihood* theme (component 3) Mainland responses display a concern for the personal economic aspects of crises, which is totally absent in the Hong Kong responses (M: 13 percent; H.K.: 0 percent). Thus, there is a strong stress on economic themes in the Mainland group's cognition of crisis phenomena. Conversely, it places little emphasis on military themes. While *military* references (component 11) account for 17 percent of the Hong Kong group's responses, such references constitute only 3 percent of the Mainland group's responses. Therefore, the proposition that Mainland Chinese tend to perceive crises more in economic than military terms is supported by our results. Lest it be thought that this response pattern is an artifact, it should be noted that Mainland responses to the stimulus "threat" *(wei-xie)* reveal fundamentally the same pattern of perception (see appendix C).

Beyond a concern with the economic aspects of crises, our documentary analysis has indicated a Chinese emphasis on the political aspects of these phenomena. This observation also receives support from the semantic response patterns. References to the *politics, political* theme (component 2) are prominent in the Mainland as well as the Hong Kong responses. Political references constitute the second largest set of references for the Mainland group, accounting for 17 percent of all the Mainland responses. The Hong Kong group accorded roughly the same emphasis to political themes (14 percent).

However, the perceptions of the Mainland and Hong Kong groups diverge considerably with regard to the question of resource crises (component 9). For the Hong Kong group, the *resources* component is the largest response category (23 percent). Prominent in this component are such energy-related responses as "oil" and "energy source." The salience of these perceptions is obviously a reflection of issues and events of recent prominence. Nonetheless, concern with resource issues is only minimal among the Mainland respondents, constituting the smallest meaning category (4 percent). This Mainland response pattern is congruent with Peking's recent public media statements, contending that the "so-called 'oil crisis' " is not a real crisis but is rather a by-product of the inevitable conflicts inherent in monopoly-capitalist systems (Ke 1975). Thus, in Peking's views, resource crises are subsumed within the framework of economic crises.

As a final point on Chinese perceptions of crisis, it is worthwhile to mention an etymological issue. From the origins of the Chinese term for "crisis" *(wei-ji),* it has been suggested that for the Chinese a crisis is a "dangerous opportunity" *(wei* referring to "danger" and *ji* referring to "opportunity") (e.g., Milburn 1972: 270). Such a notion receives no support from the data reported here. Although *danger* (component 5) is a minor theme mentioned by both groups, references to "opportunity" are totally absent. If, as the documentary analysis suggests, the Chinese do perceive that some crises pose opportunities for them, this perception is dictated more by their views on the matters at issue than the etymology of the term "crisis."

FIGURE 6-2
RELATIVE FREQUENCY OF THEMATIC RESPONSES TO THE TERM "CRISIS"

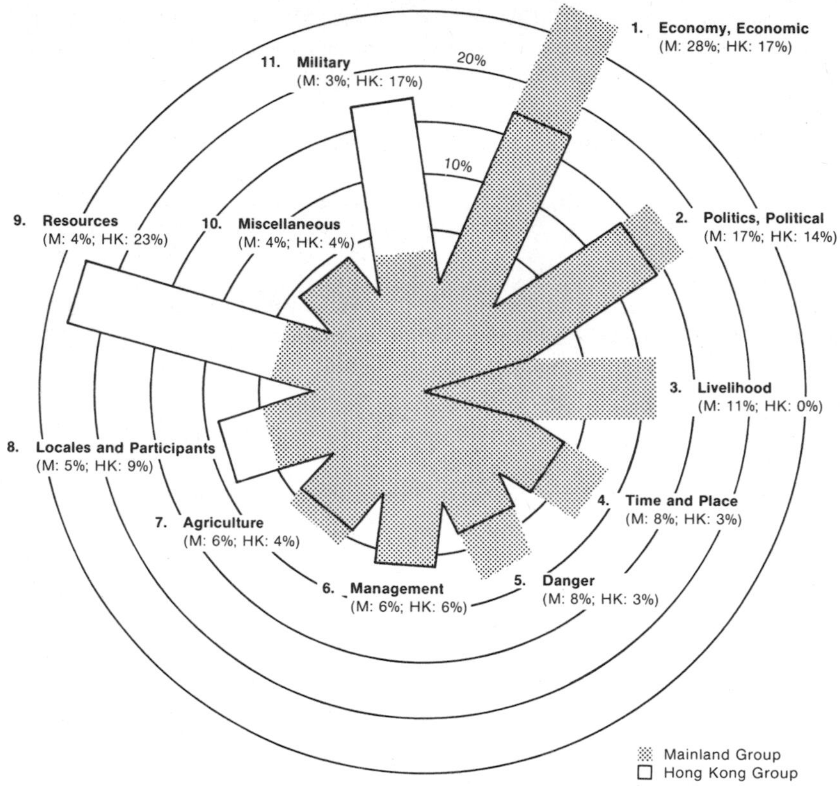

1. Economy, Economic
(M: 28%; HK: 17%)

11. Military
(M: 3%; HK: 17%)

20%

10%

9. Resources
(M: 4%; HK: 23%)

10. Miscellaneous
(M: 4%; HK: 4%)

2. Politics, Political
(M: 17%; HK: 14%)

3. Livelihood
(M: 11%; HK: 0%)

8. Locales and Participants
(M: 5%; HK: 9%)

4. Time and Place
(M: 8%; HK: 3%)

7. Agriculture
(M: 6%; HK: 4%)

6. Management
(M: 6%; HK: 6%)

5. Danger
(M: 8%; HK: 3%)

Mainland Group
Hong Kong Group

Chinese Treatment of Military Crises: Evidence from History

While the documentary and semantic analyses emphasize Chinese attention to economic factors in diagnosing international crises, their doctrine has important implications for behavior in critical incidents with ongoing or potential military confrontation. If these doctrinal precepts are in fact used by Chinese decision makers and have clear meaning, we expect the Chinese to approach those situations in certain ways, ways that are different from the standard Western views. Accordingly, we examine Chinese conduct in five cases of military confrontation: the Korean war, 1950; the Quemoy conflict, 1958; the Sino-Indian border war, 1962; the Vietnam war, 1964–1965; and the Sino-Soviet border clashes of 1969 (Chan 1978a). If our expectations are confirmed in five such diverse cases scattered over almost two decades, we can feel reasonably confident in the fruitfulness of the basic findings from our analysis of doctrinal texts. If, on the contrary, our expectations are not

TABLE 6-2

DESCRIPTION OF THEMATIC RESPONSES TO THE TERM "CRISES"*

1. **Economy, Economic** (M. 197, H.K. 127). This is the largest component for the Mainland group. The response of *economy, economic* was the one most frequently given by both groups (M. 147, H.K. 112). *Unemployment* was singled out as the most salient attribute of economic crises (M. 25, H.K. 7).

2. **Politics, Political** (M. 118, H.K. 100). The response of *politics, political* was the most salient response (M. 65, H.K. 67). *Nation-state* (M. 31, H.K. 13) and *society* (M. 22, H.K. 14) were also significant.

3. **Livelihood** (M. 80, H.K. 0). This is a totally Mainland response component, reflecting personal economic considerations. *Livelihood* (M. 38) and *work* (M. 10) were the most salient responses.

4. **Time and Place** (M. 59, H.K. 24). Both the Mainland and the Hong Kong responses reflect some concern with issues of time and place. References to the crisis *period* (M. 16, H.K. 11) and crises occurring *on all sides* (M. 18, H.K. 13) were the most prominent.

5. **Danger** (M. 59, H.K. 23). This component is somewhat more significant for the Mainland group.

6. **Management** (M. 44, H.K. 41). The most salient Mainland responses were *resolve* (M. 16) and *should not fear* (M. 13).

7. **Agriculture** (M. 42, H.K. 32). References to *food* (M. 13, H.K. 27) and *no food* (M. 14) were the most frequent.

8. **Locales and Participants** (M. 35, H.K. 32). The largest responses were *Middle East* (M. 5, H.K. 35) and *United States* (M. 12, H.K. 12).

9. **Resources** (M. 25, H.K. 173). This is the most salient component for the Hong Kong group. Energy-related concerns are the dominant ones in this theme. *Oil* (M. 14, H.K. 70) and *energy source* (M. 11, H.K. 54) were the most frequently given responses.

10. **Military** (M. 19, H.K. 121). Issues of military conflict are significantly more prominent for the Hong Kong group. *War* (M. 14, H.K. 66) was the most frequent response for both groups.

---

* Total response scores: M. (Mainland group) = 701; H.K. (Hong Kong group) = 737.

supported or we find widely different patterns of Chinese conduct in the five cases, the precepts from doctrine lose analytic importance. Descriptively, we are concerned with two questions about Chinese historical behavior in the five conflict cases. First, to what extent and in what ways did the Chinese deal with the Western trinity of crisis characteristics—high threat, short decision time, and great surprise? Second, how did they attempt to manipulate these conditions to affect the decision making of their adversaries?

Our review of Chinese conduct in the five instances shows the absence of one of the Western key concepts in crisis analysis: that of surprise. This distinctive missing ingredient is what we would expect from Chinese doctrine. To the extent that the occasions were a direct consequence of China's actions—such as Peking's intervention in the Korean war, its attempted blockade of Quemoy in 1958, and its initiation of border conflicts with India in 1962 and with the Soviet Union in 1969—attribution of surprise to the Peking elite is hardly appropriate. It is also rather uncompelling to argue that Peking was surprised by prior actions on the part of its adversaries that led to its decisions to initiate military conflict. The U.S. drive to "reunify Korea" and the Indian "forward policy" were preceded and accompanied by clear declarations of the intentions of these governments, and the implementation of these policies took place months before the Chinese responses (e.g., Whiting 1975*a*, 1960; Maxwell 1970). In the cases of Quemoy and the Sino-Soviet border conflict, while there were recurrent local clashes earlier, China's adversaries did not undertake any major policy changes that could be interpreted as being responsible for precipitating Peking's decisions to escalate the conflict. In fact, in the case of Quemoy, it was the absence of United States reactions to the initial Chinese probes that could have resulted in Peking's decision to intensify its bombardment against that island (e.g., Whiting 1975*b;* McClelland 1969). Mao did admit surprise, however, over the extreme U.S. response to the initiation of this bombardment (Whiting 1975*b*). Surprise in this sense was more a matter of a miscalculation of enemy intentions than an unawareness of a potentially dangerous situation. Finally, even in the case of second-order military crises, such as the Gulf of Tonkin incident, it is difficult to sustain the view that the Peking leaders were genuinely surprised by a new development. Chinese public media carried explicit and extensive warning of the imminent danger of conflict escalation in Vietnam prior to that incident. Event data collected from the *People's Daily* show that the Chinese reports of hostile U.S. actions and intentions toward North Vietnam increased tremendously in July 1964, one month before the Gulf of Tonkin incident (Chan 1978*b*).

Peking's behavior in past military conflicts involving China shows considerable tactical caution in efforts to control the potential for conflict escalation. This is what our doctrinal analysis leads us to expect. First, China carried out extensive probes and issued numerous verbal warnings prior to initiating military attacks in the Korea, Quemoy, and Sino-Indian cases. Probing activities are designed to determine enemy capabilities and intentions, and reflect the Maoist injunction to respect the enemy tactically. Second, the eventual Chinese attacks usually attempted to exploit the "weak links" in the enemy's defense posture (for example, the Indian outpost at Che Dong, Quemoy, Chenpao, South Korean forces near the Yalu River). The location of these combat sites gave Peking an advantage in local military capability and logistical support. The choice of conflict sites again shows tactical caution, reflecting Mao's dictum on the importance of possessing local superiority in specific military encounters. Third, in selecting the targets of the initial Chinese military actions, Peking preferred conflict through indirection. That is, the targets often were the proxies or client states of China's principal adversary, instead of the principal adversary proper. For example, in the cases of Quemoy and Korea, China's actions were directed at the Nationalist Chinese and South Korean troops rather than the United States troops in the initial military clashes. This pattern shows an expected concern to limit the risk of conflict escalation that might be triggered by a reciprocation of hostility by China's major opponent. Fourth, China's military operations were usually limited in geographical scope and temporal duration. They did not commit Peking to an irrevocable course of conflict escalation and could be terminated unilaterally (for example, the initial engagement with the U.S. troops in Korea, the bombardment of Quemoy). Fifth, China's initial military operations were usually followed by unilateral steps for arms limitation. Tactical withdrawal served as a tacit signal for conflict deescalation. Such unilateral military disengagement occurred in Korea and Quemoy as well as the Sino-Indian and Sino-Soviet border conflicts (Whiting 1975a, 1975b, 1960; Robinson 1972; Maxwell 1970). This behavior is, of course, also consonant with the Maoist injunction to deliver swift and decisive blows against the enemy and then disengage quickly before it is able to mobilize its retaliatory forces.

The timing of China's diplomatic and military moves in past armed confrontations provides some clues about how Peking manages the problem of short response time. In the Quemoy conflict of 1958, China responded very quickly to the U.S. threat of intervention. The official Newport communiqué that signaled this U.S. intention was not released until the early afternoon of September 4—which would be the morning of September 5 in Peking. On September 6, Chinese Premier Chou En-lai indicated China's intention to deescalate the conflict by publicly proposing the resumption of Sino-American ambassadorial talks in Warsaw. China's actions in the Korean and Sino-Indian wars also demonstrated rapid response to enemy moves. MacArthur's "end the war" offensive on November 24, 1950, triggered an immediate Chinese counteroffensive on November 26. Similarly, an Indian attack on Chinese border positions from Walong on November 14 resulted in a Chinese counteroffensive on November 16, which involved a major coordinated attack on Indian positions in both the eastern and western sectors of the Sino-Indian border. The scale and timing of China's counteroffensives suggest advanced planning. The promptness of Peking's responses implies that time pressure applied only to its efforts to monitor enemy actions and diagnose tactical intentions; it did not apply to its search for policy alternatives. Its policy alternatives probably were preprogramed, ready to be implemented once the significance of enemy moves could be determined.

The temporal coincidence of the Cuban missile crisis and the Sino-Indian border conflict raises important questions about Peking's ability to monitor and anticipate crisis developments involving others. Three alternative explanations of this temporal coincidence are (1) that it was accidental; (2) that the Chinese were able to anticipate the Soviet-American confrontation and schedule their military operations against India accordingly; and (3) that they were able to react quickly to the Soviet-American confrontation after it developed because they had previously established the infrastructure for military operations. The second possibility seems to us less credible than the other two alternatives, but we lack any direct evidence for testing the validity of the first and third possibilities. Some analysts are inclined to accept the first interpretation (e.g., Whiting 1975a), while others tend to favor the third interpretation. Acceptance of the latter hypothesis would, of course, imply that the Chinese were able to diagnose international relations developments, to make decisions to respond to these developments, and to implement these decisions very rapidly based on the sort of preparedness stressed in their doctrine. Short response time, in this case, involves seizing opportunities presented by one's adversaries rather than denying such opportunities to them. According to this interpretation, the timing of the Chinese military operations provides an ideal example of the boldness-caution bimodality in operation and it also fits with doctrinal injunctions to expect crises while being flexible about timing.

One additional aspect of Peking's crisis-management orientation should be noted. With regard to China's ultimate goals and principles, Peking has refused to compromise. Rigidity in China's core policy positions has accompanied a willingness to accept an extended impasse on the basic conflict issues (for example, U.S. support for Taiwan, territorial negotiations with India and the Soviet Union). This tolerance of a stalemate is in turn justified by the optimistic view that in the long run China can outwait its opposition and achieve its goals. It also conforms to the lengthy time perspective noted previously.

A policy of "standing firm" on basic principles and ultimate goals has not precluded the opportunistic tactics of detente and cooperative arrangements with China's secondary enemies in order to oppose its principal adversary more effectively. Here we see conduct in line with the flexibility component of the rigidity-flexibility maxim, as Chinese decision makers take full advantage of tactical maneuvers to reduce the threat posed by China's major opponent. As their doctrine recommends, they do indeed take the "devious road" in pursuing their basic goals and seek "temporary compromises" and "partial agreements" with China's secondary enemies (e.g., Burchett 1976). For example, detente with the United States and tacit cooperation with it in responding to critical incidents in South Asia, Southern Africa, and the Middle East are legitimate tactics to counter the Soviet threat. Various detente measures in China's first-order military incidents—such as unilateral cease-fire, negotiation proposals, and armistice talks—also manifest this concern with tactical flexibility.

Chinese doctrine stresses the irrationality of reactionaries and the importance of not letting events get out of hand. Accordingly, we expect Peking's efforts to communicate clearly with an adversary in order to reduce the chances that it will overestimate the degree of threat implied by Chinese actions and goals. The Chinese should also try to shape the adversary's perceptions of surprise and short decision time to lessen the likelihood of dangerously precipitous and extreme reactions against China.

In past instances of military confrontation, China provided ample strategic warning to its adversaries about intentions, while attempting to preserve the possibility of tactical surprise regarding the specific timing, place, and nature of China's initiatives (Chan 1978a). Chinese warning signals in the form of diplomatic threats, domestic propaganda campaigns, and military mobilization acts (for example, increased border patrols, air defense measures, troop movements, activation of military bases) could be detected long before the conflicts reached the "crisis" point (e.g., Whiting 1975a, 1960; McClelland 1969; Tretiak 1966). Peking usually did not attempt to conceal its military mobilization acts through such steps as camouflaging its troop movements and construction of military bases. In all five of the cases examined, we can be relatively confident that China's adversaries were able to monitor and detect these force displays through foreign diplomats stationed in Peking, border patrols, and such other means as electronic eavesdropping and high-altitude photography. Nonverbal warning signals were often reinforced by explicit indications of China's intentions through domestic media or international intermediaries (for example, the verbal warning conveyed through Indian Ambassador Panikkar in the Korean case). Further, Peking's warning behavior was characterized by a gradual escalation of hostility over an extended period of time. The initiation of large-scale Chinese military operations was usually preceded by a series of minor clashes (for example, border skirmishes, air combats), and Peking's demonstrative actions were often interrupted by short pauses to allow the adversary to comprehend them and to modify perception of a snowballing Chinese threat. This tendency is particularly prominent in the Korean and Sino-Indian wars; a lull in fighting of about three weeks took place in both cases before the outbreak of large-scale hostilities. The immediate precipitant for the intensification of these conflicts was the offensive by the United States on November 24, 1950, and by India on November 14, 1962.

Peking apparently has emphasized removing uncertainties about its strategic intentions on the part of its adversaries, and providing ample opportunities for adversaries to modify their policies before conflict escalation. However, once Peking decided to embark on conflict escalation, it tried to achieve tactical surprise and to restrict the opponent's ability to respond effectively to China's military initiatives. To accomplish this objective, Peking stressed quick and decisive strikes against the enemy. These operations often were terminated quickly, before the enemy could retaliate, and sometimes were followed by detente measures to discourage the possibility of further conflict escalation. For example, in 1962, after breaking through Indian defense positions in a short military campaign, Peking announced a unilateral cease-fire and withdrew its forces to the actual line of control before the outbreak of the war.

In sum, Chinese conduct in the historical cases we have examined seems compatible with the doctrinal inferences we drew earlier and in particular with the bimodal maxims. The behavioral record does support, though obviously does not prove, our contentions about Chinese perspectives and tendencies.

Conclusions

As for wisdom and efficacy, the Chinese conception of international conflicts and the implied and implemented pattern of policy actions that results have limitations as well as strengths. On source of limitations involves the extent to which Chinese strategies to control the evolution of critical international incidents depend in important ways on the perceptions of their adversaries. Another set of important considerations involves the characteristics of China and of the international context in which it operates.

Given the disparity between common Western and Chinese views addressed in this and the previous chapter, several important possibilities exist for mutual misinterpretation, creating chains of events that neither the Chinese nor a Western adversary may want.

Peking's bellicose statements, reflecting the rigidity and boldness beliefs, often result in an exaggerated estimate of the threat posed by Chinese intentions. These statements lend credibility to the view that Chinese leaders are committed to international destabilization efforts. Furthermore, given Peking's proclivity for verbal belligerency, it is difficult for opponents to discriminate between genuine threats and rhetorical assertions in actual crisis situations. The "noise" generated by routine Chinese rhetoric impedes the accurate identification and assessment of genuine threats to Peking's adversaries. Chinese rhetoric makes it especially difficult to convince opponent governments that China's objectives in crises are limited. The bimodal maxims underlying Peking's behavior can also easily result in an opposite kind of misperception. Tactical caution can be misconstrued by China's adversaries to be a sign of weak resolve and consequently embolden them, as in the Korean and Sino-Indian wars (e.g., George and Smoke 1974; Hoffmann 1972; Maxwell 1970). For example, China's detente gesture in initiating a unilateral military disengagement after the initial combat in the Korean war was misinterpreted by General MacArthur as a sign that China was merely bluffing and did not intend to intervene in the conflict.

Chinese analyses of international conflict and management preferences have obvious appeal to cope with several problems and aspirations simultaneously. On the one hand, they serve to diminish the importance of, or at least mask, military weakness. They rationalize the avoidance of full-fledged wars and the inability to mount decisive, overwhelming foreign military interventions. On the other, they buttress the attitudes and image conducive to passive deterrence. That is, they provide deterrence not by promising assured destruction but rather by promising assured resistance. And they encourage citizen and cadre assessments that the price of continuing along chosen policy lines will not be in vain by limiting the importance of short-term outcomes. Further, they encourage a form of extended defense by providing a rationale to others to engage in actions that will absorb the attention and resources of those who might otherwise be tempted by Chinese weakness. At the same time, the emphasis on internal economic and political factors warrants a policy that stops short of the automatic involvement associated with true collective security and concentrates instead on domestic development. In these and other ways, they make the most of the assets that China has and make the least of the conflict capabilities with which others are better equipped.

The efficacy of Chinese rationale depends to a significant extent on the relations between China's adversaries and third parties. A world of U.S.-Soviet animosity, where each preoccupies the other in terms of both strategic deterrence and competition for regional spheres of influence, provides a conducive context for Chinese policy. A world of U.S.-Soviet cooperation or even the lack of obsessive competition as implied by positive and minimal notions of detente, makes the success of China's preferred strategy more dubious. As the Chinese are the first to recognize, detente or even its passive aspect of withdrawal from foreign positions of strength lessens the ability of Peking to convert weakness into strength. The feasibility of the Chinese conceptions and their strategic corollaries is also seriously affected by the extent to which China becomes an attractive target for preemptive aggression. One reason why the Chinese have had relative confidence in their ability to predict critical incidents directly affecting them and to manage the resulting threats has been the fact that they posed little in the way of an objective threat to major military powers in the sense that China was likely to strike first in a major theater. And unlike the major powers, they have not had far-flung global interests or the ability to affect these interests, thus restricting Chinese crisis anticipation and management activities primarily to the region contiguous to China. Another reason has been the general consensus in a resource-abundant world that attempts to seize China, to in some sense repeat the Japanese steps of the interwar years, have little obvious economic benefit to recommend them. In the remainder of this century both of these judgments, which have aided the Chinese, are likely to become open to increasingly serious question as China's military forces modernize and acquire a substantial force-projection capability and the economic benefit from its natural resources increases in readily exploitable value. In effect, the efficacy of the Chinese views developed in the previous pages may be brought into serious question as development regains momentum and if the tension between the superpowers subsides.

For the more immediate purposes of our inquiry, it is important to note that two of our research assumptions have been supported. The first is that generalized doctrinal beliefs are not merely vague political rhetoric but do characterize important aspects of the thinking of individual Chinese and do illuminate conduct in actual historical cases. The second is that there are substantial disparities in the cognitive rules and logics used by different national foreign affairs cultures to think about and deal with international crises, and these differences matter for what governments actually do. Given the support provided by our exploration of the Chinese cognition and management of critical international incidents, we now proceed to examine the broader implications for foreign affairs decision making of the Chinese doctrinal belief system. And that, in turn, requires us to take a more comprehensive view of the rules and logics it contains.

PART III

Chinese Policy Analytics

In our discussion of Chinese perception and treatment of critical international situations, we introduced briefly a number of important beliefs and maxims. We did so in the context of the dialectical belief system that they espouse. In the next three chapters we explore the general beliefs and decision logics, both open and closed in our earlier terminology, that underlie their treatment of specific foreign affairs decision occasions. Without these general precepts, situation-specific behavior becomes largely inexplicable, defying analytic comprehension and precluding well-designed attempts to exert policy influence. Because the general cognitions we present here operate across situations, knowledge of them allows us to go beyond Chinese assessments and treatments of particular past situations.

It is important to be clear about the central concerns and limits of our analysis. First, we do not contend that all the beliefs we present are unique to the Chinese. We know from research on other national decision cultures (e.g., Brecher 1972; Leites 1953) that other national elites share some particular elements of Chinese beliefs. We are fundamentally concerned with the relative distinctiveness of Chinese policy analytics as a whole rather than with the uniqueness of particular components. And we are alert to the possibility that the Chinese may differ from those who hold some similar beliefs in terms of the conditions under which they invoke these beliefs, and the interpretations and emphases that they attach to the shared beliefs.

Second, our concern lies with general tendencies that operate in the thinking of Chinese leaders. Accordingly, we do not take the position that all members of the Peking elite hold identical beliefs. We avoid analysis of individuals or factions because, with the notable exception of a handful of leading cadres, only the most fragile and fragmentary understanding of the beliefs and roles of particular participants in Chinese foreign policy decision making is possible. We consciously sacrifice some amount of analytic precision in favor of findings more likely to be applicable to decision situations in general and to have continued importance in spite of changes in officeholders. Basic beliefs and logics inculcated by the national decision culture seem especially likely to outlast the political and natural lives of specific leaders, to characterize officials in different institutions and organizations, and to have pertinence for diagnosing and treating a wide variety of issues and problems.

Third, our view is that in the Chinese belief system—and those of most others—belief elements are not fully consistent with each other or neatly related in all respects. While these properties are attractive in terms of flexibility and creativity, they are costly in terms of decidability in the face of new and complex challenges. Accordingly, one of our major concerns in the following discussion is to locate those areas in Chinese policy analytics that suggest divergent or unclear policy implications. Intraelite policy debates are more likely to occur in these areas. From the point of view of cross-national communication, signals that impact on these "gray" areas are more likely to elicit uncertain and perhaps contradictory responses, since they are cognitively and politically more difficult for the Chinese to process.

Our findings are based on analyses dealing with two historical periods, the mid-1960s (Bobrow 1969b) and the mid-1970s (Chan et al. 1976). We are relatively confident about the stability of Chinese "core beliefs," because these analyses suggest very similar findings. To guard against source biases in our research materials, we have examined standard doctrinal treatises, cultural materials (for example, revolutionary plays), and some political-military documents with restricted access inside China. Similarity in the policy analytics articulated in these various sources increases our confidence in the validity and strength of the inferred belief elements. Disagreement between the sources suggests caution about our inferences and indicates the possibility of divergent belief elements. We will note in the following discussion areas where our inferences are relatively weak and where opposing belief elements may be operating.

We draw on findings from our semantic analysis of Mainland Chinese beliefs to further check the validity of our inferences and to explore their implications for Chinese perceptions. While these data are not without their limitations (appendix C provides a summary of the methodology and its strengths and weaknesses), they do allow us to move somewhat beyond documentary inferences by examining actual patterns of belief among a group of former residents of Mainland China.

We present the beliefs and decision logics central to Chinese policy analysis in a series of rulelike statements. These axioms organize political reality and decision processes for the Chinese. They purport not only to describe, explain, and predict political phenomena, but also to prescribe sound ways to manage them. Chapter 7 presents the "core beliefs" of Chinese doctrine—beliefs about the nature of reality (including political reality) and about change as opposed to stasis. Lying at the center of the Chinese belief system, the core elements are least likely to undergo transformation over time. If they do alter, the likely result will be substantial modification in peripheral beliefs. The following two chapters build on the foundation the core beliefs provide to develop the decision logics and precepts that underlie decision making about any particular problem. Chapter 8 presents beliefs about actors—their characteristics and the ways in which they relate to each other. Chapter 9 turns to the precepts provided by Chinese doctrine for applying the previous belief sets to estimates about and policy formation for particular issues and situations.

CHAPTER 7

CENTRAL PRECEPTS

We now turn to presenting and substantiating the major cognitive elements to which we referred in chapter 6. This chapter draws on doctrinal and socialization materials to infer Chinese precepts about what are the proper central beliefs for their citizens and officials and the key precepts dealing with change. We draw on our semantic research to check and develop the first of these—injunctions about proper articles of faith.

Precepts about Beliefs

1. The world is composed of material; its existence is objective and therefore outside and above human awareness.
   (a) Material conditions shape human thought and, consequently, human behavior.
   (b) Material conditions constrain action possibilities; only actions that are compatible with the objective laws of material conditions can succeed.
   (c) Correct understanding of social problems can only be derived through practice (that is, dealing with material conditions).
2. Human thought is the key to changing material conditions, including those governing social and political relations.
   (a) Mastery over sociopolitical conditions requires a correct understanding of their objective nature.
   (b) Only Communists possess a correct understanding of sociopolitical conditions and development.
   (c) Therefore, only Communists are capable of successfully manipulating these conditions.
3. The objective laws of sociopolitical conditions and development are contained in the works of Marx, Engels, Lenin, Stalin, and Mao.
   (a) These laws stipulate that social development is a process of struggle between opposing forces.
   (b) They also stipulate that the eventual achievement of Communist goals is inevitable.

Axiom 1(a) leads the Chinese to believe that the world views and behavior of actors are conditioned to an important extent by their class background.

Consequently, the Chinese stress the need for class analysis of actors. For example, they tend to assess political reliability on the basis of socioeconomic origin although they acknowledge the possibility that class stand and class background may not always coincide. It follows from axiom 1(a) that in the Chinese view the intentions of actors, especially those of reactionaries, are invariant. "Make trouble, fail, make trouble again, fail again ... till their doom; that is the logic of imperialists and all reactionaries the world over in dealing with the people's cause, and they will never go against this logic. This is a Marxist view. When we say 'imperialism is ferocious,' we mean that its nature will never change, that the imperialists will never lay down their butcher knives, that they will never become Buddhas, till their doom" (Mao quoted in Schram 1967: 37). Thus, in the absence of basic changes in the socioeconomic structure of capitalist societies, exploitation and conflict are inevitable. This belief also leads to the view that international conflict is primarily caused by conditions internal to the capitalist countries.

Axiom 1(b) enjoins analysts to examine objective conditions in making policy. Communists are admonished against taking wanton and reckless actions without regard for the limitations imposed by objective conditions ("leftist opportunism" and "adventurism"). "If people want to succeed in their work, that is, to achieve the anticipated results, they must make their views conform to the objective laws of the outside world; if the two are not congruent, then practice will fail" (Mao quoted in Worker-Peasant-Soldier Team 1971a: 41).

Axiom 1(c) suggests that the Chinese tend to emphasize building and confirming knowledge through practice or direct experience. According to Mao, "all true knowledge begins with direct experience" (Mao quoted in Worker-Peasant-Soldier Team 1971a: 138). This injunction implies that the Chinese will rely heavily on case-specific information acquired through firsthand observation (see the discussion in chapter 9) and assess current states of affairs in terms of past Chinese experience.

The relationship between material conditions and human thought is an interactive one. Axiom 2 and its derivatives embody the Chinese conviction in human thought as the primary determinant of material change. "Whether or not the lines of thought and policy are correct determines everything else" (Mao quoted in Tientsin Writing Group 1975: 7). Correct recognition of sociopolitical conditions is necessary for effective manipulation of these conditions. Consequently, Peking's rhetoric usually dismisses China's material inferiority, placing stress instead on the importance of spiritual superiority (for example, ideological purity, political consciousness). In this respect, Mao contended that "weapons are an important factor in wars, but not the decisive factor; the decisive factor is man and not material" (Mao quoted in Worker-Peasant-Soldier Team 1971a: 82).

Axioms 2(b) and 2(c) imply that non-Communists are inherently incapable of understanding or managing sociopolitical problems. As Mao stated, "Our enemies are regressive and corrupt reactionaries, they are destined for destruction; they do not understand the laws of the objective world, their thinking is based on subjective and metaphysical methods, and therefore their calculations are always in error" (Mao quoted in Study Team 1974: 84). Accordingly, China's enemies are intellectually impotent: " 'Lifting a rock only to drop it on one's feet' is a Chinese folk saying to describe the behavior of certain fools. The reactionaries in all countries are fools of this kind" (Mao quoted in Schram 1967: 41). Since China's enemies are irrational, one needs to stress vigilance and planning in national defense, based on "worst case" assumptions about the intentions of China's enemies. However, as we shall see in chapter 8, this view of enemy irrationality is counterbalanced by a seemingly contradictory image, which attributes a certain amount of cunning to China's enemies.

Insofar as the Chinese believe that they possess knowledge from a uniquely wise source, they are inclined to be optimistic about their role as change agents. Axiom 3(b) indicates this view by suggesting that the eventual fulfillment of Communist goals is inevitable. But axiom 3(a) cautions against undue optimism by emphasizing that Communist victory will have to be achieved through hard struggle over an undefined period of time; Communists are warned that "the imperialists and domestic reactionaries will certainly not take their defeat lying down and they will struggle to the last ditch" (Mao quoted in Schram 1967: 9). Axioms 3(a) and 3(b) therefore represent a bimodal orientation about the Chinese role as change agents. Optimism about eventual victory and pessimism about immediate success are both warranted.

These precepts have major implications for beliefs about international affairs. First, the Chinese tend to believe that reactionaries are inherently aggressive, that their hostile intentions are unlikely to change, and that their policies are determined by the socioeconomic conditions in their societies. Accordingly, the Chinese believe in the inevitability of international conflict as long as reactionaries exist, and point to socioeconomic pressures internal to the reactionary countries as the direct cause of conflict. Second, the Chinese tend to view reactionaries as both weak and dangerous. Reactionaries are weak because they are fundamentally incapable of analyzing and coping with sociopolitical problems. They are dangerous because they are by nature aggressive, because they are prone to make policy miscalculations, and because they will not give up easily without hard struggle. Third, the Chinese tend to stress dispassionate analysis of actor capabilities and, at the same time, display substantial confidence in their own capacity to cope with adversaries. As Mao recommended, "Strategically speaking, we should despise all our enemies; tactically speaking, we should treat them all seriously" (Mao quoted in Tzei 1975: 3).

Semantic Analysis: Communism and Socialism

As in chapter 6, we draw on our semantic data to check the extent to which the core precepts embodied in doctrine about the beliefs of good Communists are in fact held by Chinese and to explore their implications. We shall do so through an examination of the meanings associated with the terms "communism" and "socialism." As we shall see, the meanings attributed to these terms by Chinese socialized under the Communist regime are vastly different from those given by a linguistically similar population raised in a non-Marxist environment. After presenting the associations and their differences, we will turn to the implications of this evidence for the status of the basic precepts just discussed.

Figure 7-1 and table 7-1 summarize the responses of the Mainland and Hong Kong Chinese groups to the term "communism" *(gong-chan-zhu-yi)*. The themes of their responses are summarized in relative frequency terms in figure 7-1 and described briefly in table 7-1. Several patterns are evident in

FIGURE 7-1
RELATIVE FREQUENCY OF THEMATIC RESPONSES
TO THE TERM "COMMUNISM"

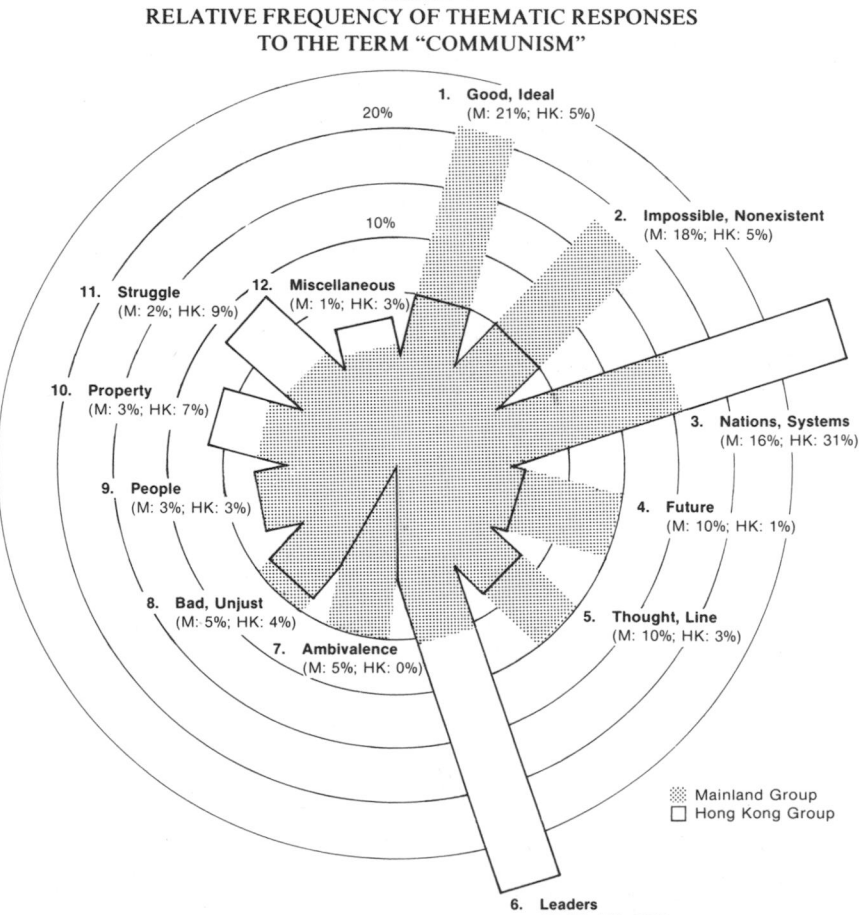

1. Good, Ideal
    (M: 21%; HK: 5%)

2. Impossible, Nonexistent
    (M: 18%; HK: 5%)

3. Nations, Systems
    (M: 16%; HK: 31%)

4. Future
    (M: 10%; HK: 1%)

5. Thought, Line
    (M: 10%; HK: 3%)

6. Leaders
    (M: 6%; HK: 29%)

7. Ambivalence
    (M: 5%; HK: 0%)

8. Bad, Unjust
    (M: 5%; HK: 4%)

9. People
    (M: 3%; HK: 3%)

10. Property
    (M: 3%; HK: 7%)

11. Struggle
    (M: 2%; HK: 9%)

12. Miscellaneous
    (M: 1%; HK: 3%)

Mainland Group
Hong Kong Group

TABLE 7-1
DESCRIPTION OF THEMATIC RESPONSES
TO THE TERM "COMMUNISM"*

1. **Good, Ideal** (M. 148, H.K. 48). The Mainland group's responses were significantly more favorable toward communism. *Good* (M. 29), *ideal* (M. 19, H.K. 16), and *everyone equal* (M. 17) were the most prominent of these favorable comments.

2. **Impossible, Nonexistent** (M. 127, H.K. 41). Although the Mainland respondents thought of communism in highly positive terms, they were also strongly inclined to express the belief that communism did not currently exist and was not likely to exist in the future. Such a belief was reflected in such responses as *cannot be realized* (M. 47, H.K. 16), *illusion* (M. 24), and *no such thing* (M. 10).

3. **Nations, Systems** (M. 115, H.K. 268). Since the Mainland group tended to believe that communism was impossible, they also tended not to apply the term to currently existing nations and systems and instead perceived communism in largely abstract terms. Thus, the Hong Kong group was more likely to apply the term "communism" to China and the Soviet Union with such replies as *China* (M. 8, H.K. 61), *Soviet Union* (H.K. 70), and *Chinese Communism* (H.K. 31) and was more likely to associate communism with *socialism* (M. 5, H.K. 36). In contrast, the most salient Mainland responses—*society* (M. 48, H.K. 10), *nations* (M. 21, H.K. 7), and *systems* (M. 14)—reflect a highly abstract orientation.

4. **Future** (M. 74, H.K. 12). To the extent that the Mainland group believed in the possibility of communism, it was relegated to the distant future. *Realization* (M. 11, H.K. 12), *possibility* (M. 11), *need a long time to realize* (M. 9), *future of socialism* (M. 8), and *successors* (M. 8) were prominent associations indicating this belief.

5. **Thought, Line** (M. 73, H.K. 27). In this largely Mainland response theme, *thought* (M. 20, H.K. 8), *style* (M. 13), *line* (M. 11), and *morality* (M. 10) were the most salient referents.

6. **Leaders** (M. 44, H.K. 254). For the Hong Kong respondents, the idea of communism was symbolized by major communist leaders. *Marx* (M. 18, H.K. 97), *Mao Tse-tung* (M. 12, H.K. 76), *Lenin* (M. 6, H.K. 57), and *Stalin* (H.K. 18) were the most important ones mentioned.

7. **Ambivalence** (M. 36, H.K. 0). Among the Mainland respondents, ambivalent feelings about communism were reflected in the associations *who knows?* (M. 17), *don't understand* (M. 18), and *is it good?* (M. 8).

8. **Bad, Unjust** (M. 34, H.K. 38). *Bad* (M. 14) was the most frequent Mainland response; *no freedom* (M. 7, H.K. 18) was the largest Hong Kong one.

9. **People** (M. 25, H.K. 22). *Proletariat* (M. 10, H.K. 12), *livelihood* (M. 10), and *classes* (H.K. 10) were the most salient replies.

10. **Property** (M. 21, H.K. 58). The Hong Kong group's responses indicated concern about the status of property under communism, with *no private property* (H.K. 17) and *common production and use* (H.K. 12) being the most significant of these.

11. **Struggle** (M. 16, H.K. 80). For the Hong Kong group in particular, communism was associated with conflict. *Struggle* (M. 9, H.K. 19), *destroy classes* (H.K. 19), and *revolution* (H.K. 13) were prominent associations.

* Total Response Scores: M. = 717; H.K. = 870.

these responses. First, contrary to the negative connotation that the term "communism" has in much of the Western political world (White 1966: 223–24), the Mainland Chinese respondents view "communism" in highly positive terms. Positive references such as "good" and "ideal" (component 1) compose approximately one-fifth of all their responses. This is, of course, particularly noteworthy in view of the refugee status of the Mainland respondents. Second, the positive image of "communism" does not imply endorsement by the Mainland Chinese of political or economic arrangements currently existing in China or any other nations. In terms of historical stages, China is regarded in official ideology as a "socialist" state; the stage of communism is not expected to be realized for some time (e.g., Mao quoted in Schram 1975: 174). The Mainland respondents have adopted this viewpoint at least partially. As indicated by the responses listed in component 3 (table 7-1), the Mainland Chinese group does not use the term "communism" to refer to existing nations (for example, China and the Soviet Union), in contrast to the usage by the Hong Kong group. Rather, the Mainland respondents refer abstractly to "societies," "nations," and "systems." Indeed, for the Mainland Chinese group, the referent "communism" is simply not a central part of their political vocabulary (Kringen 1978: 145–50). When they think of communism

FIGURE 7-2
RELATIVE FREQUENCY OF THEMATIC RESPONSES
TO THE TERM "SOCIALISM"

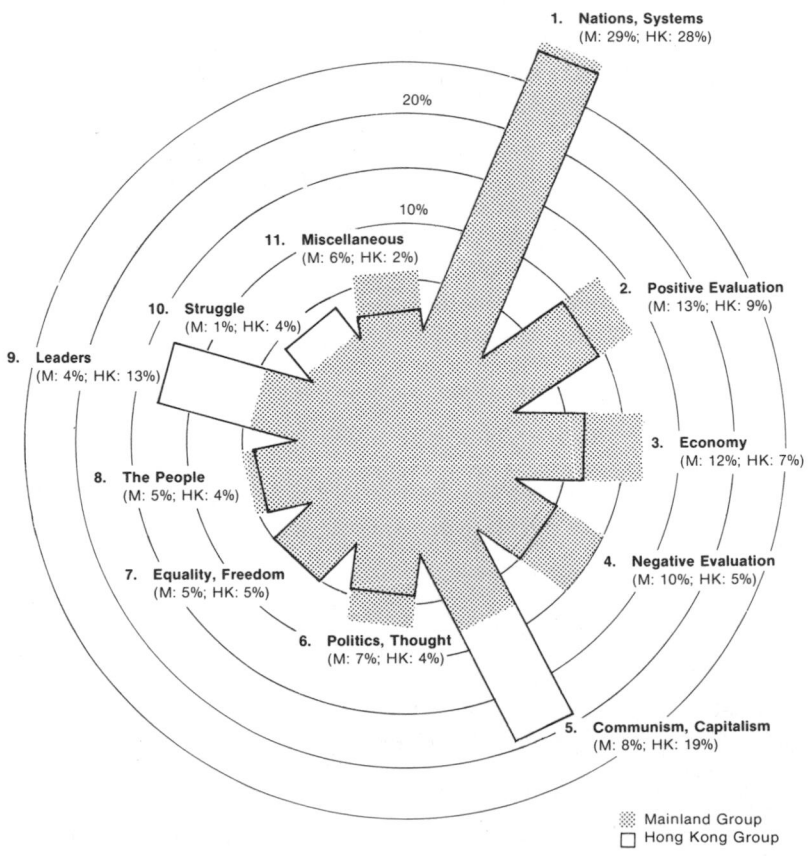

TABLE 7-2
DESCRIPTION OF THEMATIC RESPONSES
TO THE TERM "SOCIALISM"*

1. **Nations, Systems** (M. 176, H.K. 215). Both groups indicated that the term "socialism" was one that applied to various *nations* (M. 30, H.K. 16), *systems* (M. 33), and *societies* (M. 11, H.K. 27). The specific nations receiving prominent attention from both groups were *China* (M. 53, H.K. 50) and the *Soviet Union* (M. 20, H.K. 60). In addition, the Hong Kong group made marked reference to *England* (H.K. 29).

2. **Positive Evaluation** (M. 82, H.K. 72). *Good* (M. 44, H.K. 13) was the largest Mainland response; *ideal* (H.K. 36) was the largest Hong Kong one.

3. **Economy** (M. 70, H.K. 58). The Mainland group was somewhat more inclined to make economic references. *Economy* (M. 18, H.K. 15), *livelihood* (M. 13), and *construction* (M. 10, H.K. 23) were the most salient replies.

4. **Negative Evaluation** (M. 63, H.K. 37). Just as the Mainland respondents were somewhat more inclined to make positive comments, they were also more inclined to make negative ones. *Bad* (M. 29) and *not free* (M. 29) were the largest of these negative responses.

5. **Communism, Capitalism** (M. 49, H.K. 149). The Hong Kong group saw a considerably greater degree of association between socialism on the one hand and communism and capitalism on the other hand. *Communism* (M. 27, H.K. 78), *Chinese Communism* (H.K. 19), *Communist party* (M. 17, H.K. 18), and *capitalism* (M. 5, H.K. 18) were the most salient of these associations.

6. **Politics, Thought** (M. 42, H.K. 33). *Government* (M. 10), *politics* (M. 9, H.K. 11), *line* (M. 9), and *thought* (H.K. 9) were the most significant replies.

7. **Equality, Freedom** (M. 28, H.K. 38). *Equality* was the single largest response for both groups (M. 14, H.K. 18).

8. **The People** (M. 28, H.K. 31). The most frequent association for both groups was *the people* (M. 28, H.K. 16).

9. **Leaders** (M. 24, H.K. 102). The Hong Kong associations revealed a strong tendency to think in terms of individual leaders. The familiar trinity of *Marx* (M. 11, H.K. 52), *Lenin* (M. 6, H.K. 19), and *Mao Tse-tung* (M. 7, H.K. 14) received the greatest attention.

10. **Struggle** (M. 6, H.K. 30). *Struggle* (M. 6, H.K. 7) and *revolution* (H.K. 17) were the most prominent replies.

* Total Response Scores: M. = 606; H.K. = 778.

at all they tend either to relegate it to some future time period (component 4) or to express doubt about its eventual occurrence (component 2).

Much more important to Chinese classification of the current political world is the referent "socialism" (Kringen 1978: 145–50). Figure 7-2 and table 7-2 report the Mainland and Hong Kong Chinese responses to the term "socialism" *(she-hui-zhu-yi)*. As can be seen from the responses listed in component 1 of table 7-2, the Mainland Chinese group clearly identifies China as a "socialist" country. The contrast with their responses to the stimulus "communism" is apparent. And, significantly, for some members of the Mainland Chinese group the Soviet Union is still regarded as a "socialist" country. The presence of these responses may be indicative of the lag involved in adapting Chinese public opinion to changes in policy line. Finally, we can note in the Hong Kong responses a tendency that is absent in the Mainland responses—a tendency to treat socialism as a category applicable to European nations as well (for example, the number of references to England). Beyond the classification of actors, it is apparent that Mainland Chinese views of "socialism" are distinctive in other respects. First, as indicated in component 5, the Mainland respondents are significantly less likely to see an association between socialism, on the one hand, and either communism or capitalism, on the other. Second, there is also a tendency to view socialism less in terms of particular political leaders (component 9) and more as a particular type of economic system (component 3).

Obviously, these patterns of semantic association do not allow us to confidently infer internalization of the core precepts presented at the beginning of this chapter. However, they are related to them in three interesting ways. The first is the internalization of basic philosophy as a description of an ideal state to be aspired to. The second is the lack of confidence in its ever being realized—that is, less than complete acceptance of the inevitability of success embodied in axiom 3(b). The third is the emphasis on economic features (material conditions) as the hallmarks of a social system and on China as unique in that respect. While Western usage of terms such as "communism" and "socialism" may refer to countries that take a particular internal and external policy line (White 1966), it seems that for the Chinese socialized in the People's Republic they refer instead to the combination of ideal norms and economic realities stressed in the doctrinal precepts.

Beliefs about the Nature of Change

The universal, comprehensive nature of the core precepts we have just discussed means that in and of themselves they are of little value for illuminating how the Chinese think about dynamics that require adjustment in their judgments and actions. To understand both their expectations about the need for adaptation and their interpretive mechanisms, we now turn to a set of generalized beliefs about the nature of change and the portents of the need for policy vigilance and adjustment.

4. The world is constantly changing; the history of material, personal, or social development is a continuous series of contradictions and resolutions of contradictions.
    (a) Social development passes through distinct historical stages, with each successive stage taking place on a higher dialectical plateau.
    (b) The transition between these stages is a wavelike or screwlike rather than a straight progression. Temporary reversals of historical processes are inevitable, but in the long term these processes cannot be blocked or deflected.
5. So long as they correctly grasp and act in accordance with the laws of social development, Communist actors will be successful change agents. While current international conditions and their development in the

immediate future may be unfavorable to the Communist cause, the long-term trend is always favorable.

6. In order to become successful change agents, Communist actors must achieve a basic understanding of the nature and bases of change.
    (a) Factors internal to things are the causes of their change, while factors external to things are the facilitators of their change.
    (b) There is usually a considerable time lag between the development of conditions for change and visible results of change.
    (c) Small incremental changes in the capabilities of actors may in the long term lead to a significant structural change in their relationship.
    (d) However, quantitative changes in actor capabilities (that is, marginal revisions in the gap between the superior and inferior parties) are inherently unstable and transient and can be easily compensated for or reversed by the opposing party.
    (e) Qualitative changes in actor capabilities (that is, the attainment of parity between actor capabilities or the reversal of positions between the superior and inferior party) indicate that a structural transformation in actor relationships has taken place.
    (f) The transition from quantitative change to qualitative change is likely to be turbulent because the parties involved will be more prone to take risks either to promote or prevent the new stage.
    (g) Confrontation is especially likely under conditions of parity, and the ensuing struggle will eventually lead to the subjugation of one of the parties.
    (h) Structural change in actor relationships accomplished through qualitative change is more enduring than the fluctuations from quantitative adjustments.
    (i) However, this change is not always conclusive and may be challenged by the newly inferior party, thus renewing the cycle of contention.

Axiom 4 rules out the possibility that the status quo can continue indefinitely. Belief in the permanence of change in turn calls for capabilities to monitor and forecast environmental change, to update knowledge constantly, and to adjust policy. Change stems from contradictions—that is, from confrontation and struggle between opposing forces. "Contradictions take place constantly and are resolved constantly; this is the dialectical law of material development" (Mao quoted in Worker-Peasant-Soldier Team 1971*b:* 8). Mao explained that "the generality and absoluteness of contradictions have two meanings. First, it means that contradictions exist in the development of all things. Second, it means that the development process is a series of contradictions from beginning to end" (Mao quoted in Tientsin Writing Group 1975: 41–42). Notions of "contradiction" and "change" are closely related in the Chinese world views: contradictions generate change, and change produces new contradictions. The Chinese assert that they are present in all things and at all times.

Axiom 4(a) treats the development process as unfolding in distinct "stages" marked by some basic transformation in actor relationships. Stages are distinguished by changes in the nature of the main contradiction among the actors or massive changes in their capabilities or behavior. Shifts in actor capabilities, especially qualitative leaps (axioms 6e–6h), indicate the imminent resolution of contradictions. A change in strategy is called for to deal with the new situation.

Parenthetically, we expect that disagreements among the Chinese leaders are more likely during the transition periods between stages because of differences in the assessment of the nature and degree of changes and of their policy implications. Also, new policy objectives and strategies are likely to impact differentially on the power and interests of groups in the Chinese leadership. Historically, periods of major policy review have been accompanied by leadership dissent. Those who continue to apply methods or views that are no longer appropriate for the new stage are indicted for "defeatism" and "tail-ism," while those who attempt to apply methods or views that are not yet warranted by altered objective conditions are accused of "adventurism" and "leftist opportunism."

While axiom 4(b) suggests that setbacks in the Communist cause are inevitable, these setbacks are manageable with only temporary adverse effects. "The setbacks, failures, and deaths of socialism are temporary phenomena, and it will be able to recover quickly. Even in case of total failure, the setbacks are temporary and could be recovered" (Mao 1969: 268). As long as the Communist cause represents the laws of objective social development, ultimate victory is assured (axiom 5). "The socialist system will eventually replace the capitalist system; this is an objective law that cannot be altered by people's wishes" (Mao quoted in Study Team 1974: 48).

Axiom 6 makes effective control of change contingent on proper causal analysis. Specifically, it should be kept in mind that internal factors are the primary cause of change (6a). In Mao's words, "dialectical materialism recognizes external causes as conditions for change and internal causes as bases for change; external causes would have effect only if they operate through internal causes" (Mao quoted in Worker-Peasant-Soldier Team 1971a: 9). This axiom underlies the previously noted Chinese tendency to explain the behavior of foreign governments primarily in terms of domestic pressures. It also implies the judgment that domestic political and social conditions, especially the political consciousness of the people, determine the success or failure of a nation's efforts to develop its capabilities. Correct political thought provides the key to manipulate material conditions; therefore, changing the political thought of people makes possible all other kinds of changes. Concomitantly, "self-reliance" becomes a hallmark of Chinese domestic and foreign policies.

Of course, change requires a considerable period of gestation and development (6b). Successful transformation of external attributes, such as economic and technological capabilities, will lag behind successful transformation of internal attributes (for example, political consciousness). Socioeconomic changes are expected to call for long, hard struggle. During this struggle visible accomplishments are incomplete and tentative (6i).

This is not to dismiss small and often latent changes over a protracted period of time as unimportant (6c). Incremental quantitative changes provide the basis for qualitative changes. As Mao explained,

> Change in all things takes two forms: the form of [apparent] opposing stagnation and the form of manifest change. . . . When things are in the first form, there is only quantitative change and no qualitative change and, therefore, they give the appearance of stagnation. When things are in the second form, the quantitative change in the first form has reached a certain high point, causing the breakup of the unified existence [of their elements] and creating qualitative change. . . . Things are constantly changing from the first form to the second form. The struggles between contradictions take place in both of these two forms, but the resolutions of contradictions are reached through the second form [quoted in Tientsin Writing Group 1975: 87, 90].

This reasoning leads to the possible reversion associated with quantitative changes that leave intact the basic power relationship between the opposing forces (6d). Qualitative breakthroughs are far more stable and ongoing because of the decisively changed distribution of power associated with them (6e, 6g, 6h).

These premises lead to the expectation of intensified conflict between actors when their capabilities undergo qualitative change (6f). The Chinese will attend closely to developments in other countries that suggest basic changes in their capabilities. They are not likely to make significant policy realignments when only quantitative changes in actor capabilities occur. They will reexamine major policies if they perceive that qualitative changes favoring them or their opponents are taking or have taken place. The Chinese will expect their opponents to launch foreign "adventures" if the qualitative change is adverse to China; they themselves will act more boldly when they perceive such a change in China's favor.

In the context of these beliefs, it becomes clear why the Chinese attach particularly high probabilities to the outbreak of major international conflicts in a period where power disparities have been shrinking and approaching parity. Each party to the power relationship is particularly likely to perceive an imminent qualitative change and thus to engage in what it hopes will be decisive action.

Conclusions

The core precepts introduced in the first part of this chapter seem to offer generally applicable closed beliefs—whatever their correlation with objective circumstances. The beliefs about change instead provide more open heuristics. They only make decisions easy if the assessments required for their application can be readily made—for example, about the magnitude of disparity in power relationships and the nature of approaching or recently realized changes in these relationships. Consensus on such matters is more likely to be on a post hoc than anticipatory basis. Accordingly, adjustments before the fact seem likely to be the focus of substantial policy debate within the Chinese elite. Major changes in policy are stressful for most national elites, and the Chinese are no exception. Given the especially high stakes they associate with the prospect of qualitative change and their expectations that others do so as well, their prescription for relative stability and order in international affairs takes a form different from that of some Western formulations. Parity and balance through some variant of "essential equivalence" simply imply that the regimes involved will act as if they are on the brink of some turning point in their power relationships. Marked imbalance, one-sided superiority, has the opposite implication and thus restrains tendencies to take highly committing, potentially extremely costly, and damage-inflicting actions. One example of this tendency in Chinese interpretation can be found in their current assessment of the shifts in the U.S.-Soviet military relationship and the expectations of severe violence they associate with the loss of U.S. military supremacy.

CHAPTER 8

ACTOR CHARACTERISTICS AND RELATIONSHIPS

Policy judgments and actions by the Chinese necessarily involve some image of the parties involved (including the Chinese themselves). In order to offer decidability, belief systems have to provide some limited set of roles, each with its particular profile, and some structure of relationships between the occupants of the major roles. The other desirable belief-system property, flexibility, in turn requires that each role be associated with some repertoire of actions rather than a particularly stereotypic and shallow character. By analogy, the core precepts presented in chapter 7 provide the basic orientation to bring to the drama of international affairs, and the actor profile and relationship possibilities shown in this chapter present the characters and the credible plot lines about how they will interact. To explore these aspects of Chinese policy analytics, we first present the basic set of roles and some semantic data pertinent to the particularly interesting role of the enemy. We then turn to the relationship between these types of participants in international affairs and some semantic data about two salient relationship patterns: contradiction and class struggle. We conclude the chapter with a discussion of ambiguities raised by the set of beliefs presented here by themselves and when combined with those about change introduced previously.

Major Roles: Contrasting Profiles

In reviewing Chinese conceptions of critical international incidents and beliefs about change, we found a basic theme of conflict and opposition, which the Chinese style as "antagonistic contradiction." The relational implications of this concept and alternatives to it will be dealt with in a subsequent part of this chapter. For now we will introduce the three major roles used by the Chinese in discussing such zero-sum relationships. The protagonist role is assigned to the "progressive" actor, the enemy role to the "reactionary" actor, and the waiverer role to intermediate parties whose basic interests do not coincide with either of the other two actors. In cultural materials (for example, plays and operas), the Chinese place great stress on striking differences in the major attributes of these roles to develop widespread, internalized recognition of these differences. The role images are intended to provide a model of good decision making and shared expectations about the likely behavior of antagonists in zero-sum conflicts.

The Protagonist.   Occupants of this role

1. Possess indomitable courage and cannot be threatened into submission or dissuaded from pursuit of their goals;
2. Hold deep feelings of affection for the working people and of hatred for the enemy;
3. Make decisions quickly and decisively and can immediately assess situations when surprised, thus quickly identifying the enemy's weak points;
4. Encourage group participation in decision making;
5. Engage in bold decision making when threatened and manifest caution when circumstances warrant;
6. Rely heavily on class analysis;
7. Employ stratagems of deception and surprise attack in situations of temporary inferiority.

Characteristics 1 and 2 suggest that defiance is part of the proper attitude set in dealing with the enemy. Threats made by the enemy should not sway one's firm resolve to pursue one's goals; one must be ready to make whatever sacrifices are necessary. Struggle is the only appropriate mode for dealing with the enemy; sacrifice and striving are inevitable costs that have to be borne.

Characteristics 3 and 5 reflect standard Chinese maxims regarding the need for acting decisively and the need for acting cautiously. Situations of unexpected threat must be dealt with decisively and rapidly. The description of Red Army cadre Hung Chang-ching in *Red Detachment of Women* is typical in this regard: "Hung swiftly emerges from the hall and calmly prepares to cope with the unexpected change. He makes a rapid appraisal, then orders Pang and the others to kill the 'civil guards' in coordination with the Red Army's assault from the outside" (Ebon 1975: 140). However, the need for rapid, decisive decision making does not invalidate the requirement for the appropriate amount of caution. Decision makers need to keep in mind that "one wrong move can lose the whole game" (Ebon 1975: 298).

Characteristic 6 reaffirms the important role of class analysis noted in our presentation of core precepts. Class analysis is particularly important to assess political reliability. Persons, groups, and regimes with appropriate class backgrounds are more likely to be committed to "progressive" goals. The importance of class analysis in Chinese decision making follows from their previously noted views on the importance of material factors in shaping human thought and behavior.

With respect to decision process, characteristic 4 suggests the important role of group deliberation, not only as a possible mechanism to solicit opinion conducive to "sound" choices but also as a device to build consensual support for decisions. With respect to policy options, characteristic 7 suggests that decision makers should consider strategies of deception and surprise as opposed to obvious, straightforward ways to deal with situations of temporary inferiority. Strong, well-defended enemy positions should be seized by "strategy."

The Enemy. Occupants of this role

1. Have an insatiable appetite and make demands that are nothing less than total;
2. Possess a dual nature, feigning good intentions but plotting secretly on the sly;
3. Manifest cunning;
4. Engage in shrewd class analysis to identify and cultivate "enemies within" the protagonist's camp;
5. Launch surprise attacks and lay "traps" for the overly trusting;
6. Lack sufficient shrewdness to match the skill of the protagonist.

These characteristics of the enemy support the oft-quoted maxim about despising the enemy strategically, but respecting him tactically. Clearly, the enemy has substantial ability (3, 4, and 5), and it is only prudent to respect him accordingly. Just as class analysis aids the protagonist in decision making, it also helps the enemy. In *Red Lantern,* Japanese imperialist Hatoyama used such an approach:

> *Hatoyama:* How about Inspector Wang?
> *Hou* [collaborator]: He was shot in the left arm, but the bone . . .
> *Hatoyama:* That's not what I was asking. Tell me his background.
> *Hou:* Very good, sir. His name is Wang Hung-chang, otherwise known as Wang Lien-chu. His grandfather used to sell opium, his father kept a tavern, and he was one of the first graduates from the Manchukuo police school. He has one wife, one son, and one father.
> *Hatoyama:* So he comes from a good family.
>
> [Ebon 1975: 227]

On the basis of his class analysis, the enemy can be expected to identify actors that can be threatened or bribed into supporting his cause. Further, he may use them to implement sabotage and surprise attacks. An enemy with these abilities is obviously formidable. Nevertheless, because ultimately the enemy's abilities are not equal to those of the protagonist (6), one can be confident of ultimate victory after an intervening period of protracted struggle.

The rapacity of the enemy (1) constitutes a key weak point. For example, in *Taking Tiger Mountain by Strategy* the bandit leaders engaged in this dialogue:

Bandit Chief Adjutant: On our way back this time we've made off with quite a pile, Chief. The village is right on our doorstep. We ought to leave it alone.

Bandit Chief of Staff: That's right, as the saying goes, "A rabbit doesn't foul its own hole."

Vulture: Who cares? Chief of Staff, go and grab me some of those paupers. We'll put them to work building fortifications. Men and women—both of them.

[*Peking Review,* December 26, 1969: 14]

The complete rapacity of the enemy eventually will alienate most other actors. Such alienation makes coalitions possible between the protagonist and third parties, even though their basic interests may not be identical.

The insatiable demands of the enemy may be masked by professed good intentions and a willingness to compromise (2). Statements of good intention do not preclude efforts to cultivate "enemies within" and planning and preparation for surprise attack. Accordingly, the wise protagonist should discount sharply the enemy's verbal behavior and make plans for dealing with him on the basis of "worst case" assumptions, including the likely violation of formal agreements.

The Waiverer.   The waiverer role applies to actors peripherally involved in the protagonist-enemy conflict. Because of its less direct involvement and the Chinese predilection to avoid emphasizing "middle characters," the profile of the waiverer is less completely developed. Essentially, occupants of this role

1. Hold intermediate class positions, being neither at the top nor at the bottom of a predominant class system;
2. Hold interests not identical with those of the protagonist or those of the enemy;
3. Cannot be fully relied upon, because their marginal status makes them susceptible to the threats and rewards of the enemy;
4. Can on occasion be mobilized by promises and threats from the protagonist.

On the basis of this image, the Chinese view actors occupying marginal status positions (whether these actors be states, groups, or individuals) as potential sources of both support and danger (1, 2). Insofar as waiverers represent assets or resources that can be marshaled in the struggle with the enemy, the impact of Chinese behavior on their relationship with the enemy receives consideration. Further, efforts to enlist their support should be made (4). However, because they cannot be fully relied upon, efforts to enlist their support should be limited to relatively low-cost, easily terminated sorts of arrangements; long-term, binding commitments with large, irretrievable "sunk cost" investments are unwise (3).

The role set with its associated images supports a number of basic orientations to the conduct of foreign affairs, many of which were illustrated in our discussion of Chinese critical incident behavior and conceptions. First, the Chinese qua protagonists should maintain a high degree of readiness and vigilance, because their enemies are constantly alert to opportunities to damage China and to launch troublesome surprises. "Whether or not we succeed in preventing a sudden attack is the pivot for deciding the next step of our success. . . . Every unit must have a specialist to take charge of that matter and to study the enemy seriously. Enemies have special techniques for launching surprise attacks" (Cheng 1966: 544). Readiness and anticipation are but one of a three-pronged strategy to deal with inevitable threats. A second ingredient is to make salient the commitment to assured resistance we introduced in our previous discussion of Chinese deterrence style. Standing firm and a psychology of defiance are essential because "capitulationist" moves will neither avoid nor terminate conflict with the enemy, but will instead increase vulnerability to attack and harassment. And supposedly mutual compromises will be voided by the enemy at the first convenient time. The third technique is to manipulate conflicts of interest between the enemy and waiverers to lessen the possibility of coalitions against China and to divert enemy resources from opposition to China to the pursuit of antagonisms with third parties. Chinese support for a militarily strong NATO and vigorous U.S. opposition to Cuban activities in Africa are illustrative. However, in the last analysis, the protagonist must be self-reliant. While China should be alert to the possibility of inducing waiverer-enemy conflict and engendering supportive behavior by waiverers, the foreign and defense policy of the People's Republic must never assume that third-party support is reliable.

Semantic Evidence: Images of Enemies

It would be naive to assume that Chinese perceptions of "real-world" adversaries simply mirror the stereotypic image calculatingly presented in plays, movies, and other media. No one expects that the Chinese regard their adversaries homogeneously as incessantly cunning, back-stabbing oppressors driven by insatiable desires. On the other hand, it is reasonable to expect images of stereotyped characters to bear some general resemblance to perceptions of actual adversaries. It seems worthwhile to explore Chinese images of enemies at several symbolic levels. The first level, that most directly related to the images presented in cultural media, concerns the characteristics Chinese attribute to enemies generically. We explore this level by examining responses to the term "enemy" *(di-ren)*. The second, somewhat more concrete symbolic level, deals with labels the Chinese documents use to identify "real-world" adversaries. The Chinese make heavy use of the term "imperialism" in portraying their enemies. Accordingly, we examine associations with it *(di-guo-zhu-yi)*. Finally, enemies are ultimately represented in the form of specific national actors, and we analyze Mainland and Hong Kong Chinese images of the Soviet Union and Japan. By comparing images of the two countries, we hope to clarify the distinguishing features of the country (the Soviet Union) currently identified as the main enemy. We do not expect isomorphism across these different symbolic levels but rather some general similarities.

To review, Chinese media portray enemies as treacherous and prone to violate agreements. Driven by an insatiable appetite for dominance, their demands will be nothing less than total. Given no possibility for conciliation, hatred of the enemy can powerfully motivate "struggle" to defeat him. This struggle will culminate in victory because enemy capabilities, while substantial, are no match for the superior organizational and decision skills of "progressive" forces. Class analysis to identify friends and enemies is one major decision skill.

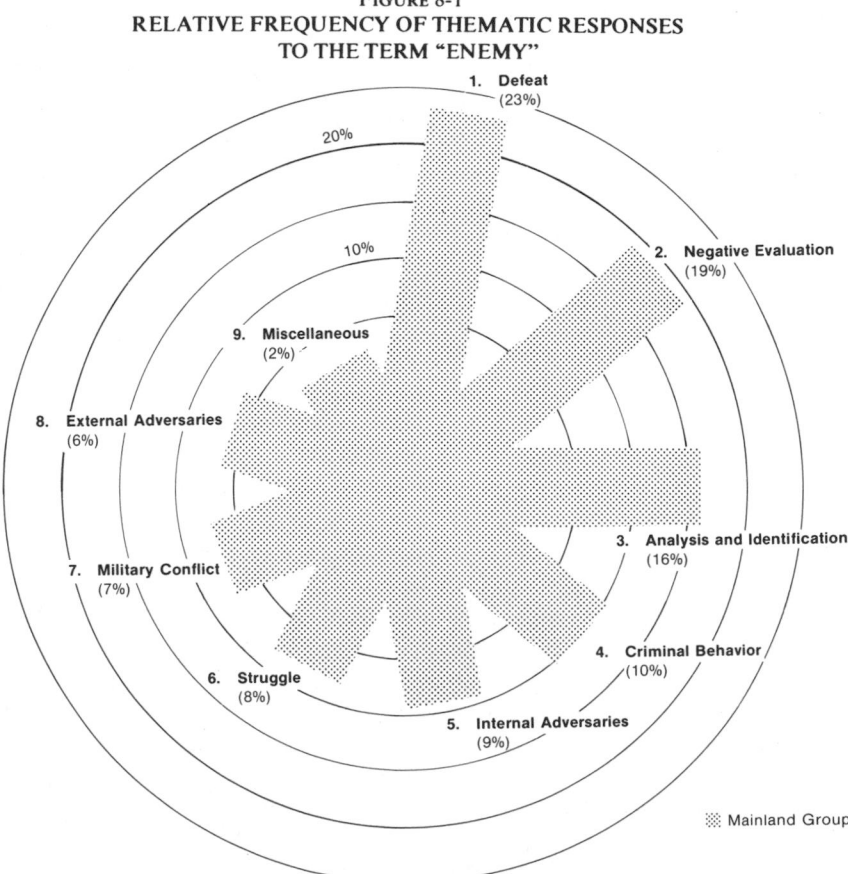

FIGURE 8-1
RELATIVE FREQUENCY OF THEMATIC RESPONSES
TO THE TERM "ENEMY"

1. Defeat (23%)
2. Negative Evaluation (19%)
3. Analysis and Identification (16%)
4. Criminal Behavior (10%)
5. Internal Adversaries (9%)
6. Struggle (8%)
7. Military Conflict (7%)
8. External Adversaries (6%)
9. Miscellaneous (2%)

Mainland Group

The pattern of Mainland responses to the stimulus "enemy" (reported in figure 8-1 and table 8-1) generally resembles the image we drew from the media. In these responses, negative references are very prominent. *Negative evaluation* (component 2) constitutes the second largest response category (19 percent); responses mentioning *criminal behavior* (component 4) are also significant (10 percent). An equally prominent theme in the Mainland responses is the *defeat* of the enemy (component 1). This set of references constitutes the single largest category, accounting for 23 percent of all responses. Having a somewhat lesser degree of prominence are those responses (in component 3) dealing with the *analysis and identification* of enemies (16 percent). In line with documentary materials, the major emphasis here is on identification of "class" enemies.

The remaining 30 percent of the coded responses are distributed across four categories: *internal adversaries* (9 percent); *struggle* (8 percent); *military conflict* (7 percent); and *external adversaries* (6 percent). Mainland references to struggle and military conflict in this connection are not unexpected. Similarly, the minor references to the United States and the Soviet Union as *external adversaries* are unremarkable. However, the inclusion of "Mao Tsu-tung" and the "Communist Party" in the listing of *internal adversaries* is obviously a reflection of distinctively refugee perceptions.

TABLE 8-1

DESCRIPTION OF THEMATIC RESPONSES
TO THE TERM "ENEMY"*

1. **Defeat** (M. 129). *Annihilate, annihilation* (M. 53) and *strike down, be struck down* (M. 42) were the most frequent responses in this component. Also significant were references to the enemy's *escape* (M. 13) and *surrender* (M. 14).
2. **Negative evaluation** (M. 103). The enemy is seen in highly negative terms. *Bad* (M. 24) and *bad person* (M. 14) were the largest of these negative responses.
3. **Analysis and Identification** (M. 90). *Class* (M. 39) was elicited as the major identifying attribute of enemies. Enemies were also seen as those who *oppose oneself* (M. 13), are *harmful to oneself* (M. 8), or are *injurious to oneself* (M. 8). Enemies were distinguished in opposition to *friends* (M. 16).
4. **Criminal Behavior** (M. 55). Enemies were associated with criminal behavior such as *murder* (M. 19) and *sabotage* (M. 13).
5. **Internal Adversaries** (M. 53). References to the *Communist party* (M. 16) and *Mao Tse-tung* (M. 6) reflect refugee dispositions of antipathy toward some aspects of the homeland regime. The *Kuomintang* (M. 10), *landlords* (M. 8), *bureaucrats* (M. 8), and *reactionaries* (M. 5) were also mentioned.
6. **Struggle** (M. 42). *Struggle* (M. 23) was the single largest response in this component.
7. **Military Conflict** (M. 39). *Aggression* (M. 14) and *war* (M. 11) were the largest responses dealing with military conflict.
8. **External Adversaries** (M. 35). *United States* (M. 11) and *Soviet Union* (M. 6) were the only specific nation responses.

* Total Response Score: M. = 555.

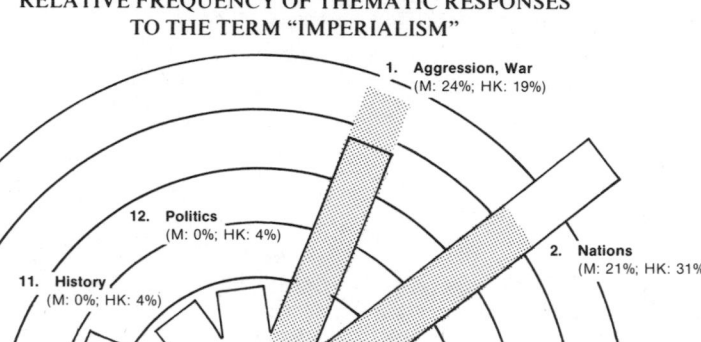

FIGURE 8-2
RELATIVE FREQUENCY OF THEMATIC RESPONSES
TO THE TERM "IMPERIALISM"

Turning to perceptions of "imperialism," we can see in figure 8-2 (and table 8-2) that the image of imperialism held by the Mainland Chinese group is also highly negative. Imperialism is primarily associated in Mainland perceptions with *aggression* and *war* (component 1). Almost one-fourth (24 pecent) of all the Mainland responses reflect this association. Other Mainland associations also indicate intensely negative perceptions of imperialism, with a large proportion of replies stressing *negative evaluation* (component 3), *oppression* (component 6), and efforts to *resist* and *defeat* imperialism (component 5). While the Hong Kong perceptions are also intensely negative, it is important to note their tendency to treat imperialism as a historical phenomenon. This is evidenced by their explicit reference to *history* (component 11) and their frequent mention of England as an imperialist power (in component 2).

The Mainland emphasis on the theme of *good, powerful* (component 3) is sufficiently anomalous to deserve some discussion. Obviously, some of the

TABLE 8-2

DESCRIPTION OF THEMATIC RESPONSES
TO THE TERM "IMPERIALISM"*

1. **Aggression, War** (M. 158, H.K. 174). For both groups, war and aggression were the predominant attributes of imperialism. Comparatively, the Hong Kong group tended to emphasize *aggression* (M. 82, H.K. 126) while the Mainland group tended to emphasize *war* (M. 55, H.K. 19).

2. **Nations** (M. 136, H.K. 276). Hong Kong responses made more mention of specific nations as imperialist actors. For the Mainland group, the three most frequently mentioned nations were the *United States* (M. 46, H.K. 78), the *Soviet Union* (M. 25, H.K. 40), and *Japan* (M. 17, H.K. 31). Not unexpectedly, the most salient imperialist power in the Hong Kong group's perceptions was *England* (M. 5, H.K. 81).

3. **Negative Evaluation** (M. 87, H.K. 69). The most salient negative references from the Mainland respondents were *bad* (M. 23, H.K. 10) and *unreasonable* (M. 21).

4. **Good, Powerful** (M. 87, H.K. 6). The Mainland group was significantly more likely to describe imperialism as good and powerful. The three largest responses were *good* (M. 24), *powerful* (M. 24, H.K. 6), and *have freedom* (M. 12). Undoubtedly, situational bias is partially responsible for the favorable responses of the Mainland group; however, such responses also seem to reflect some perception that the imperialist nations are more "free" and more "developed."

5. **Resist, Defeat** (M. 61, H.K. 14). For the Mainland group, responses mentioning resistance to imperialism and the defeat of imperialism were significant. The single largest response was *defeat* (M. 15, H.K. 7).

6. **Oppression** (M. 49, H.K. 44). Significant Mainland responses were *plunder* (M. 14) and *bandit* (M. 12); the largest Hong Kong response was *exploitation* (H.K. 31).

7. **System Types** (M. 44, H.K. 88). With regard to identification of types of imperialism, the largest references of the Mainland group were *social-imperialism* (M. 18, H.K. 8) and *the highest stage of capitalism* (M. 18, H.K. 9). Most salient for the Hong Kong group was *capitalism* (M. 8, H.K. 59).

8. **Society, Culture** (M. 10, H.K. 14). References to social and cultural aspects of imperialism were insignificant for both groups.

9. **Economy** (M. 9, H.K. 63). This response component was more significant for the Hong Kong group. The most frequent responses were *economy, economic* (M. 9, H.K. 18) and *economic aggression* (H.K. 21).

10. **Territorial Expansion** (M. 9, H.K. 86). This theme was salient only for the Hong Kong group; *colony* (M. 9, H.K. 53) was the largest response.

11. **History** (M. 0, H.K. 32). This solely Hong Kong component indicates that the Hong Kong respondents see imperialism, at least partially, as a historical phenomenon.

12. **Politics** (M. 0, H.K. 32). Explicit reference to politics was made only by the Hong Kong group. *Power* (H.K. 17) was the most salient response.

---

* Total response scores: M. = 650; H.K. = 898.

positive responses reflect bias effects operating on the Mainland refugee responses. However, some of the positive response may be linked to the association of imperialism with the developed world. As indicated in component 2, the United States, the Soviet Union, and Japan are seen, in that order, to be the major imperialist actors. Perhaps some of the positive economic and modernity image of these countries has been transferred in a modest fashion to the image of imperialism itself.

Since the United States, the Soviet Union, and Japan are the most prominently mentioned imperialist countries, an analysis of salient enemy nations ought to include all three. Unfortunately, refugee responses to the stimulus of the United States were so biased as to preclude meaningful analysis.[1] Accordingly, we limit our analysis to the different images of the Soviet Union and Japan. As will be reported in chapter 11, the differences in semantic references to these two countries coincide strongly with Chinese media references to them.

FIGURE 8-3
RELATIVE FREQUENCY OF THEMATIC RESPONSES
TO THE TERM "SOVIET UNION"

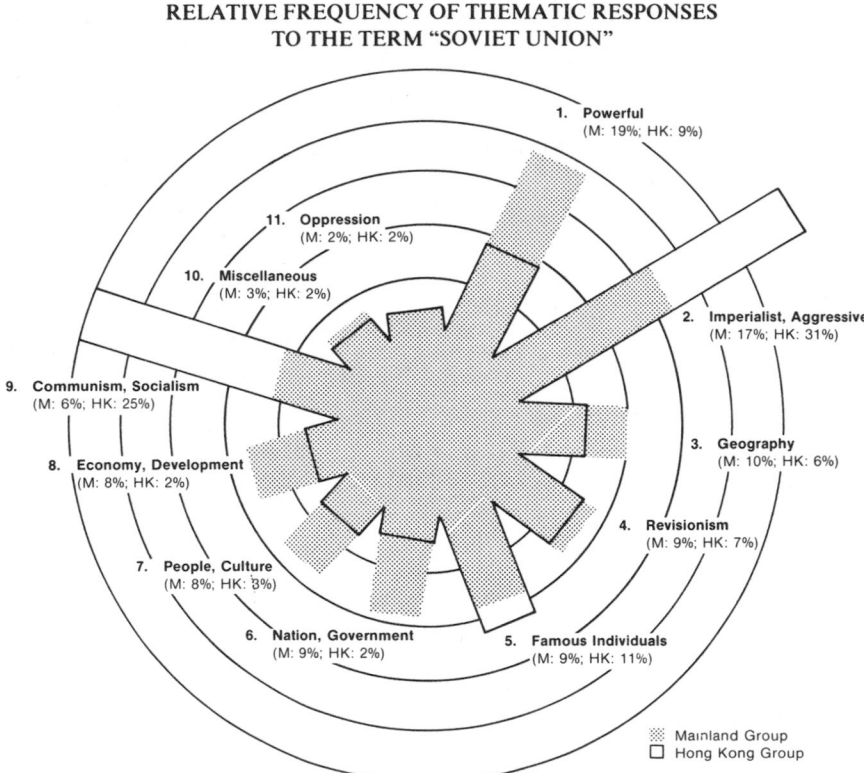

1. Powerful
(M: 19%; HK: 9%)

11. Oppression
(M: 2%; HK: 2%)

10. Miscellaneous
(M: 3%; HK: 2%)

2. Imperialist, Aggressive
(M: 17%; HK: 31%)

9. Communism, Socialism
(M: 6%; HK: 25%)

8. Economy, Development
(M: 8%; HK: 2%)

3. Geography
(M: 10%; HK: 6%)

4. Revisionism
(M: 9%; HK: 7%)

7. People, Culture
(M: 8%; HK: 3%)

6. Nation, Government
(M: 9%; HK: 2%)

5. Famous Individuals
(M: 9%; HK: 11%)

░ Mainland Group
☐ Hong Kong Group

Examination of the Mainland Chinese perceptions revealed in figure 8-3 (and table 8-3) indicates that the Soviet Union is seen as highly threatening—*imperialist, aggressive* (component 2,) *revisionist* (component 4), and *oppressive* (component 11). References to these negative characteristics account for 28 percent of all the Mainland responses. Additionally, the Main-

1. Most of the refugee interviews were conducted at a research institution composed largely of Americans. Additionally, the refugees were aware that the researcher was an American.

TABLE 8-3
DESCRIPTION OF THEMATIC RESPONSES
TO THE TERM "SOVIET UNION"*

1. **Powerful** (M. 150, H.K. 81). References describing the Soviet Union as powerful were particularly prominent in the Mainland group's responses. *Powerful country* (M. 61, H.K. 15), *great power* (M. 33), *superpower* (M. 26, H.K. 12) and *army* (M. 24) were the most prominent Mainland associations. The Hong Kong group gave particular emphasis to possession of the *nuclear bomb* (H.K. 23).

2. **Imperialist, Aggressive** (M. 134, H.K. 282). While attention to this theme was significant for both groups, the Hong Kong group's attention was considerably greater. *Aggression* (H.K. 59), *polar bear* (H.K. 36), *ambitious* (M. 14, H.K. 27), and *social-imperialism* (M. 16, H.K. 19) were the significant Hong Kong responses. *War* (M. 21) and *Sino-Soviet conflict* (M. 19) were the most prominent Mainland associations.

3. **Geography** (M. 76, H.K. 58). *Largest territory* (M. 26) and *Moscow* (M. 21) were the most salient Mainland referents; *biggest country* (H.K. 23) and *icy cold* (M. 6, H.K. 14) were the most significant Hong Kong ones.

4. **Revisionism** (M. 69, H.K. 61). Mention of Soviet *revisionism* was prominent in the responses of both groups (M. 62, H.K. 61).

5. **Famous Individuals** (M. 69, H.K. 98). *Lenin* (M. 27, H.K. 32) and *Stalin* (M. 27, H.K. 23) were the individuals most frequently named.

6. **Nation, Government** (M. 68, H.K. 17). The response *nation* was by far the most prominent one (M. 33, H.K. 17).

7. **People, Culture** (M. 65, H.K. 27). Attention to *the people* of the Soviet Union was far greater in the Mainland group's responses (M. 47, H.K. 11).

8. **Economy, Development** (M. 60, H.K. 15). The Mainland group also gave more emphasis to issues involving the Soviet economy and its development. *Science* (M. 15, H.K. 6) and *advanced* (M. 9) were the most salient responses.

9. **Communism, Socialism** (M. 47, H.K. 224). Association of the Soviet Union with communism and socialism was a major theme for the Hong Kong group, with *communism* (H.K. 79), *Communist party* (H.K. 30), and *communist great power* (H.K. 20) being the most significant responses. Reference to communism was absent in the Mainland associations, but *socialism* (M. 38, H.K. 19) was a significant response.

11. **Oppression** (M. 12, H.K. 21). Reference to Soviet oppression constituted only a minor theme for either group.

* Total Response Scores: M. = 775; H.K. = 908.

land associations show sensitivity to the capability of the Soviet Union, describing it as *powerful* (component 1) and as possessing a significant economic base (component 8). This emphasis on the threatening posture of the Soviet Union is congruent with the image of the Soviet Union that the Chinese present in public forums (see chapter 11). Interestingly, this threatening image is shared by the Hong Kong respondents, although, as might be expected from our earlier Associative Group Analysis results, the Hong Kong respondents also strongly associate the Soviet Union with *communism* and *socialism* (component 9). Parenthetically, we can note in component 9 some Mainland references to "socialism." This "lag" in public opinion behind policy change is probably facilitated by the association of the Soviet Union with revolutionary heroes such as Lenin and Stalin (component 5).

FIGURE 8-4
RELATIVE FREQUENCY OF THEMATIC RESPONSES TO THE TERM "JAPAN"

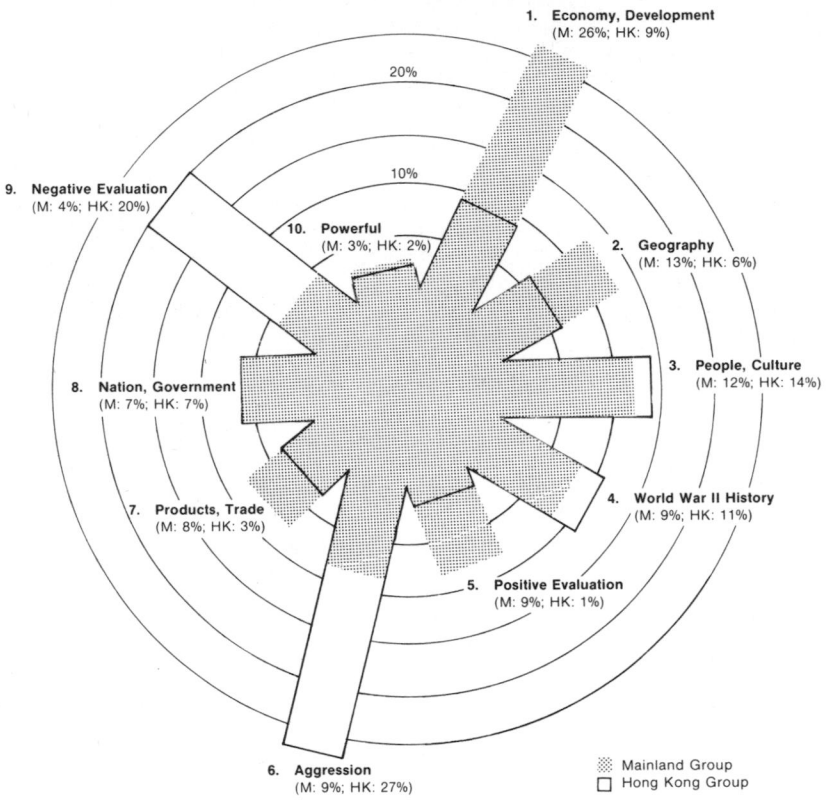

Looking at the image of Japan held by the Mainland Chinese (figure 8-4 and table 8-4), the differences relative to the Soviet Union are apparent. Most obviously, Japan is seen in less threatening terms. References to Japanese aggression are relatively infrequent (components 4 and 6), and at least half of those references treat Japanese aggressive behavior in historical terms (component 4). There is little perception that Japan is a powerful nation that needs to be feared. In contrast to perceptions of the Soviet Union, Mainland responses about Japan clearly emphasize economic development rather than military threat (components 1, 7, and 10). And, the presence of a large number of associations stressing *positive evaluation* (component 5) relative to those stressing *negative evaluation* (component 9) is significant. With respect to negative comments, the relative absence of Mainland responses dealing with national stereotypes is particularly noteworthy. Finally, the absence of references to Japan as a "capitalist" system should be noted. While Mainland respondents readily categorized the Soviet Union as "revisionist" or

TABLE 8-4
DESCRIPTION OF THEMATIC RESPONSES
TO THE TERM "JAPAN"*

1. **Economy, Development** (M. 204, H.K. 89). The responses of the Mainland group placed great umphasis on Japan's economic development. The largest Mainland responses were *industrial development* (M. 48), *industry* (M. 29, H.K. 33), *rapid development* (M. 28), and *development* (M. 21).

2. **Geography** (M. 101, H.K. 56). Reference to aspects of Japan's geography was also significant in the Mainland group's responses. Mention of Japan as an *island nation* (M. 34, H.K. 17) was particularly prominent.

3. **People, Culture** (M. 90, H.K. 127). Mainland and Hong Kong responses show roughly comparable attention to the Japanese people and their culture. By far the most frequent Mainland reference was *the people* (M. 42, H.K. 7). Hong Kong responses were considerably less focused, mentioning various aspects of Japanese culture such as Japanese *national character* (H.K. 12), *samurai spirit* (H.K. 12), and *the Emperor* (M. 15, H.K. 11).

4. **World War II History** (M. 70, H.K. 99). Both groups made reference to World War II history in their responses. Particular attention to the Sino-Japanese war was revealed in such responses as *invaded China* (M. 14, H.K. 29) and *anti-Japanese war of resistance* (M. 13, H.K. 19). Two other prominent responses were *vanquished nation* (M. 18) and *World War II* (H.K. 17).

5. **Positive Evaluation** (M. 69, H.K. 11). Responses reflecting positive evaluation of Japan were more significant for the Mainland respondents. In particular, Japan was described as *prosperous* (M. 17) and *advanced* (M. 13).

6. **Aggression** (M. 67, H.K. 252). In the Hong Kong group's responses, tremendous emphasis was placed on references to Japanese aggression and aggressiveness. The most prominent of these references were *aggression* (M. 7, H.K. 84), *militarism* (H.K. 43), *ambitious* (H.K. 39), and *economic aggressor* (H.K. 16).

7. **Products, Trade** (M. 63, H.K. 25). Just as it stressed Japanese economic development (component 1), the Mainland group made more frequent reference to Japanese products and trade.

8. **Nation, Government** (M. 54, H.K. 70). The largest Mainland responses were *nation* (M. 18) and *established diplomatic relations with China* (M. 14); the largest Hong Kong responses were *China* (H.K. 19) and *name of a nation* (H.K. 12).

9. **Negative Evaluation** (M. 29, H.K. 191). Negative references were significantly greater for the Hong Kong group, and they tended to deal with personal characteristics of Japanese people. Most prominently, Japanese people were described as *imitators* (H.K. 48), *dwarfs* (H.K. 25), *cunning* (H.K. 19), and *selfish* (H.K. 14).

10. **Powerful** (M. 25, H.K. 21). Descriptions of Japan as a powerful nation were infrequent for both groups. Rather, Japan tended to be described as *an economic power* (M. 11, H.K. 7) or as an *Asian power* (H.K. 14).

* Total Response Scores: M. = 772; H.K. = 941.

"socialist," this labeling of system types was not salient in perceptions of Japan.

In comparing the differences between the images of the Soviet Union and Japan and in assessing similarities in the perception of enemies at several symbolic levels, what patterns emerge? The marked hostility in perceptions of adversaries is evident. Of course, strongly negative evaluation of enemies is common throughout the world, although differences may exist in the degree to which groups conceive of enemies as "middle characters" with both positive and negative attributes. Clearly, Mainland perceptions of enemies do not emphasize such a mixture of attributes. More significantly, Mainland perceptions of enemies stress strongly both their actively aggressive nature and their substantial capacity to do mischief. This is particularly marked for their current officially recognized main enemy, the Soviet Union. While these images are hardly unique to Chinese foreign affairs perceptions, they do seem to be exaggerated to a greater degree. For example, verbal association data on American perceptions of "communism," the U.S. analogue to "imperialism," indicate considerable negative evaluation but hardly involve attribution of the same degree of either activity or potency (Szalay et al. 1971). Similar results have been found for American perceptions of the Soviet Union (Szalay et al. 1973). Any such tendency for the Chinese to emphasize the activity and capability of adversaries is likely to strengthen their emphasis on "worst case" reasoning about their principal adversary in foreign affairs. Whether or not the image of the Soviet Union is realistic is not a matter we wish to judge. It is clear that the images of the two national adversaries just discussed differ from each other in ways that most neutral observers would find reasonable.

Our semantic data clearly suggest some Chinese internalization of the beliefs provided by authorized publications and cultural materials. We find convergence in this aspect of Chinese policy analytics as we did with respect to beliefs explored earlier through both qualitative content analysis and semantic association methods.

Relationships between Actors

The dynamics of foreign affairs, and of politics more generally, are dealt with by means of beliefs about how actors relate to each other and about the "laws" that apply to their interactions. Some of these refer to relationships of antagonistic contradiction, whose three roles we have just examined. Others deal with alternative connections between parties. As we shall see, a number of the beliefs and conceptions discussed in terms of Chinese views of international conflict follow from the axioms below.

1. Contradictions are central to every relationship.
   (a) Every actor relationship can be characterized in terms of a set of contradictions; however, at any given moment, there is a principal contradiction.
   (b) Contradictions can be antagonistic or nonantagonistic. In antagonistic relationships the interests of the actors are fundamentally opposed; in nonantagonistic relationships the actors share a basic identity of interests.
   (c) In international affairs, nonantagonistic contradictions are relative, conditional, and temporary while antagonistic contradictions are absolute and protracted.

    (d) The nature of contradictions characteristic of an actor relationship changes over time; therefore, primary contradictions can become secondary contradictions and antagonistic contradictions can become nonantagonistic contradictions (and vice versa).
2. The resolution of contradictions is reached through struggle between the relevant actors.
    (a) Action strategies to cope with contradictions are contingent upon the nature of the principal contradiction.
    (b) Antagonistic contradictions can only be resolved through violence and coercion, although violent and coercive means can be temporarily deferred because the particular contradiction in question is not the primary one at the moment.
    (c) The resolution of antagonistic contradictions is achieved when one actor dominates or subjugates another actor.
    (d) The resolution of contradictions is always temporary and unstable; it only leads to the emergence of new contradictions of a higher order.
3. The resolution of contradictions is determined by the relative capabilities of the actors.
    (a) The actors have what are in reality unequal capabilities.
    (b) The balance of capabilities between the actors is always changing.
    (c) Quantitative changes in the balance will lead to qualitative changes.
    (d) Effecting internal changes within the actors is the key to effecting external changes in the balance between the actors.

These notions about antagonistic and nonantagonistic contradictions limit as well as open up feasible foreign policy options. On the one hand, cooperative arrangements are viewed as temporary and unstable; basic differences in interests can only be resolved through struggle. "Unity of opposites is conditional, temporary and transient; while struggle between opposites is absolute" (Mao quoted in Tientsin Writing Group 1975: 47). On the other hand, all international relations are viewed to have both antagonistic and nonantagonistic aspects. This indicates the need to discriminate between the different aspects of actor relationships and suggests the possibility of exploiting these differences. "United front" tactics are therefore a legitimate and important part of Chinese strategy. "The enemies of the revolutionary forces are definitely not monolithic. Their class nature determines that they contend as well as collude with one another. Their collusion serves the purpose of more intensified contention. Contention is absolute and protracted, whereas collusion is relative and temporary. This being the case, the revolutionary forces can make use of their contradictions" (Hung 1973: 11).

Differentiating the principal contradiction from secondary contradictions (1a), discriminating antagonistic contradictions from nonantagonistic contradictions (1b), and recognizing possible permutations in actor relationships

(1d) all operate against rigid policy. Furthermore, the distinctions between primary and secondary contradictions and between antagonistic and non-antagonistic contradictions enable the Chinese to pursue a "principled stance" while allowing for tactical flexibility. They allow them to "be unyielding on principles, and . . . also maintain flexibility in order to realize all that is allowed and required by principles" (Mao quoted in Study Team 1974: 27).

The generalizations in the first axiom lead to an emphasis on struggle (2), both with respect to China's direct relations with others and the relationships between second and third parties. For China itself, they lead to the previously mentioned view of conflict in international relations as the norm rather than the exception ("one divides into two, while two cannot be combined into one"). For Chinese analysis of situations primarily involving relations between other nations and foreign groups, emphasis goes to detecting antagonistic contradictions, which can then be manipulated and exploited to China's advantage. This calls for careful discrimination between different actor relationships, and adaptation of Chinese policy accordingly. In doing so, decision making should give priority to treating the principal contradiction, since it provides the key to resolving the other, secondary contradictions (2a). Concentrating on the enemy who is the current principal adversary makes possible the mobilization of the greatest amount of resources to defeat it. Hence,

> Chairman Mao criticized the wrong practice of striking with two "fists" in two directions at the same time. In a certain period of time, there are always main and secondary enemies. In order to isolate the main enemy to the greatest extent and concentrate all forces to strike it, the revolutionary forces enter into certain necessary compromises with some other enemies at a given time. . . . "Make use of contradictions, win over the many, oppose the few, and crush our enemies one by one" [Hung 1973: 12].

Differences between the basic interests of actors can only be resolved through armed struggle (2b). "The central task and the highest form of revolution is the armed seizure of political power, that is, resorting to war to solve problems" (Mao quoted in Study Team 1974: 83). Only power backed up by coercive capabilities is credible and efficacious ("political power grows out of the barrel of a gun"), and only the use or threat of use of coercive capabilities will achieve fundamental social reforms. Intermediate political measures to resolve differences in interests will not suffice, because they will not lead to any fundamental change in the conditions responsible for the actors' basic antagonism. For example, arms-control agreements between the superpowers cannot reduce international tension because they do not change the intention of each superpower to dominate all others. And the Chinese see antagonistic relations in terms of zero-sum games (2c). In East-West relations, "either the east wind prevails over the west wind, or the west wind prevails over the east wind; on this issue there is no other alternative" (Mao quoted in Study Team 1974: 35). Compromise and moderation can only encourage aggression and undermine one's own position. "With regard to reactionary lines and with regard to erroneous things, if you do not struggle against them, they will struggle against you; if you yield to them, they will spread freely; if you tolerate them, they will become ever more aggressive; if you seek accommodations with them, they will devour you" (Study Team 1974: 34–35).

Beliefs about the permanence of contradictions (1) and the constant change in actor relationships (1d) preclude a static view of conflict resolution. Therefore, the resolution of contradictions is always unstable (2d). The defeat of reactionary elements by progressive elements is never complete; the remnants of the defeated elements will attempt to "reverse history." Vigilance including military preparedness is a continuing necessity.

The stress on struggle and coercive change (2) naturally leads to concerns about actor capabilities (3). Unequal capabilities are to be expected (3a). This inequality leads the dominant party to try to exploit the inferior party and encourages international conflict. Parity or equilibrium arrangements will not deter conflict (3b). Arrangements to freeze actor capability are illusory because of inevitable change and are undesirable because they only help to perpetuate existing dominance and subservience relationships.

The emphasis on capability changes from "quantitative" to "qualitative" transformation in actor relationships was referred to in chapter 7. They underwrite expectations of a reversal of power relationships with the progressive forces or the Chinese eventually overcoming initial inferiority in capability. Also, they imply that international conflicts and critical incidents are especially likely in the context of marked changes in the capability ratio, whether the change is caused by a relative improvement in protagonist or enemy posture.

The importance given to the internal properties of participants in international affairs (3d) helps put military force ratios in perspective and makes the capabilities they imply also a factor of the wisdom of national officials and mobilization of human resources. It also leads to an emphasis on internal development in contrast to a reliance on external alliances. This perspective manifests itself in Chinese contentions that national liberation movements must depend on indigenous support and leadership rather than external military assistance, and that domestic socioeconomic development must not involve dependence on foreign aid. Diagnostically, economic and political instability are seen as sources of reactionary aggression and as opportunities for revolutionary action. Increases in internal instability in reactionary societies are likely then to be followed in relatively short order by stepped-up reactionary aggression (unjust wars) and resistance by the external and internal victims of reactionary regimes (just wars). Given the importance of internal politics, Chinese policy should attend to and manipulate political differences in enemy and waiverer nations. Important instruments for the latter purpose are people-to-people diplomacy and support for insurgent groups (Van Ness 1970).

It follows from the three major axioms that effective policy involves implementing several general maxims. We turn to these now:

4. The inferior party can only survive and become dominant through struggle.
   (a) Psychologically, the inferior party must possess attitudes of defiance, determination, and perseverance.
   (b) Long-run victory against a currently superior enemy follows from skillful manipulation of the balance of capabilities.
5. The inferior party must shape the behavior of intermediate actors (the waiverers mentioned previously) in order to achieve and maintain dominance.
   (a) The inferior party should form a "united front" with other parties to compensate for his own weaknesses and to deny the dominant party additional increments of capability.
   (b) Even after achieving dominance, the protagonist should continue to form coalitions with others to bar adversaries from reversing the situation.
   (c) The protagonist should pursue a strategy of "divide and rule," fragmenting enemy alliances to weaken and then overcome his adversaries and creating the preconditions for the two previous injunctions.
   (d) In carrying out coalition tactics, the protagonist should make timely and appropriate concessions to intermediate actors and secondary enemies.

In applying these maxims, the Chinese consistently cast themselves as the inferior party and the protagonist. The prospect of dominance and subjugation precludes passive acceptance of the status quo. "When facing reactionary counter currents, 'if we do not struggle, we will be put to death; and if we do not wage bloody wars, we will be destroyed' " (Study Team 1974: 25). Autonomy and eventual dominance sustain the will to struggle against a superior foe (4a). "As long as the peoples of small countries dare to struggle, dare to pick up weapons, dare to command the destiny of their own countries, they can certainly defeat the aggression of large countries. This is a historical law" (Mao quoted in Worker-Peasant-Soldier Team 1971b: 84). The adversity the inferior party must undergo calls for a willingness to endure hardships and setbacks, bolstered by faith in the righteousness of his cause and the infallibility of his action principles.

Because the policy of self-reliance is unlikely to improve significantly China's inferiority in the near term, coalition formation and fragmentation tactics can help compensate for China's relative weaknesses in international affairs (5). The inferior party should form a "united front" with intermediate groups in order to defeat the superior party (5a). He should also exploit contradictions between the primary enemy and intermediate groups so as to attract membership to his camp and divert pressure from China to other targets (5b, 5c). Under certain circumstances, the inferior party should be willing to make concessions to secondary enemies to gain time to develop his capabilities (5d). As mentioned in chapter 4, the Brest-Litovsk treaty provides for the Chinese an exemplar of how to temporize conflict. Even after attaining superiority the protagonist should continue to pursue coalition formation to isolate prospective challengers to this position (5b, 5c). He should strive to convert the intermediate parties into his genuine supporters, forming coalitions sequentially to absorb or eliminate these parties.

The coalition formation tactics of the protagonist serve to: (1) provide winning coalitions on particular issues, (2) neutralize potential members of the enemy's coalition, and (3) undermine the solidarity of the enemy's existing coalition. Several considerations are germane to attempts to forge winning coalitions on particular issues. The friendship or hostility of an actor to China's main enemy basically determines acceptability as a coalition partner (the enemy of my enemy is my friend) (Burchett 1976; Cleveland 1976). For example, Chinese policies toward Angola and Bangladesh supported "bourgeois" actors in order to oppose the Soviet Union. China should strive for maximum winning coalitions ("unite the middle, isolate the extremes"). Of course, since the class standpoint of an actor indicates his fidelity to coalition goals, Communists were told that "To distinguish real friends from real enemies, we must make a general analysis of the economic status of the various classes in Chinese society and of their respective attitudes towards the revolution" (Mao quoted in Schram 1967: 7).

The Chinese should exploit contradictions within and between opponents ("sit on the mountain, and watch the tigers fight"). Efforts that concentrate on enemy weak links provide the greatest chance for success. These may be domestic political opposition, nonconforming members of the enemy coalition, members vulnerable to internal or external pressure, and issues and places ignored or uncontested by the main enemy. Chinese efforts can also be effective by providing critical support in contests between third parties, one of whom is supported by the main enemy. An example of this policy is Peking's support for one of the contestants in stalemated disputes such as in the Indian-Pakistani conflict. Another Chinese coalition tactic encourages opposing power centers to distract China's main enemy. In this respect, a militarily strong and united Western Europe can alleviate Soviet pressure on China. Finally, confrontation by proxies provides a low-cost and low-risk approach to sap the resources and energy of China's main adversary. It reduces his threat to China and allows additional time to augment Chinese capabilities.

Coalition formation requires careful analysis of the impact of China's policies and the policies of other parties on the intermediate groups. Cooperation with the intermediate parties may have undesirable contamination effects on domestic groups within China. Because intermediate groups cannot be trusted to come to China's aid at critical moments, policy makers must be alert to the prospect that coalitions will disintegrate. The injunction to form a "united front" and defeat "our enemies one by one" calls for an ability to control the focus and timing of conflict. Policy makers should thus be able to seize the main contradiction of the moment and suppress and delay confrontation with the secondary enemies until conditions are ripe.

As discussed earlier, international relations persistently change and international coalitions are inherently unstable. The Chinese view three factors as triggering the breakup of coalitions. First, victory over the common enemy precipitates conflict between the coalition partners. Second, changes in the capabilities of coalition members or changes in the capabilities between opposing coalitions attenuate coalition ties. Third, high threat from the opposition or setbacks to the protagonist encourage defection by third parties. These parties are by nature opportunistic, and they will "bend in the direction the prevailing wind blows."

Accordingly, the Chinese believe that coalitions are particularly fragile under conditions of active or imminent war and crisis. When these conditions create dissent within the reactionary camp and reveal the true nature of the reactionaries (aggressive, unreliable, and "weak-kneed"), they provide opportunities for China to mobilize opposition against them. When these events involve the reactionaries and third parties, China can benefit because reactionary aggression will antagonize intermediate parties and alienate the aggressors' own coalition partners. By the same token, when China or its close associates are heavily involved, Peking should guard against reactionary attempts to divide the socialist or progressive camp. The rationale becomes stronger for China to make considerable concessions to the intermediate actors and even secondary enemies to neutralize and, if possible, attract them to join in a struggle against the main enemy.

Semantic Evidence: Images of Contradiction and Class Struggle

If documentary injunctions about actor relationships have been accepted by the population of the People's Republic, they should be reflected in the associations with the key terms of "contradiction," "struggle," and "class." Sound analysis doctrinally follows from correct assessment of the relevant contradiction in a situation (for example, as primary or secondary, antagonistic or nonantagonistic). For antagonistic contradiction, the correct response is that of struggle. And both the diagnosis of contradictions and the response strategy should reflect sound analysis of the class stands of the pertinent groups.

Figure 8-5 and table 8-5 summarize the themes associated by Mainland and Hong Kong respondents with the stimulus "contradiction" (*mao-dun*). The Mainland group's responses emphasize the use of contradictions in problem solving; the three largest Mainland response categories are *resolution, diagnosis,* and *existence and development.* Mainland attention to the resolution of contradictions is considerably greater than that of the Hong Kong group (16 to 6 percent), with the responses "resolve" and "unite" being the most salient. The differences in emphasis with regard to the *diagnosis, existence and development,* and *progress* themes (components 2, 3, and 9) are not as great, but again indicate greater salience for the Mainland respondents. Comparison of the relative stress on the aggregate categories probably understates the divergence in perceptions. The responses within these categories also reveal important differences. For example, the Mainland responses in the *diagnosis* category are considerably more complex and differentiated. [2]

In contrast, the responses of the Hong Kong group focus on theory and particular theoreticians (Mao, for example). This greater emphasis (H.K. 23 percent; M. 6 percent) indicates some knowledge of Mainland politics among

FIGURE 8-5
RELATIVE FREQUENCY OF THEMATIC RESPONSE
TO THE TERM "CONTRADICTION"

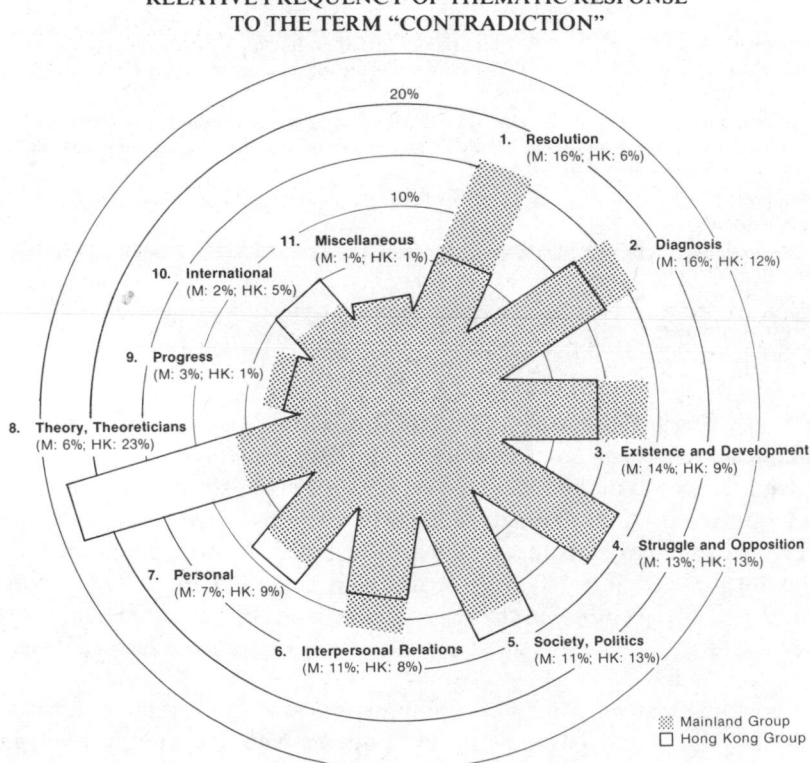

2. Mainland references included the following: "thought," "complex," "internal," "discuss," "problem," "issue," "within," "primary," "secondary," "specification," "empirical." Hong Kong responses were limited to the replies of "thought," "discuss," and "heart" (of a problem).

TABLE 8-5
DESCRIPTION OF THEMATIC RESPONSES
TO THE TERM "CONTRADICTION"*

---

1. **Resolution** (M. 125, H.K. 33). This is the most salient component for the Mainland group. In comparison, Hong Kong references are infrequent. *Resolve* (M. 74, H.K. 7) and *unite* (M. 34) are the most salient responses for the Mainland group.

2. **Diagnosis** (M. 123, H.K. 67). The response *thought* was a significant one for both groups (M. 25, H.K. 38). Mainland responses also stressed that contradictions were *complex* (M. 21).

3. **Existence and Development** (M. 111, H.K. 50). This theme was stressed somewhat more in the Mainland responses. Both groups emphasized the *existence* (M. 23, H.K. 22) and *occurrence* (M. 18, H.K. 10) of contradictions. In addition, significant Mainland responses were *sharpening* (M. 14) and *cannot be eliminated* (M. 20).

4. **Struggle and Opposition** (M. 101, H.K. 76). This theme was emphasized by both groups. *Struggle* (M. 33, H.K. 25) was the most frequent response. *Conflict* was a significant response for the Hong Kong group (H.K. 26); *enemy and us* was a significant response for the Mainland group (M. 21, H.K. 7).

5. **Society, Politics** (M. 86, H.K. 73). *Politics* was a significant response for the Hong Kong group (H.K. 28). *Society* (M. 18, H.K. 5) and *class* (M. 16, H.K. 21) were mentioned by both groups.

6. **Interpersonal Relations** (M. 86, H.K. 47). *Interpersonal* (M. 15, H.K. 17) was the largest single response.

7. **Personal** (M. 56, H.K. 55). *Self*-(contradiction) was the most frequent response for the Mainland group (M. 16, H.K. 7); *psychology* was the most frequent for the Hong Kong group (H.K. 23).

8. **Theory, Theoreticians** (M. 47, H.K. 134). This is the largest component for the Hong Kong respondents. *Mao Tse-tung* (M. 7, H.K. 37) and Mao's essay, *"On Contradiction"* (M. 40, H.K. 36) were the most frequent responses.

9. **Progress** (M. 21, H.K. 6). This is a minor theme for both the Mainland and the Hong Kong respondents.

10. **International** (M. 19, H.K. 32). *War* is the most significant response for the Hong Kong group (H.K. 14).

---

* Total Response Scores: M. = 784; H.K. = 581.

the Hong Kong group. But it is important to note that this type of response does not indicate the use of "contradictions" as a problem-solving tool.

We have noted that Chinese doctrine emphasizes struggle as the appropriate means to handle antagonistic contradictions—that is, contradictions involving conflict with an enemy. Since antagonistic contradictions are based on conflicts of class interest, "class struggle" is the dominant form of conflict. Struggle between conflicting classes ends in victory for one and defeat for the other. Thus cadres are urged to pay careful attention to class analysis in decision situations.

Figures 8-6 and 8-7 (and the accompanying tables) report the associations of the Mainland and Hong Kong respondents with the stimuli "struggle" (*dou-zheng*) and "class" (*jie-ji*). The data clearly indicate that the notion of "class struggle" is embedded in Mainland perceptions. *Class* constitutes the largest set of responses to the stimulus "struggle"; references to *struggle, conflict* constitute the second largest group of Mainland replies to the stimulus "class." The preceived linkage between the two terms is strong. Somewhat surprisingly, references by the Hong Kong group stress the notion of "class struggle" as well. As we shall see later, this emphasis relates to their views about communism and socialism.

Beyond the evident internalization of the concept of "class struggle," several Mainland response patterns are congruent with documentary injunctions about struggle. The Mainland group perceived struggle as conflict with an enemy (component 8), which results in either victory or defeat (component 2). Further, as indicated in the theme indentified as *correct attitudes* (component 3), the Mainland subjects were more inclined to see struggle as necessary (for example, "must," "sacrifice") or beneficial (for example, "can temper," "advance"). Concomitantly, they were less likely than the Hong Kong subjects to view struggle in negative terms (component 5). This is significant in view of the severe personal experiences of members of the Mainland group in struggle contexts. Finally, with respect to the stimulus "class," the extensive development of the vocabulary of *class analysis* should

FIGURE 8-6
RELATIVE FREQUENCY OF THEMATIC RESPONSE
TO THE TERM "STRUGGLE"

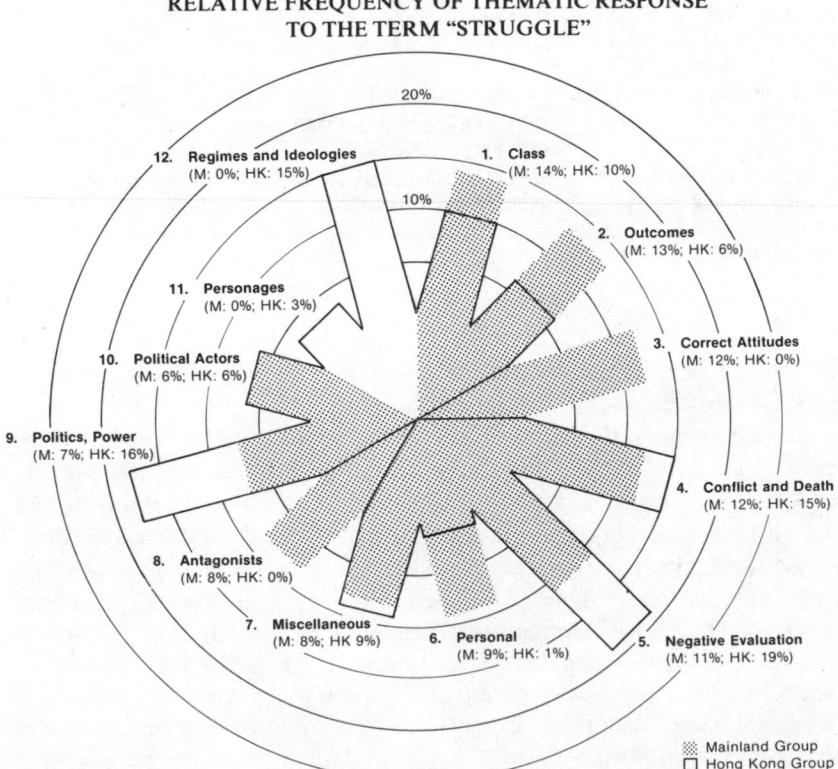

TABLE 8-6
DESCRIPTION OF THEMATIC RESPONSES
TO THE TERM "STRUGGLE"*

1. **Class** (M. 105, H.K. 65). This is the single largest component of the Mainland group's responses. The response *class* (M. 99, H.K. 60) was the most frequent one for both groups.

2. **Outcomes** (M. 97, H.K. 38). Mainland responses focused strongly on *victory* (M. 50, H.K. 10) and *defeat* (M. 23). Other Mainland responses centered on favorable struggle outcomes—*creates peace* (M. 13), *success* (M. 6), and *fruitful* (M. 5). The most salient Hong Kong response was *continuous* (H.K. 19).

3. **Correct Attitudes** (M. 91, H.K. 0). This component reflects Mainland regime efforts to develop "correct attitudes" toward struggle. The most significant responses were *must* (M. 13), *can temper* (M. 11), *sacrifice* (M. 11), *complex* (M. 11), and *advance* (M. 9).

4. **Conflict and Death** (M. 89, H.K. 96). Both groups see struggle as involving conflict and death. *Bloodshed* (M. 22, H.K. 21), *armed force* (H.K. 18), *war* (M. 10, H.K. 11), and *death* (M. 11, H.K. 6) were the largest responses.

5. **Negative Evaluation** (M. 88, H.K. 122). Somewhat more emphasis on negative evaluation was made in the Hong Kong group's responses. *Cruel* (H.K. 35), *brutal* (H.K. 23), and *pain* (H.K. 16) were the largest Hong Kong responses; *very painful* (M. 30), *unreasonable* (M. 13), and *terrible* (M. 11) were the largest Mainland responses.

6. **Personal** (M. 68, H.K. 7). Personal references were limited almost exclusively to the Mainland group. *Livelihood* (M. 12) and *self-* (M. 9) were the most salient ones.

8. **Antagonists** (M. 61, H.K. 0). This Mainland component reflects references to *enemy* (M. 25) and *bad person* (M. 15) in particular.

9. **Politics, Power** (M. 51, H.K. 100). Mainland responses centered on *politics, political* (M. 24, H.K. 15), and *policy line* (M. 13). The most salient Hong Kong references were *power* (H.K. 54) and *power struggle* (H.K. 20).

10. **Political Actors** (M. 49, H.K. 40). *Communist party* (M. 10, H.K. 16), *the people* (M. 17, H.K. 5), and *cadres* (M. 13, H.K. 6) were the most significant responses.

11. **Personages** (M. 0, H.K. 21). This theme received slight mention by the Hong Kong group only.

12. **Regimes and Ideologies** (M. 0, H.K. 94). This solely Hong Kong component centered on *Chinese communism* (H.K. 37), *communism* (H.K. 20), and the *Soviet Union* (H.K. 18).

* Total response scores: M. = 764; H.K. = 638.

be noted. The more numerous and finely differentiated Mainland associations suggest a sophisticated class-analysis vocabulary.

In comparison with the Mainland respondents, Hong Kong perceptions of "class struggle" are distinctive in two respects. Most obviously, the Hong Kong group associated "class struggle" with socialism, communism, and communist countries. For the stimulus "struggle" (figure 8-6), these associations account for 15 percent of all the responses given by the Hong Kong group. For the stimulus "class" (figure 8-7), such references constitute 12 percent of all replies. In both cases, Mainland references of this sort are insignificant. In other words, while the Hong Kong respondents interpreted "class struggle" to be a distinctive feature of communist or socialist systems, the Mainland respondents treated it more as a universal. Second, Hong Kong perceptions of "struggle" were colored strongly by the notion of "power struggle"

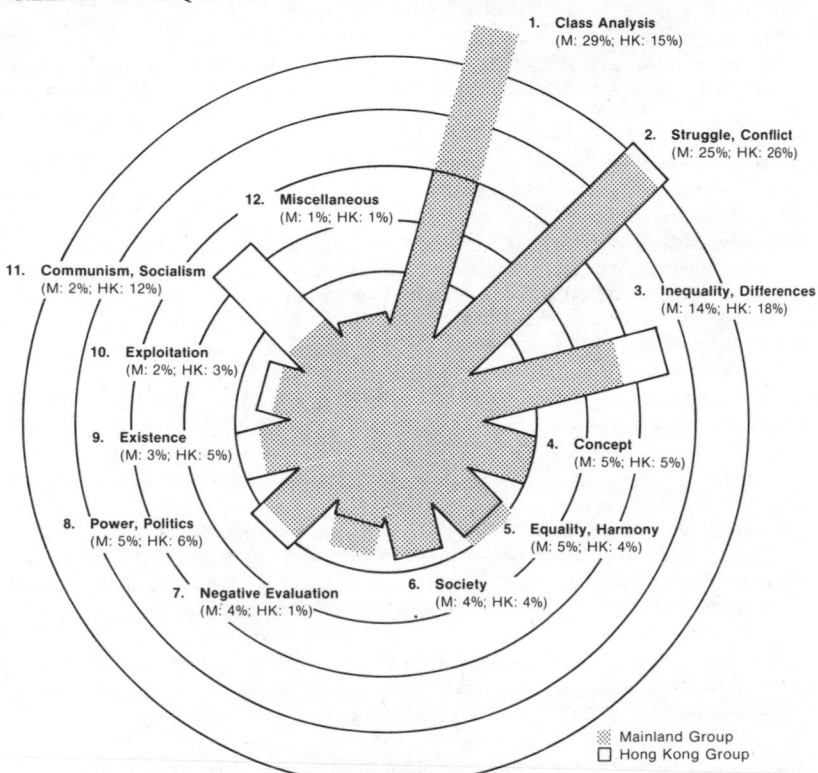

1. Class Analysis
    (M: 29%; HK: 15%)

2. Struggle, Conflict
    (M: 25%; HK: 26%)

12. Miscellaneous
     (M: 1%; HK: 1%)

11. Communism, Socialism
     (M: 2%; HK: 12%)

3. Inequality, Differences
    (M: 14%; HK: 18%)

10. Exploitation
     (M: 2%; HK: 3%)

9. Existence
    (M: 3%; HK: 5%)

4. Concept
    (M: 5%; HK: 5%)

8. Power, Politics
    (M: 5%; HK: 6%)

5. Equality, Harmony
    (M: 5%; HK: 4%)

7. Negative Evaluation
    (M: 4%; HK: 1%)

6. Society
    (M: 4%; HK: 4%)

Mainland Group
Hong Kong Group

(component 9). As indicated elsewhere (Kringen 1978: 164), power as a concept does not seem to be important to Mainland perceptions of politics.

To summarize, the above patterns indicate substantial congruence between documentary injunctions about contradictions and struggle and the views held by persons who lived until recently in Mainland China. Such similarity does not directly confirm our inferences about the decision logics used by the Chinese to make foreign policy choices, but it does give us confidence that the views in documentary sources represent something far more important than mere public rationalization.

Universal Clarity and Situational Ambiguity

The beliefs introduced in this and the previous chapter provide a clear set of precepts for Chinese officials to follow in foreign affairs. Basically, they should retain autonomy about the timing of their actions and not let themselves be

TABLE 8-7
DESCRIPTION OF THEMATIC RESPONSES
TO THE TERM "CLASS"*

1. **Class Analysis** (M. 259, H.K. 112). The Mainland responses reveal a considerably more extensive and richer set of class-analysis terminology. The largest Mainland responses were *bourgeoisie* (M. 65, H.K. 13), *proletariat* (M. 42, H.K. 34), *worker* (M. 33, H.K. 17), *landlord* (M. 30), *peasant* (M. 19), *poor peasant* (M. 15), and *rich peasant* (M. 12).

2. **Struggle, Conflict** (M. 229, H.K. 194). References to class struggle and class conflict were prominent for both groups. The response *struggle* (M. 149, H.K. 160) was by far the most frequent.

3. **Inequality, Differences** (M. 131, H.K. 131). To a significant extent, class was associated by both groups with inequality or differences in wealth and status. *Difference* (M. 32, H.K. 12) and *segregate* (M. 18) were the most salient Mainland responses; *rich and poor* (H.K. 28) and *inequality* (M. 14, H.K. 17) were the most salient Hong Kong responses.

4. **Concept** (M. 49, H.K. 37). *Concept* (H.K. 21) was the largest Hong Kong response; *elements* (M. 16) was the largest Mainland response.

5. **Equality, Harmony** (M. 47, H.K. 26). The most significant Mainland responses were *solidarity* (M. 13) and *brothers* (M. 11); the most significant Hong Kong responses were *equality* (M. 9, H.K. 11) and *harmony* (H.K. 10).

6. **Society** (M. 39, H.K. 28). References to *society* (M. 34, H.K. 28) compose almost all the responses in this component.

7. **Negative Evaluation** (M. 34, H.K. 16). Comments reflecting negative evaluation were more significant for the Mainland group. *Hatred* (M. 16) was the most prominent response.

8. **Power, Politics** (M. 43, H.K. 43). The Mainland responses placed more emphasis on *policy line* (M. 14) and *politics* (M. 10), while the Hong Kong responses emphasized *power* (H.K. 8) and *force* (H.K. 8).

9. **Existence** (M. 25, H.K. 37). Both the Mainland and Hong Kong respondents called attention to the objective existence of class divisions.

10. **Exploitation** (M. 21, H.K. 25). Class exploitation was a minor theme in the responses of both groups.

11. **Communism, Socialism** (M. 19, H.K. 92). The responses of the Hong Kong group emphasized the particular significance of class divisions for communism and socialism. *Communist party* (M. 10, H.K. 24) and *Marx* (H.K. 24) were the most frequently given responses.

* Total response scores: M. = 908; H.K. = 740.

trapped in a simple action-reaction process. To do so is to cede control of their future to their enemies. Instead, Communists must control the initiative and act at a time and place and in a manner of their own choosing. "When the enemy advances, we retreat; when the enemy halts, we harass; when the enemy seeks to avoid battle, we attack; when the enemy retreats, we pursue" (Mao quoted in Griffith 1963: 51). Effective deterrence lies in following four injunctions. First, never communicate weakness to the reactionaries. A posture of vigilance, strength, and determination deters attacks; a posture of indecisiveness, military unpreparedness, and domestic economic and social disarray encourages them. Second, raise the perceived costs of aggression against China far beyond the likely benefits through a two-pronged strategy of self-reliance and united action with intermediate actors. Third, divert pressure away from China by exacerbating contradictions within the reactionary world, by confronting the main enemy with other power centers of vigorous opposition, and by supporting protracted confrontation with the main enemy and its "running dogs" through proxies. In this sense, Peking might well conceive of U.S. involvement in Africa in opposition to regimes and groups supported by the Soviet Union as "playing the American card." Fourth, compromise with secondary enemies and intermediate participants in order to reserve energy for the main enemy. Sometimes even temporary concessions to the main enemy would be warranted, if they are conducive to subsequent efforts to reverse the balance of power in China's favor. Should deterrence fail or seem to waste an opportunity, China must pursue overt conflict in a highly conscious manner, seeking immediate finite gains but without triggering a cataclysmic response.

In contrast, application of the rules we attribute to the Chinese to particular situations is much less clear and calls for many complex judgments. Problems in situational application follow from many of the precepts introduced here and in chapter 7. They also stem from the bimodal maxims introduced in chapter 6: optimism-pessimism; rigidity-flexibility; boldness-caution; and emotional arousal–analytic distance.

It seems clear from the preceding pages that Chinese assessment of foreign affairs situations rests on identification of the main contradiction, estimates about the nature and timing of changes—especially qualitative change—and attributions of class composition and stand. Because these three sets of judgments are strongly interrelated, ambiguity about how to arrive at a conclusion about any one of them makes it harder to do so for the others. For example, if the main contradiction is unclear or the class stand of major parties cloudy, it is impossible to assess the impact of particular changes on the progressive forces. In the absence of a firm grasp of the nature of the main contradiction and the impact of changes on it, class analysis drifts aimlessly. After all, an actor is "progressive" or "reactionary" primarily because of its behavior in relation to the protagonist and the enemy in the main contradiction. To illustrate further, class analysis can be applied to international relations or to domestic politics. Depending on the level, conclusions may well differ. Some actors, such as major oil-producing Arab countries, can play a "progressive" role in international affairs but adopt a "reactionary" stand in domestic politics. Conversely, it is possible for some actors, such as the Portuguese Communist party and the Popular Movement for the Liberation of Angola, to play a "progressive" role in domestic politics but to be aligned closely with China's adversaries internationally. Class analysis of particular actors does not provide policy guidance until it is related to the current main contradiction of international relations.

Because the precepts introduced so far are not particularly helpful in determining basic judgments about the definition of the situation, it seems that the Chinese themselves may well disagree about the future of their foreign policy environment. Obviously, it will be very difficult for external analysts to predict if and when the Chinese will change what they identify as the main contradiction, or will conclude that a qualitative change has just occurred or can be expected at a particular point in the near future. Nevertheless, within an established Chinese position on these matters we have the core of the Chinese definition of the international environment. Barring changes on that score, we can be reasonably clear about their processing of information about particular governments, issues, and local incidents. If we know them to believe that a qualitative change has taken place in their favor, we can expect them to show heightened boldness in their foreign policy. If we know them to believe that quantitative changes are fast approaching the threshold of a qualitative change, we can expect them to redouble efforts at building a united front and inducing the other actions necessary to drain the resources and momentum of their main enemy.

Beyond the basic assessment problems just discussed, the set of attributes the Chinese attach to the primary roles in international affairs pose decision problems and doubts for them. Three areas seem to have particular policy importance. First, there are clashing Chinese beliefs about the rationality or irrationality of China's opponents. On the one hand, reactionaries are by nature aggressive, irrational madmen prone to miscalculate their own and others' strengths and intentions. If this is true, then obviously the Chinese should make "worst case" assumptions about enemy intentions and plan to cope with the enemy on that basis. On the other hand, reactionaries can make rational cost–benefit calculations. Therefore, as long as China can convince the reactionaries that the costs of attacking China outweigh the benefits, they will be deterred from aggression. If this is true, then China can minimize the probability of enemy attack by increasing the perceived costs of such attack. Policy planning should therefore be based on the relative probability of the various negative contingencies, and not on the worst contingency.

Second, coalitions with intermediate actors are of value against the main enemy, yet the coalition allies are unreliable when the chips are down. Chinese statements yield unclear implications for the emphasis to be placed on self-reliance versus external coalition in foreign policy. We infer that disagreements among Chinese leaders are likely to occur on this issue because of different appraisals of the costs and risks in pursuing these two policy lines.

Third, the Chinese are very ambivalent about the use and costs of compromises with the enemy. On the one hand, compromises are futile because the enemy is inherently aggressive and cannot be expected to abide by agreements. More significantly, compromises with the enemy are dangerous because appeasement will only whet the enemy's appetite (that is, the enemy is likely to misperceive Communist concessions as a sign of weakness). If this diagnosis is correct, the only viable and effective deterrent is to "stand firm" and "get tough." On the other hand, compromise with the enemy can buy China valuable time to develop its capabilities. Therefore, Communists should participate in "temporary truces" and "partial agreements" with the enemy to avoid an untimely, premature showdown. Again, we believe that policy disagreements among the Chinese leaders are likely on this question.

CHAPTER 9

RULES FOR POLICY DESIGN

The beliefs discussed in chapters 7 and 8 establish basic orientations toward foreign policy problems and solutions. To draw policy-specific conclusions, Chinese officials use them in combination with a third set of precepts: rules for policy design. These rules suggest good practice to Chinese officials as they engage in the ongoing foreign affairs reporting, estimation, and policy planning process. We will present and discuss them in terms of some common tasks in decision making: framing problems and information requirements, collecting and evaluating pertinent data, and applying decision logics to convert information into policy. To the extent that these rules involve the ambiguities just discussed, applying them poses similar problems for Chinese officials.

Framing Problems and Information Requirements

1. Helpful statements of policy problems are based on accurately locating the main contradiction, and then identifying actors and their relations accordingly.
   (a) Correct analysis of the main contradiction is the key to policy analysis. In its absence, relationships between parties are incomprehensible or misunderstood, with the result that policies cannot have the desired impact.
   (b) The class stand of actors should be determined in the context of the main contradiction. Particular attention should go to antagonistic and nonantagonistic aspects of their relations with China and its principal adversary.
   (c) Relations between secondary parties should be assessed, again with emphasis on distinguishing between antagonistic and nonantagonistic contradictions in their relations with each other.
2. In general, the knowledge required is that from a full systems analysis involving a "comprehensive" examination of the "general situation." Accordingly, analysts should
   (a) Take into account all relevant factors that affect actor relationships and capabilities. Isolated attention to selective factors produces erroneous conclusions.

(b) Evaluate the implications of isolated pieces of information in terms of a body of systematically collected data. This evaluation must be based on the general framework of core beliefs, beliefs about change, and precepts about actors and their relations provided by communist doctrine.

(c) Examine the general policy situation and its relationship to the specific problems at hand before drawing conclusions about a policy problem. Simplistic extrapolation of general policies to cope with particular problems and ad hoc decision making based on isolated attention to particular problems yield poor policy analyses.

3. The systems-analysis approach requires decomposing the relevant universe into a number of subsystems (that is, particular contradictions) and examining each systematically and comprehensively.

(a) For each subsystem, the analyst must again locate the main contradiction, identify the relevant actors, and determine the nature of their relations. Main contradictions, relevant actors, and actor relationships vary across subsystems and over time.

(b) The analyst must also determine the linkages between the various subsystems.

4. The systems analysis should be based on specific knowledge about attributes of the relevant actors. In order to arrive at useful conclusions, analysts need to:

(a) Determine the basic character of actors (for example, revolutionary, reactionary). The nature of an actor should not be inferred simply on the basis of his statements, behavior, or external attributes.

(b) Understand the internal characteristics of actors (for example, the interest alignments among domestic groups and institutions) and the manner in which these characteristics may influence their foreign policy behavior.

(c) Estimate the capabilities of actors. Analysts should not equate the external attributes of capability of an actor with his real or inherent strength or treat actor capabilities in isolation without analyzing relative positions in specific contexts.

(d) Establish the objectives and motives of actors and, therefore, their likely responses to Chinese policies. Error results if analysts mechanically project their own views and motives onto others.

5. The systems analysis must be based on specific knowledge of past and likely future changes in the properties and behavior of the relevant actors. Accordingly, analysts should:

(a) Use relevant case histories to find patterns of actor behavior, characteristics, and capabilities.

(b) Identify trends in the development of the internal characteristics and policy activities of relevant parties without confusing the "main current" with "secondary currents."

In applying these principles of good policy analysis, Chinese officials are obviously limited by the categories and relations introduced in our previous discussions of the authorized belief system. To violate these precepts is to fall outside the range of acceptable reasoning. However, within that framework the principles encourage flexible and complex intelligence estimates and policy appraisals. They lower the chances of metaphysical approaches, which "look at things as if they were absolute, static, isolated, and unchanging" (Mao quoted in Worker-Peasant-Soldier Team, 1971*b*: 92). Indeed, they can be seen as a conscious effort to avoid such tendencies and the loss of policy effectiveness associated with them.

> Metaphysics has several characteristics. First, it looks at problems in isolation and in a partial manner. It does not look at the world as a unified entity with mutually interrelated parts, and instead it looks at the world in terms of isolated entities and unrelated parts like sand. Second, it looks at problems through superficial appearances and not through their inherent qualities; it looks at the forms of problems and not at their substance. Third, it takes a static view of problems, and does not look at them from a developmental viewpoint. It does not penetrate the forms to look at the substance, and it does not penetrate the surface to look at the nature of things [Mao 1969: 272].

To the extent that the rules introduced in this section are followed in practice, they provide the Chinese with basic guidelines to treat international events and situations as important or unimportant in terms of active involvement or mere observation and in terms of major policy review or continuing along established lines. If the Chinese perceive a particular development as a sharpening of the main contradiction, they will take active measures to meet it and, as the direction of change warrants, to exploit or damp it. If they view it as peripheral to the main contradiction, they are likely to refrain from any major action. Involvement and intervention in the latter kind of situation only divert attention and scarce resources away from tackling the cardinal problems posed by the main contradiction. If the Chinese perceive some development in international relations as suggesting fundamental and lasting changes in actor relationships or capabilities, they will adjust their policies accordingly. On the other hand, they will not significantly alter their policies if they view these developments as only transient phenomena. Nor are they likely to alter apparently "unsuccessful" policies if they perceive that adverse developments constitute only isolated and temporary setbacks rather than systemwide and continuing failures. Similarly, developments in any one geographical or issue area of international affairs are treated as serious only if they will matter in ways related to the main contradiction. Finally, they will engage in major policy reviews when they perceive international developments as accelerating or postponing their general timetable for achieving a new stage of domestic development and international relations. And this timetable is a matter of decades that does not need to be reexamined because of short-lived perturbations.

Data Collection and Evaluation

6. Data acquired through direct experience are the most useful and reliable. They can be collected through firsthand field observation and personal contact with relevant participants.

7. The knowledge required for sound policy analysis cannot be provided by applying doctrinal axioms dogmatically, or by reading reports and conducting abstract analyses. On-the-spot examination of concrete and specific problems is essential.

8. General knowledge about problems can be achieved through careful analysis of information based on small samples. In particular, purposive sampling of "good" and "bad" units provides comparison useful for pinpointing problem areas and identifying appropriate responses.

9. Historical experience, particularly that of the Chinese Communist Party, provides valuable analogies that illuminate current situations.

10. Systematically collected and organized quantitative data are valuable; however, one should not ignore the qualitative aspects of problems.

11. Group "discussions" provide a valuable medium for "exchange of ideas" and serve to expose differences in views. Confrontation of experts drawn from different occupational groups is particularly valuable in flushing out implicit assumptions and biases.

12. When engaged in data analysis, analysts should remember that:
    (a) Specialists always weigh the parts of the problem in their jurisdiction too heavily;
    (b) Situations of extreme adversity or stress reveal the essential traits of actors normally hidden;
    (c) Any change in the behavior of anticommunist actors indicates weakness; and
    (d) Both increases and decreases in enemy strength will produce increased enemy aggressiveness.

13. In evaluating reports from external sources, analysts should consider the context of the statement or document and the personal attributes of the source. In particular:
    (a) The more politically progressive, the more reliable is the source;
    (b) The more anticommunist, the more inaccurate is the source.

14. Analysts should give special importance to some kinds of information about reactionaries.
    (a) Data about actual behavior of these actors ought to be emphasized more than data about policy statements.
    (b) Data about their capabilities should be emphasized more than data about their intentions.

Because a correct understanding of policy problems must be based on firsthand knowledge (6), "leadership cadres should take the lead in going to the primary level, to the most problematic places, to the backward units and isolated areas, should personally 'make a postmortem examination of the bird' so as to acquire firsthand experience, should not only remain at the key posts but also cover the entire area, should make investigations and studies right at the place, and should solve the problems there" (Cheng 1966: 93). This emphasis is related to the belief that the masses constitute a uniquely wise and abundant source of knowledge. "The masses are the real heroes, while we ourselves are often childish and ignorant, and without this understanding it is impossible to acquire even the most rudimentary knowledge" (Mao quoted in Schram 1967: 65).[2] Therefore, through interactions with the people, the participant observer may gain valuable insights.

Officebound staff studies divorced from the "real world" are useless (7). As Mao put it, "Only idiots will alone or with a group of others attempt to look for 'methods' and 'solutions' in the abstract without conducting empirical investigation" (Mao quoted in Worker-Peasant-Soldier Team 1971a: 62). He argued instead that "all practical workers must go down to investigate." Directives from authorities or reports from subordinates are not by themselves adequate sources of information for policy analysis. The leadership is enjoined to make "direct contact" with the lower ranks and examine concrete problem areas.

A general understanding of problems can be derived from intensive analyses of a few specific cases, especially if they illustrate success and failure (8). "Catch a sparrow, and dissect it; although the sparrow is a small animal, it has a complete set of internal organs. Chinese and foreign sparrows are alike, and therefore we do not need to dissect each one" (Mao 1969: 19). For example, military commanders are urged to "lay emphasis on the actual and personal investigation of one or two company units—one good and one bad" (Cheng 1966: 410). The historical experience of the Chinese Communist Party provides both cases to follow and ones to avoid (9). Systematic observation should be used to secure quantitative and qualitative information. Quantitative data are especially valuable. Analysts should " 'have a head for figures.' That is to say, we must attend to the quantitative aspect of a situation or problem and make a basic quantitative analysis" (Mao quoted in Schram 1967: 61). However, analysts are not to neglect qualitative matters. For example, when estimating actor capabilities, quantitative data about force levels should be supplemented by information on relatively nonquantifiable factors such as morale, terrain, and leadership.

The Chinese emphasize group decision making with "discussion" meetings to elicit, circulate, test, and evaluate ideas and information (11). The practice of "three-in-one" brings together experts drawn from at least three different specialties. For example, after each combat operation military

2. Semantic analysis of Mainland Chinese perceptions of "the people" indicates that they do see the masses in heroic, creative terms (Kringen 1978: 160–61).

commanders should call together "persons from three areas, i.e., pilots, commanding and navigating officers of the ground command posts, and radar observers, to discuss, face to face, their own feelings, opinions, and experiences" (Cheng 1966: 266). Of course, discussion must be carried out in strict observance of the bounds imposed by the central belief axioms. Otherwise, there will only be "reckless and dangerous talk."

The remaining rules (12–14) suggest adjustments to recognize and compensate for biased information. The distrust of specialists in part underlies the benefits attributed earlier to heterogeneous decision groups. The revelation of essential qualities under stress is obviously compatible with the expectation of the Chinese that intermediate parties are unreliable in crises. The two rules about enemy activity (12c, 12d) are apparently paradoxical, and we will return to them later. The first follows from the view that enemy hostility is invariant; therefore the enemy only alters policy because of a deterioration in relative capability. The second includes this expectation but adds to it the likelihood of increased enemy aggression when the capability balance shifts against China.

It is especially important to conduct a class analysis of any non-Chinese information source (13). In a "class society where class struggle still exists, all social phenomena are closely linked with class struggle. From their varied social stands, people view and analyze problems from different points of departure and use different methods. This is why different and even diametrically opposite conclusions may be reached on the same question or about the same material" (Chiang 1973: 13). Noncommunist sources are fundamentally incapable of understanding social phenomena, and reactionary sources are particularly prone to miscalculate because "their thinking is based on subjective and metaphysical methods" (Mao quoted in Study Team 1974: 84–85). When the discounting of "reactionary" sources is combined with the dismissal of nonhostile statements and reassurances (14), the information considered seriously by Chinese analysts deals with only one question about China's adversaries: the question of their capacity to coerce China and other progressive forces. Similarly, with regard to secondary enemies and other reactionaries potentially mobilizable against the main enemy, Chinese analysts will be less concerned with declaratory policy than with actions and capabilities.

Within the bounds imposed by their belief system, Chinese doctrine advocates a number of measures to reduce bias and noise in their information about China and the external environment. The stress on direct observation and personal involvement minimizes possible distortion introduced by intervening levels of organization. The use of group discussion and debate helps to encourage exchange of ideas and ventilation of diverse views. The stress on synthesizing data interpretations operates against being misled by unrepresentative fragments of information and overgeneralizing from specific incidences. The summation of experiences and generalization of historical lessons from natural experiments help to detect faulty applications and facilitate institutional learning. Finally, the injunction to engage in systematic observation and careful evaluation of the credibility of information sources helps to guard against undue reliance on biased information.

However, there are several weaknesses in the Chinese approach to data collection and evaluation. First, the Chinese tend to rely heavily on knowledge from specific case studies, which they generalize to other situations, asserting that "generality exists only through individuality" (Lenin quoted in Tientsin Writing Group 1975: 60). If these experiences are inapplicable or unrepresentative, the generalizations drawn will be misleading. This danger seems particularly likely with respect to international affairs, in which until recently the Chinese leadership has had very limited experience and is especially likely to fall back on examples from the bipolar years after World War II and the experience of the Chinese revolution. In addition, the rules used to recognize bias in information and for weighing different indicators about the main enemy and other reactionaries are likely to increase rather than reduce the resulting errors in analysis. Because the Chinese are likely to interpret any change in the foreign policy posture of an enemy as a sign of his weakness, both escalation and deescalation of enemy hostility can be read as a deterioration of his position. Paradoxically, increased militancy of an opponent may indicate either increased weakness or increased strength. Further, since the Chinese tend to be more receptive to information from sources that are sympathetic to them and dismiss sources that are hostile to them, they are more likely to accept foreign information about an opponent's weakness than strength. Finally, because they assume that the intentions of the enemy are invariably hostile and expect his behavior to reflect his capability to damage China, the Chinese are prone to "worst case" planning while dismissing conciliatory declarations of intent.

A number of perplexing questions arise as to how China's adversaries can communicate their intentions to Peking. First, verbal declarations of conciliation or belligerence by China's adversaries will not in themselves have a significant impact on Chinese leaders. Signals have to be communicated through actual behavior to demonstrate and back up declared intentions. Second, for China's adversaries the task of signaling a willingness to deescalate conflict is complicated by the Chinese predisposition to perceive any change by China's opponents as a sign of their weakness. A conciliatory gesture may well be misinterpreted as an indication of vulnerability, which may in turn encourage a more militant Chinese stand. Third, conciliatory gestures are not likely to alter Chinese views about the basic hostility of their adversaries; they can be interpreted as enemy "feigning" and dismissed as "sugar-coated" tactics. Fourth, a show of strength by China's adversaries is also insufficient to alter Chinese views. Under the rules provided by Chinese doctrine, China's enemies overestimate their own capability and underestimate Chinese capability, and therefore their views and actions do not reflect the real power balance. Further, China may reciprocate hostility because of the Chinese belief that the inferior party can survive only through "struggle." Fifth, increased militancy on the part of China's adversaries can be interpreted alternatively as signs of weakness or strength.

In sum, a major weakness of the rules about information collection and evaluation is that they make it well-nigh impossible for governments and political movements that Peking has categorized as hostile to successfully communicate positive intentions or credible coercive will without engaging in major physical actions. If an improvement in relations requires some reciprocation by Peking before a sometime enemy government can take concrete steps, it is unlikely to be forthcoming or recommended in the Chinese policy process. And with respect to enemy resolve to engage in coercion if necessary, the Chinese are unlikely to be convinced short of military moves, which can readily get out of control and in any event can trigger Chinese actions conducive to escalation or at least a hardening of hostile postures. As a result, the Chinese may well miss opportunities for coalitions useful to them and approach closer to the brink of conflicts not yet in their interest than situations warrant.

Relating Information to Policy Alternatives

We conclude our discussion of Chinese policy analytics with the doctrinal recommendations for relating information to policy alternatives. These recommendations follow from all the sets of axiomatic beliefs, including the bimodal maxims, introduced in this and the preceding chapters.

15. Good analysis presents a summary of the "good" and "bad" aspects of situations and policy alternatives; they always have both aspects. Negative conclusions are important, and even alternatives with nothing to recommend them have the "good" aspect of providing a clear example of what not to do.

16. Judgments regarding what are "good" and "bad" aspects are to be made in relation to the impact of policy alternatives on the "main contradiction" and also on "secondary contradictions." Consequences that aid "progressive" forces in these contradictions are "good"; those that benefit their adversaries are "bad."

17. Summaries of the "good" and "bad" aspects are the key to evaluating probable net results from policy alternatives. Summaries of the "good" and "bad" aspects of situations in a historical context are the key to determining whether current trends are favorable or unfavorable.

18. Consequences need to be evaluated in terms of both the short and the long run. "Long-term" impact should weigh much more heavily in assessing the net benefit from situations and policy alternatives than "short-term" impact.

Obviously, policy choices rest on assessments of available information rather than on the information in and of itself. Equally obviously, Chinese doctrine calls for rather complex assessments. In Mao's words, "We must learn to look at problems all-sidedly, seeing the reverse as well as the obverse side of things. In given conditions, a bad thing can lead to good results and a good thing to bad results" (Mao quoted in Fan 1972: 190). These enjoinders to summarize "pro" and "con" impacts and to project them over time are not dissimilar from Western policy-analysis principles. However, in following the Chinese principles, analysts are asked to apply vague distinctions to specific situations that may not be categorized easily.

To illustrate, the assignment of values to consequences hinges on the identification of the main contradiction and of the progressive forces (16). Both change according to historical circumstances. Who is progressive and who is not also depends on numerous and possibly even less stable secondary contradictions. The summarization of situations as indicative of positive ("revolutionary tide") and negative ("adverse current") trends poses similar problems (17). The Chinese are not particularly explicit about the rules for making such an assessment, only linking the direction of trends to shifts in the policies and capabilities of major actors in the international system. For example, "the appearance of Soviet revisionist social-imperialism is an adverse current in the advance of the history of world proletarian revolution" (Chang 1973: 9). Yet identifying these shifts depends upon an assessment of their impact on "progressive" forces, and that assessment is hard to make. What is clear, however, is that the appearance of an "adverse current" increases the attractiveness of cautious policy alternatives to deal with the increased dangers that accompany it. Conversely, the advent of a "revolutionary tide" period implies a heightened robustness on the part of the progressive forces and enhances the attractiveness of bold and rather unilateral policy options. The weighing of good and bad consequences depends on whether they are treated as short- or long-term (18). Yet Chinese doctrine does not clearly distinguish between the two and, as we have seen, takes it as an article of faith that the ultimate long-term outcomes will be good from a communist perspective.

For the Chinese, policy making is an ongoing process in which courses of action are tried and modified in the light of experience. Policy evaluation and development are iterative and, because of the inevitable nature of change, never completed processes. The following principles should govern the conduct of and inferences from evaluation of policy alternatives.

19. Policies are best evaluated through "practice" — that is, validation is most appropriately determined through selective implementation and field experiments. However, in "social affairs" (for example, defense policy), the results can be unsuccessful and the policy still be correct because of "temporary inferiority" in the progressive's capability.
20. The results of experimental policy applications should be evaluated in

accord with principles 15–18 and in the light of the response of reactionaries. A hostile enemy response confirms the desirability of one's policy.
21. Strongly positive results should be recognized as "models" to emulate; strongly negative results as "negative examples" to avoid.
22. When policies cannot be tried out experimentally or the results are not yet in, past successes of the general policy line constitute sufficient supporting evidence. Successful forecasts in the past based on the general policy line lend credence to that line.

These principles provide for caution in implementation but do not require that the policies being tried out be incremental. Policies are to be tested in one area or sector, evaluated and appropriately modified, and only then considered for more general application. Decision makers would be well informed about the negative or marginal consequences of a policy and could adapt accordingly. Adherence to such a procedure would result in alternating periods of activity (field trials) and inactivity for the evaluation of results (pauses). The pattern of preferred Chinese international conflict behavior discussed in chapter 6 shows such tendencies.

However, the empirical, almost classically scientific, approach this ideal implies is open to substantial modification by some of the other principles just discussed. The first is the assumption that enemy denigration confirms one's policy wisdom, as in Lin Piao's "evaluation" of the Cultural Revolution: "The imperialists headed by the United States and their lackeys the modern revisionists and all the reactionaries have taken great pains to curse and vilify our great proletarian revolution. This proves by negative example that our victory has dealt the enemy a very heavy blow and they are nothing but a bunch of vampires that are bound to be destroyed" (Lin quoted in Fan 1972: 500). Similarly, Mao argued that

> I hold that it is bad as far as we are concerned if a person, a political party, an army or a school is not attacked by the enemy, for in that case it would definitely mean that we have sunk to the level of the enemy. It is good if we are attacked by the enemy, since it proves that we have drawn a clear line of demarcation between the enemy and ourselves. It is still better if the enemy attacks us wildly and paints us as utterly black and without a single virtue: it demonstrates that we have not only drawn a clear line of demarcation between the enemy and ourselves but achieved a great deal in our work [Mao quoted in Schram 1967: 8].

Conceptions of the enemy can clearly introduce and reinforce error in Chinese policy analysis. The second source of distortion is reliance on the established general policy line as the great simplifier of information and the guide for policy commitments. The Chinese, like decision makers in other cultures, endeavor to avoid excessive information and decision-making costs. Accordingly, the principles introduced in this chapter should not, cadres are told, be taken to mean "that every detail of the objective process must be taken into account; this would be both impossible and unnecessary. It is possible and most necessary, however, to take stock of the basic situation, basic character-istics, and basic tendencies of the development of a thing at the time" (Chiang 1973: 13). The prevailing general policy line offers a legitimate conception of what those basics are and of policies compatible with them. This adaptation to the costs of complex, open analysis tends to obstruct recognition of anomalies with the general line and of changes from the context in which it was initially promulgated. Disconfirmation of the general policy line becomes even more unlikely with the major exception to policy validation incorporated in axiom 19:

> In social struggle the forces representing the advanced class sometimes suffer defeat not because their ideas are incorrect but because, in the balance of forces engaged in struggle, they are not as powerful for the time being as the forces of reaction; they are therefore temporarily defeated, but they are bound to triumph sooner or later [Mao quoted in Schram 1967: 117].

As a result of the above tendency, the Chinese often may not recognize the need for major policy shifts until unwanted developments seem to have substantial momentum. The burden of evidence must be substantial to merit attention and for it to be reasonable to question the general policy line rooted in the experience of the Chinese Communist Party and its leaders. The effort and urgency required to turn institutions and the populace around quickly then lead to a radical policy shift and reinterpretation of the domestic and international environment. From the manifestations visible to outside ob-servers of China, major policy lines and campaigns seem to begin at full speed and to terminate abruptly without incremental change at either end of their life. Perhaps this is why Western China scholars have found it easy and fitting to classify Chinese foreign policy into major "periods."

PART IV

Empirical Tests

In our introductory chapter, we stressed the importance of relating opera-tional-code beliefs to policy actions. Can we better explain and predict what governments do if we understand their policy analytics? We also attached considerable importance to deducing empirically falsifiable propositions about policy activities from a national elite's belief system. Can we use policy analytics to make predictions that cannot be compatible with all possible patterns of policy behavior, instead of using them to construct plausible, after-the-fact explanations? The work to which we now turn presents a crucial part of our answers to these questions for the Chinese case. To the extent that our answers are positive, our approach has strong potential, and perhaps even current value, for the practice of foreign affairs in general and estimates about and policies toward the People's Republic of China in particular.

In earlier parts of this book, we have worked with only one or two parts of the four-element cybernetic conception of decision making advocated in chapter 1. Since we want to link beliefs to policy practice in real-world foreign affairs contexts, we now work with all four elements: external environment, information assessment, decision making, and policy implementation. In evaluating the empirical tests in the next two chapters, two points should be kept in mind. First, they in no sense check the predictive value of all the policy-analytic beliefs introduced earlier. To do so lies well beyond our research ability and available information. We do test important pieces of each of these sets. Accordingly, predictive success is only encouraging and, since the pieces we work with are some of the best understood, predictive failure is rather discouraging. Second, this does not mean that success and failure should be assessed solely in terms of the confirmation of particular propositions or hypotheses drawn from our understanding of the Chinese elite belief system. As we have discussed on several occasions, belief systems are not equally closed and consistent with respect to all decision problems, parties, and events. Instead they are highly closed in some respects and open in others to offer the desirable properties of decidability and flexibility. For the Chinese, we begin with a general proposition that some matters are more predictable from their belief system than others, and that understanding their belief system helps us to differentiate areas where policy activity should be predictably patterned from areas where it may well be erratic or anomalous. While we will use empirical procedures of hypothesis testing to try to lessen the scope of foreign affairs decisions and policy actions that are unpatterned and elusive, unsuccessful hypotheses are also useful for pointing out where our understanding is weak.

Chapters 10 and 11 report statistical tests of propositions about how the Chinese treat foreign affairs events and actors. Obviously, events do not come without participants, and participants do not come without some involvement in events. Policies must deal concurrently with both, and our discussion will link them as appropriate.

CHAPTER 10

TREATMENTS OF FOREIGN AFFAIRS EVENTS: A QUASI-EXPERIMENTAL ANALYSIS

To understand our approach to Chinese responses to foreign affairs events, it seems helpful to introduce the familiar mediated stimulus-response model developed by the Stanford group (Holsti et al. 1968). A foreign policy decision process has for them four elements: (1) the big S refers to "objectively" defined international relations occurrences; (2) the little r, to the characterization of these occurrences by the decision makers under analysis; (3) the little s, to the intentions of these decision makers; and (4) the big R, to the responses actually carried out by them as "objectively" defined. In relation to this $S:r–s:R$ framework, foreign policy researchers have only fragmentary, nonrandom profiles of the big S and R elements. The little s is almost totally hidden from direct observation. In the case of the little r, scholars can only infer it from the regime's public statements, post hoc reconstructions, and self-reports.

On the basis of our work on the "$r–s$" region presented in part III, we hypothesize and then test relationships between the big S and big R elements. The beliefs elucidated in chapters 7, 8, and 9 lead us to expect particular little r interpretations for different big S events. They also connect particular little r classification decisions with different little s reactions. Since there are usually prevailing views in policy circles about the proper use of particular instruments, implementing organizations, and foreign and domestic perceptions about the use of each instrument, the chains of reasoning that result from our "$r–s$" inferences are thus combined with a set of views about the policy instrument with which we deal here: public posture in *People's Daily*. We then infer hypotheses about the big R behavior associated with various big S events. We choose big S events reasonably viewed as important at least for the foreign affairs of the relevant regions. We expect on the basis of Chinese decision logics that media response manifested in the *People's Daily* will differ in certain ways for particular subsets of these events. To test our predictions, we use an interrupted time-series approach and engage in a quasi-experimental analysis in which big S events play the role of experimental treatments.[1]

1. We have used the same approach elsewhere with a smaller set of events amd different time periods for aggregating media coverage (Bobrow et al. 1976).

Rules for Policy Interpretation

The policy analytics in part III suggest that the Chinese encode international events in terms of the following dimensions:

1. The role of China's principal adversary (currently, the Soviet Union);
2. The location of the participants toward opposite poles of a progressive-to-reactionary continuum in terms of their domestic characteristics;
3. The degree to which an event signals fundamental changes in an actor's international role because of possible effects on its internal political economy;
4. The degree to which an event provides an example extremely supportive of or incompatible with stated Chinese policy; and
5. The degree to which an event is extremely sensitive or serious for China's territorial security.

To review, according to the Chinese operational code, Peking's policy selection will focus on the current "main contradiction" in international relations. It will also involve the class stand and domestic situation of particular actors, and the implications of particular developments for China as well as others, especially as those developments signal approaching "qualitative changes." Assessments of the current international trend as a "revolutionary tide" or "adverse current," and of recent experience in terms of particularly positive and negative examples, are important as well. Finally, possible signs of aggression by hostile reactionaries against China must be considered. In dealing with potentially grave national security events for China, "one wrong move can lose the whole game" (Ebon 1975: 298).

The implications of these rules may clash in actual policy application. For instance, a participant in an event could be domestically progressive *and* allied with the Soviet Union. Accordingly, we try to establish the relative priority of these rules in situations where they indicate divergent conclusions about an event. The rules for policy treatment may also clash with the rules for media treatment to be discussed next. For example, while decision makers are enjoined to attend to negative examples, public media attention to them may be at least temporarily curtailed lest it adversely affect the domestic audience. In short, media treatment does not relate in any neat, linear way to particular rules for policy interpretation.

Rules for Media Use

In chapter 2, we argued that the linkage between operational codes and policy behavior reflects the elite's views about the relevant policy instruments. Accordingly, we need to evaluate the event-related material in the context of the policy purposes the official media serve for the Chinese elite. This concern is particularly crucial because of elite manipulation of reporting. More specifically, the mass media of countries like China offer official interpretations of history. As such, they are shaped by elite policy assessments, even though the public treatment of issues is unlikely to relate in any exact way to the private attention and concerns of the elite. Since mass media are used to communicate policies to domestic as well as foreign audiences, coverage in these sources forms an important part of the regime's policy behavior. This coverage is used to propagate the elite's policy rationales, to mobilize support for them, and to convey warnings to potential adversaries. Valid inferences from state-controlled public media require an understanding of the general rules applied to them as a policy instrument. For the Chinese elite, the major rules for media coverage age as follows:

1. The extent of news coverage should reflect importance for the core Chinese policy agenda, although temporary lags in this coverage are possible (see 4 below). Continuing importance warrants substantial continuing coverage.

2. Attention should reflect support for the prevailing, declared policy line of the regime. Given the tutorial role of the official media vis-à-vis the population, events that clash with the dominant line should not be salient in public discussion, although they may be used later as "negative examples" to educate the masses. For example, reporting of regime changes with adverse implications for China can usefully be deferred.

3. Attention should support elite policy interpretations. If these indicate the wisdom of awaiting further developments, public discussion should be avoided until things have taken shape.

4. Self-imposed restraint to avoid publicity is necessary when dealing with highly fragile events having significant national security implications for China. Media attention should be deferred to avoid unwanted countermoves by adversaries as the price of premature disclosure.

5. The status of media treatment as "declared" policy requires consideration of how foreign audiences may interpret coverage. For example, "friends" expect that some attention should be paid to them in cases where they are severely threatened by events or incurring grave costs due to events. Adversaries, potential adversaries, and empathetic third parties will look for clues as to Chinese policy stands and firmness of intention. Withholding expected coverage can thus have important foreign affairs consequences. Accordingly, even in the absence of significant concern with an event per se, some temporary media attention may be appropriate.

6. Finally, a finite amount of space must be allocated to numerous subjects competing for attention. In a world of numerous fresh events, there is an inherent tendency for decay in the amount of attention given to any particular event and the parties associated with it, unless the previous rules maintain its priority.

Selecting Events for Comparison

Our analysis faces two problems common in decision-making research. First, the same policy can be "explained" by several decision logics (that is, different decision logics are compatible with the same behavior). Second, the size of the available sample of pertinent historical cases limits the possiblity of controlling for the influence of these alternative explanations.

To lessen these problems, we employ comparative analysis of Chinese treatment of the events listed in table 10-1. To expand and diversify our sample for the period covered by our Chinese media data, we draw on different chronologies (e.g., Blechman and Kaplan 1976; Phillips and Moore 1975; Writing Team 1974) as well as the *New York Times Index* and the *Peking Review* for pertinent events during 1972-1974. We select events likely to be

TABLE 10-1
QUASI-EXPERIMENTAL TREATMENTS

Test Event	Date
Nixon's Peking visit	Feb. 21, 1972
U.S. mining of Haiphong	May 8, 1972
Nixon's Moscow visit (SALT agreement)	May 22, 1972
Sato resignation in Japan	Jun. 17, 1972
Egypt-U.S.S.R. dispute	Jul. 18, 1972
Uganda-Tanzania dispute	Sep. 17, 1972
U.S.-U.S.S.R. nuclear tests	Sep. 21, 1972
U.S. bombing of Hanoi	Oct. 11, 1972
U.S. bombing of Hanoi	Dec. 18, 1972
Rhodesia-Zambia dispute	Jan. 9, 1973
Western monetary crisis	Mar. 3, 1973
Iraq-Kuwait dispute	Mar. 20, 1973
Attempted Chilean coup	Jun. 29, 1973
Coup overthrowing Zahir Shah in Afghanistan	Jul. 17, 1973
Coup overthrowing Allende in Chile	Sep. 11, 1973
South Korean student demonstration	Oct. 2, 1973
Coup overthrowing Kittikachorn in Thailand	Oct. 6, 1973
Mideast war	Oct. 6, 1973
Chinese invasion of the Paracels	Jan. 14, 1974
Israeli-Egyptian disengagement	Jan. 18, 1974
P.R.C.-U.S.S.R. diplomatic dispute	Jan. 19, 1974
U.S.S.R. helicopter intrusion into P.R.C.	Mar. 14, 1974
Dismissal of de Costa Gomes and de Spinola in Portugal	Mar. 14, 1974
Coup overthrowing Caetano in Portugal	Apr. 25, 1974
Ethiopian mutiny leading to the overthrow of Haile Selassie	Apr. 26, 1974
Sikkim election leading to the annexation by India	Apr. 30, 1974
First Indian nuclear test	May 18, 1974
Turkish invasion of Cyprus	Jul. 20, 1974
Nixon resignation	Aug. 8, 1974
Overthrow of Haile Selassie in Ethiopia	Sep. 12, 1974

assigned to polar positions on the Chinese encoding dimensions suggested earlier in order to increase the chances for contrast in media coverage. In interpreting Chinese behavior, we stress comparisons of responses to different events rather than the handling of any particular episode. That is, we examine several cases that we expect to receive similar coverage and contrast them with other cases for which we expect a different pattern. This allows us to put a given event into several categories and examine it in terms of several competing hypotheses. Different results clarify the relevance of the alternative hypotheses to the event response in question.

Problems of the Quasi-Experimental Method

The events in table 10-1 are treated as quasi-experimental stimuli to Chinese media behavior. Their effects are explored through an interrupted time-series approach (e.g., Caporaso and Roos 1973; Caporaso and Pelowski 1971; Campbell and Ross 1968; Campbell and Stanley 1966). We check the magnitude, direction, and timing of changes in *People's Daily* news coverage between two time spans separated by the occurrence of the big S event of interest.[2] The observed changes in this coverage between the preevent and postevent periods are attributed to the intervention of the event. We expect that the events in our inventory will induce different Chinese interpretations and decisions, and the nature of the interruptions in the time series of coverage should differ accordingly.

The literature suggests problems in this type of analysis, which, if not handled properly, can lead to unwarranted conclusions. Observed changes may result from: (1) *history* (events other than the one being examined); (2) *maturation* (a running process unrelated to the experimental treatment in question); (3) *testing* (the pretest experience unaffected by the nature or presence of subsequent treatments); (4) *instrumentation* (changes in measuring instruments and/or the reporting organizations); (5) *instability* (an inherently unstable process, especially with inferences from a small number of observation points); (6) *regression* (the extreme values of the pretest observations, which can be expected to return to the mean even in the absence of posttest treatments); and (7) *idiosyncrasy* or *irrelevance* (changes may be unrelated to the test treatment in question because similar treatments have produced different results or because dissimilar treatments have produced the same results).

---

2. For some of the events, it is difficult to specify exactly when they occurred. Often they involve long, drawn-out development (for example, the Watergate affair leading to Nixon's resignation). It is also difficult to determine to what extent they represent the end or the beginning of an important series of foreign policy developments. In these cases, significant "turning points" in these developments have been used (for example, Nixon's actual resignation).

Some of these problems are more tractable than others. Testing, instrumentation, and regression do not pose significant threats to our inferences. Any adjustment by the editors of the *People's Daily* to foreign observation would have happened long before our analysis. There is also no reason to expect changes during the period under examination with regard to Peking's decision logics, its rules for relating policy treatment to media treatment, or the coding procedures for our data base. We have not selected countries on the basis of their extreme values in Chinese media treatment. Therefore, regression toward the mean is not a problem. We will try to control the problem of idiosyncrasy and irrelevance by stressing event comparisons. That is, we will check for idiosyncrasy by examining responses to similar events and for irrelevance by examining events with similar responses.

The problems of maturation, instability, and history are more intractable. They impinge on the mundane considerations concerning the unit and number of observation points available for the regression estimates used to make interrupted time-series inferences. Specifically, we can reduce the possible distorting effects of maturation by using small observation units over a short time period. By shortening the observation period, we can also minimize the chances of intervention by events other than the one being examined, thereby relaxing the threat posed by the history problem. However, the more we use small temporal units and a limited number of these units for our analysis, the more we compound the problem of data instability. Consequently, confidence in the reliability of regression estimates will suffer. In the absence of any strong theoretical or substantive rationale, we compromise. The observation units used in the following analysis are fifteen-day periods and, unless noted otherwise, our pretest and posttest regression estimates are computed on the basis of ten units before and after the event occurrence respectively. We reason that ten observation points are large enough to permit relatively stable regression estimates and yet small enough to avoid major complications with regard to "history." One hundred and fifty days also seem adequate to capture any lags in Chinese media response to events and to reveal any new trends in media coverage.

To assess possible distortions introduced by maturation and instability, we compare the results of the subsequent analyses with those of our earlier study (Bobrow et al. 1976), which used a different number of observation units. If the results are "fragile" in the sense that they fluctuate according to different temporal specifications they merit less confidence. If they are relatively unaffected by the rather major changes in periodization between the two analyses, confidence in their validity is enhanced.

Finally, to ameliorate the dangers posed by the problem of history, we examine patterns across events rather than focusing on particular cases in isolation. Patterns across events are less likely to be artifacts of unrecognized "history" than the results associated with any single stimulus. It is important

table, the border dispute between Rhodesia and Zambia, has single-mood test results that are all significant at the .01 level. These results gain greater weight when we compare them with the results for another African dispute, the Uganda-Tanzania border conflict, also reported in table 10-3. Although the Chinese had closer relations with Uganda and Tanzania, the single-mood tests show no significant changes. In contrast to the Rhodesia-Zambia case, the absence of an easy propaganda target—or conversely, the desire to avoid damaging relations with either of the two conflict parties—curtailed immediate Chinese press reaction.

Our previous analysis included only events pertinent to hypothesis 2 (Mideast war, Iraq-Kuwait border dispute, and Turkish invasion of Cyprus). In all cases Chinese responses supported the hypothesis, in spite of the substantial differences in data periodization used in that analysis and the present one.

HYPOTHESIS 5: *For second-order domestic political crises, immediate Chinese media response is more likely if, in the following order of importance, (a) there is significant foreign involvement, (b) at least one of the conflict parties is a "polar" character in terms of its ideological background or political alignment, and (c) the event produces clear changes in regime characteristics.*

HYPOTHESIS 6: *Successful second-order regime changes with significant transformation of elite characteristics or major realignment of the regime in international politics are more likely to result in enduring changes in Chinese media treatment than unsuccessful threats to regimes or successful threats that did not bring about fundamental changes in the elite's characteristics or policies.*

Our expectations in hypothesis 5 are based on the Chinese injunctions to examine local developments in terms of their global implications (particularly as these local developments impact on the "main contraction") and to avoid policy comment or disclosure in uncertain situations where the probable outcome of the domestic contest for power or the characteristics of the contestants cannot be clearly determined. Accordingly, the media response is more immediate when the Chinese perceive that the event is an extension of the global contest between the major powers, that the local conflict parties clearly represent "progressive" or "reactionary" forces, and that the local developments have brought about relatively conclusive and unambiguous changes in the nature of the dominant elite. Figure 10-1 provides a summary of how these considerations should influence Chinese reactions to the pertinent historical events included in table 10-4. We expect that events in cells with lower roman numerals are more likely to produce immediate Chinese media response than events in cells with higher roman numerals. However, according to hypothesis 6, the increase in Chinese media coverage will be rather transient unless there are "genuine" changes in the victorious elite's commitment to domestic policy programs or international alignment.

For ease of interpretation, we group the pertinent events into four general

TABLE 10-3

TREATMENT OF SECOND-ORDER MILITARY CRISES

Event/Actor		Single-Mood	Double-Mood	Walker-Lev Test 1	Walker-Lev Test 3
I. Involvement and Noninvolvement by Main Enemy					
Mideast War					
Egypt:	CM	2.359*	0.280	9.343†	0.265
	IT	4.106†	0.694	9.360†	0.952
Syria:	CM	49.442†	1.732	-2.524	-61.121†
	IT	44.899†	1.727	0.776	-3.911
Israel:	CM	25.616†	2.220*	6.293*	9.943†
	IT	32.641†	2.275*	7.135*	10.958†
Iraq-Kuwait Dispute					
Iraq:	CM	2.745*	0.806	0.039	0.734
	IT	0.964	0.086	0.060	0.003
Kuwait:	CM	0.724	0.243	0.281	0.050
	IT	1.238	0.854	0.193	0.765
Cyprus Invasion‡					
Turkey:	CM	-0.338	-0.410	0.049	1.234
	IT	0.315	0.098	0.607	0.345
Cyprus:	CM	0.953	0.783	1.630	0.011
	IT	2.037*	1.244	2.041	0.922
Greece:	CM	-0.091	-0.317	0.052	0.131
	IT	0.191	-0.709	0.055	0.378
Uganda-Tanzania Dispute					
Uganda:	CM	0.032	1.240	0.018	2.281
	IT	-0.262	0.951	0.145	1.511
Tanzania:	CM	-0.907	-1.133	0.333	1.707
	IT	-0.947	-1.106	0.949	1.638

II. Involvement by P.R.C. Ally

Escalation of U.S. bombing (Oct. 1972)					
North Vietnam:	CM	0.054	1.187	0.111	1.908
	IT	0.494	1.290	0.193	2.230
U.S.:	CM	2.046*	2.405*	0.176	10.018†
	IT	2.236*	2.423*	0.432	10.102†
Escalation of U.S. bombing (Dec. 1972)					
North Vietnam:	CM	2.058*	0.967	8.413*	1.772
	IT	1.426	0.875	7.517*	1.560
U.S.:	CM	2.977*	0.733	15.220†	1.128
	IT	4.560†	1.059	11.230†	2.087
Mining of Haiphong (May 1972)‡					
North Vietnam:	CM	-0.288	0.287	1.071	5.366*
	IT	1.764	0.313	3.469	13.648†
U.S.:	CM	2.993*	0.279	0.229	0.059
	IT	3.168*	0.061	0.738	2.298

III. Involvement of International "Pariah"

Rhodesian–Zambian Disupte					
Rhodesia:	CM	5.937†	2.279*	1.273	9.651†
	IT	7.129†	2.156*	1.263	8.483†
Zambia:	CM	6.167†	1.215	0.638	2.248
	IT	7.407†	1.305	1.612	2.706

* Significant at 0.05 level.   † Significant at 0.01 level.

‡ Since this event took place within 150 days of the temporal bounds of our data coverage, we do not have ten data points for either the pre- or the posttest period. The findings reported for this event are based on *all* available data points over a thirty-four-month period, partitioned into the pre- and posttest periods according to the date of the test-event occurrence. Thus, unlike the other findings reported in this table, the number of data points for the pre- and posttest periods for this event is not comparable, and it is not held constant to ten.

151

FIGURE 10-1

EXPECTATIONS REGARDING P.R.C. TREATMENT OF THREATS TO OTHERS'
REGIMES: SINGLE-MOOD TEST

	Involvement by Polar Character(s)		Involvement by Middle Character(s)	
	Clear Changes in Regime Characteristics	Fluid Situation	Clear Changes in Regime Characteristics	Fluid Situation
Foreign Involvement	I India's annexation of Sikkim Overthrow of Allende	II	III Overthrow of Makarios	IV
No Foreign Involvement	V Overthrow of Kitti-kachorn Overthrow of Caetano	VI Dismissal of de Costa Gomes and de Spinola	VII Overthrow of Haile Selassie Overthrow of Zahir Shah	VIII Ethiopian mutiny leading to eventual regime change

IX Situations where the regime changes involve only changes in the representatives of the same elite, and thus do not involve any basic break with the policies of the previous administration: Unsuccessful coup against Allende; South Korean student demonstration; Sato resignation; Nixon resignation.

categories in table 10-4. Since hypothesis 5 suggests that foreign involvement in domestic political crises is the most important determinant of short-term changes in Chinese media attention, we first use this criterion to sort the events. In contrast to the other three groups, the three events included in group A share the common characteristic of significant foreign involvement, even though such partisan support by foreign countries might not have involved the superpowers. They are the Sikkim election leading to the annexation of that country by India, the overthrow of Allende by the Chilean military, and the overthrow of Makarios by the Cypriot National Guard. They show immediate Chinese media response, as indicated by the significant results of the single-mood tests. Hypothesis 5 is substantially confirmed with respect to foreign involvement.

However, hypothesis 6 does not receive strong support from the events in group A. One of these events—the overthrow of Allende—produced a basic change in the ruling elite's characteristics and in its domestic and foreign policies. Yet the Walker-Lev tests 1 and 3 did not produce significant findings—that is, show basic changes in Chinese coverage of Chile.[4] The results for the other two events in group A—which, compared to the Chilean case, do not clearly involve fundamental departures in pertinent regime characteristics or policies—fit with our expectations. None of the test results suggests lasting changes in Chinese media patterns. The occurrence of only a temporary increase in Chinese attention in the immediate posttest period follows from the double-mood test, which indicates no significant change at the .05 level for any of the three events.

Unlike group A, we control for the nature of actors involved in the power contest in creating group B. The events in this group do not indicate significant foreign involvement, but they are relatively clear in terms of policy implications for the Chinese because of the involvement of "polar" characters. If hypothesis 5 is correct, this group is more likely to receive immediate posttest increase in Chinese media attention than events involving "middle" characters, particularly if they also suggest ambiguous outcomes (which constitute group C in table 10-4). This expectation is strongly supported by the results. The three events in group B—the overthrow of Kittikachorn of Thailand, the dismissal of de Costa Gomes and de Spinola in Portugal, and the subsequent coup against Caetano—produced immediate and major increases in Chinese press attention to these countries. On the other hand, none of the events in group C—which consists of the overthrow of Haile Selassie of Ethiopia and of Zahir Shah of Afghanistan (Entessar 1978) and the Ethiopian military mutiny—produced any significant single-mood findings. Thus, controlling for the presence or absence of foreign involvement, situations that involve

---

4. China continued its normal relations with Chile after the anti-Allende coup (Burchett 1976), a fact that may be due to the junta's anti-Soviet views.

TABLE 10-4

TREATMENT OF THREATS TO OTHER REGIMES

Event/Actor		Single-Mood	Double-Mood	Walker-Lev Test 1	Walker-Lev Test 3
A. Situations Implying Foreign Involvement					
India's Annexation of Sikkim					
Sikkim:	CM	NA§	NA§	2.902	0.196
	IT	NA§	NA§	3.428	0.135
India:	CM	2.314*	0.546	1.903	0.233
	IT	1.761	0.704	2.742	0.444
Overthrow of Allende					
Chile:	CM	6.347†	0.569	3.170	0.610
	IT	4.662†	0.385	2.693	-0.339
Overthrow of Makarios‡					
Cyprus:	CM	0.953	0.783	1.630	0.011
	IT	2.037*	1.244	2.041	0.922
Turkey:	CM	-0.338	-0.410	0.049	1.234
	IT	0.315	0.098	0.607	0.345
B. Situations Implying No Foreign Involvement, but Involving Polar Characters					
Overthrow of Kittikachorn					
Thailand:	CM	3.393†	1.015	0.950	1.438
	IT	4.247†	1.190	0.663	1.986
Dismissal of de Costa Gomes and de Spinola					
Portugal:	CM	2.058*	0.487	0.467	0.262
	IT	2.462*	0.850	2.081	0.838
Overthrow of Caetano					
Portugal:	CM	2.618*	1.487	0.654	3.846
	IT	4.918†	2.008*	0.529	9.488†

C. Situations Implying No Foreign Involvement, and Involving Middle Characters with Uncertain Outcomes

Overthrow of Haile Selassie‡				
Ethiopia:	CM	-0.026	-0.079	0.047	0.135
	IT	-0.140	-0.192	0.040	0.375
Overthrow of Zahir Shah				
Afghanistan:	CM	0.039	0.294	1.874	0.054
	IT	0.085	0.557	2.377	0.297
Ethiopian Mutiny				
Ethiopia:	CM	0.565	0.566	3.079	0.260
	IT	0.438	0.115	1.581	0.003

D. Situations Resulting in Status Quo Ante

Unsuccessful Coup against Allende				
Chile:	CM	1.460	1.198	0.029	1.767
	IT	1.314	1.156	0.060	1.772
South Korean Student Demonstration				
South Korea:	CM	-0.585	-0.247	0.195	0.070
	IT	-0.182	0.120	0.005	0.029
Sato Resignation				
Japan:	CM	-0.254	0.544	1.021	0.259
	IT	3.256†	3.601†	0.002	1.595
Nixon Resignation‡				
U.S.:	CM	0.271	0.137	0.548	1.733
	IT	0.105	0.004	0.533	0.822

* Significant at 0.05 level.   † Significant at 0.01 level.

‡ Since this event took place within 150 days of the temporal bounds of our data coverage, we do not have ten data points for either the pre- or the posttest period. The findings reported for this event are based on all available data points over a thirty-four-month period, partitioned into the pre- and posttest periods according to the date of the test-event occurrence. Thus, unlike the other findings reported in this table, the number of data points for the pre- and posttest periods for this event is not comparable, and it is not held constant to ten. In addition, it should be noted that the results of the case of the overthrow of Makarios may be distorted by the subsequent Turkish invasion of Cyprus. Since these two events were only four days apart, no separate analysis was conducted for them. The results presented here are based on changes surrounding the Turkish invasion.

§ Since all the data points in the pretest period are zero values, no single- or double-mood tests can be conducted. However, the data do indicate an increase in Chinese media attention to Sikkim immediately after the test event.

155

"middle" characters with ambiguous or fluid outcomes are likely to restrain Chinese media reaction immediately after the event occurrence, a pattern also evident in initial Chinese silence about the Thai coups in 1957, 1958, and 1971.[5] We also expect that immediate Chinese media response is more likely to be forthcoming—as in the case of the Thai and Portuguese events included in group B—if the events signal victories of "progressive" forces.

Hypothesis 6 receives much stronger support from the results for groups B and C than those for group A. With the single exception of the overthrow of Caetano, all the events considered would not represent basic regime changes in the Chinese view.[6] Hence, we expect the Walker-Lev tests and the double-mood test to produce no significant results for all the events in groups B and C except the Caetano case. This expectation is borne out. Only with respect to this case did the results of our tests indicate lasting changes in Chinese media coverage. The double-mood test and the Walker-Lev test 3 show significant (at the .05 and .01 levels respectively) increases in Chinese media coverage of that country on our item-frequency measure following the overthrow of Caetano.

Group D includes events—such as the Sato and Nixon resignations—that did not produce basic changes in elite characteristics or policies. These situations are least likely to trigger immediate comment and to result in long-term changes in Chinese media attention. Except for the Sato case, the test results support hypothesis 5. All events in group D support hypothesis 6.

The results of our previous analysis (Bobrow et al. 1976) supported hypothesis 5 for groups C and D and for three of the six cases in groups A and B. That is, we found immediate posttest increases in Chinese media attention in the instances of the overthrow of Allende, Kittikachorn, and the dismissal of de Costa Gomes and de Spinola. In the other three cases the previous findings ran contrary to our expectations (the annexation of Sikkim and the overthrow of Makarios and Caetano). We have no ready explanation for these

---

5. "In September 1957, Field Marshal Sarit, claiming that the government had lost popular support, carried out a sudden coup. Sarit's seizure of power went unreported in Peking, as it was far from clear that he intended to reverse Thailand's development of friendly relations. . . . On November 17 1971, however, Thanom and a junta of generals, in a repeat of Sarit's 1958 coup against his own government, dissolved the cabinet, abolished Parliament, suspended the constitution, and declared martial law. Responsibility for foreign affairs was taken away from Thanat. . . . Consequently, the generals did not intend to end the exploration of a dialogue with China, but rather they wished to keep tight control over the development of this major policy change. Elimination of public pressure on the issue would allow the generals to continue at a more measured and cautious pace. Indeed, 10 months later, the Thai government accepted a ping pong invitation to Peking and sent along a government official to sound out the Chinese on their attitude toward Thailand. *Interestingly, Peking, as in 1958, did not directly comment on the military takeover in Bangkok"* (Taylor 1974: 175, 353–54; emphasis added).

6. The orientation of the Ethiopian military government had not clarified during our data-coverage period.

TABLE 10-5
SIGNALING TO THIRD PARTIES

Event/Actor	Single-Mood: CM	Single-Mood: IT
I. Supporting Friends		
India's Annexation of Sikkim:		
Pakistan	22.109[†]	8.493[†]
India's Initial Nuclear Test:		
Pakistan	–1.235	–1.131
South Korean Student Demonstrations:		
North Korea	–0.786	–1.221
II. Warning, Criticizing, or Embarrassing Enemies		
Mining of Haiphong[‡]:		
U.S.S.R.	–2.013	–2.109
South Vietnam	–1.688	–1.506
Paracels Invasion:		
North Vietnam	1.399	–0.451
U.S.	0.040	–0.320
U.S.S.R.	3.612[†]	2.645[*]
Overthrow of Zahir Shah:		
India	–0.075	0.650
U.S.S.R.	3.082[*]	4.660[†]

[*] Significant at 0.05 level.   [†] Significant at 0.01 level.
[‡] Since this event took place within 150 days of the temporal bounds of our data coverage, we do not have ten data points for either the pre- or the posttest period. The findings reported for this event are based on *all* available data points over a thirty-four-month period, partitioned into the pre- and posttest periods according to the date of the test-event occurrence. Thus, unlike the other findings reported in this table, the number of data points for the pre- and posttest periods for this event is not comparable, and it is not held constant to ten.

divergent findings other than the effects of different periodization. The findings derived from our previous analysis generally support hypothesis 6. Two of the three exceptions (the Ethiopian mutiny and the Nixon resignation) are suspect because of the very small number of observation points available.

HYPOTHESIS 7: *In situations involving China's "main enemy" or its proxy and in situations involving the interests of China's close allies, Chinese media coverage for third parties increases.*

Hypothesis 7 is based on the role of media as an official policy declaration instrument and on the Chinese emphasis on "whole system" analysis. Given the Chinese emphasis on the implications of specific developments for third parties and on the use of media to publicize policy intentions, we expect to find evidence of Chinese signaling to parties not directly engaged in the events.

Table 10-5 reports six pertinent events. On three of these occasions, we expect the *People's Daily* to increase its coverage of China's allies in order to bolster their morale. These events are India's annexation of Sikkim and its first nuclear detonation (for Pakistan), and the anti-Park demonstrations in South

Korea (for North Korea). Only with regard to the annexation of Sikkim did we find significant and immediate increases (at the .01 level) for coverage of Pakistan after the event.

Three events in table 10-5 seem to have presented occasions for the Chinese to warn against, criticize, or embarrass adversaries. Since the U.S. mining of Haiphong was followed in about two weeks by Nixon's Moscow visit, we thought it provided a timely opportunity for the Chinese to embarrass the Soviets. Also, we thought that the Chinese would engage in warnings to potential adversaries on the occasions of the Chinese invasion of the Paracels and the abolition of the Afghan monarchy. With the exception of the media coverage of the Soviet Union in the Paracels and Afghan cases, our evidence does not support hypothesis 7. The escalation of Chinese media attention to the Soviet Union in the immediate aftermath of the invasion of the Paracel Islands is somewhat surprising, since, compared with North Vietnam and the United States, the Soviet Union did not appear to pose a threat to local Chinese aims in this instance. Distortion due to other concurrent events involving the Soviet Union may be the problem.[7]

With one exception (the U.S. mining of the Haiphong Harbor), our previous analysis covered all the events presented in table 10-5. The results of that analysis also were generally negative about Chinese media signaling to indirect conflict participants other than the Soviet "main enemy."

HYPOTHESIS 8: *Major changes in the economic or military capability of leading nations or in their internal or external balance of power will produce major sustained changes in media treatment, although such changes may not be manifest immediately after a key event occurs.*

Our analyses of the Chinese belief system attributed great importance to what they would view as "qualitative changes"—that is, basic changes in the relative capabilities and power positions of major participants in world politics. Unfortunately, as we pointed out earlier, the Chinese are much less than clear about what are or are not qualitative changes except from the perspective of many years later. What we propose to do is to use eight events that conceivably might be treated by the Chinese as signs of qualitative change. If we are correct about their perceiving these events in such a manner, we expect their treatment to have the patterning stated in hypothesis 8. Under Chinese policy analytics, events marking qualitative change induce massive policy reexamination and thus should be associated with long-term changes in media attention patterns. Also, they are fraught with importance and sensitivity, and thus we expect them to be associated with a lower level of media

---

7. There are two sources for potential distortion. Both the Israeli-Egyptian military disengagement and the Sino-Soviet diplomatic dispute happened close to the Paracels invasion. Also, as indicated previously, the PAMIS coding rules do not permit a sensitive assessment of the general question of changes in media attention to the indirect participants in the event treatments.

attention immediately after they occur. Basic changes in media-coverage posture will be delayed until the implications of events can be fully understood. Because the implications of major setbacks to the "main enemy" are clear, the coverage associated with such events differs in that there will be immediate media exploitation for domestic and international purposes.

The events in table 10-6 help us explore these expectations and interests. Short-term behavior supports hypothesis 8. There were no statistically significant immediate changes for four of the eight events. For the four where such changes appear, three involved the Soviet Union. Two of these events (the Egyptian-Israeli accord to disengage militarily in the Sinai and the Egyptian-Soviet diplomatic dispute resulting in the explusion of Soviet advisers from Egypt) signaled major setbacks to Soviet influence in the Mideast. The third event indicated a strong possibility of Soviet-American confrontation (the Mideast war of 1973). The fourth case where the single-mood test produced a significant finding is the occasion of the first Indian nuclear test.[8] However, in this instance the change involved only the number of news items about India (and not the space of coverage) and it was relatively short-lived, as indicated by the nonsignificant findings of the double-mood test. The four cases with no immediate posttest increase in Chinese media coverage are: the Western monetary crisis, Nixon's Peking visit, Nixon's Moscow visit, and the resumption of nuclear tests by the United States and the Soviet Union. The implications of these events are less clear than in the four cases where we did find significant single-mood results.

While our expectations of *delayed* change generally received little support (the single exception being item frequencies for the Common Market and Japan after the Western monetary events), we did find major and continuing changes in the handling of Egypt in the aftermath of the Egyptian-Soviet diplomatic dispute and of the Soviet Union subsequent to the Mideast war and military disengagement (see the Walker-Lev test 3 findings). The Egyptian finding is particularly interesting in that it shows a Chinese policy interpretation of a substantial foreign affairs change based solely on the alignment of a government with the "main enemy." The puzzling absence of long-term changes associated with either Nixon's visit to Peking or that to Moscow (and the concomitant SALT agreement) may reflect a substantive uncertainty, dispute on the part of the Chinese elite, or simply data limitations on our analysis.[9] Perhaps more interesting is the general contrast in the prevalence of

8. Actually, the Chinese did not report this event in their press at the time (Cleveland 1976: 17). We are, however, interested in testing the general changes in the attention level to an actor, and not necessarily the explicit mention of the event that induced these changes.

9. Both Nixon visits took place near the beginning of our data set, so that we have very few observations in the pretest period.

TABLE 10-6

TREATMENT OF POTENTIAL "QUALITATIVE CHANGES"

Event/Actor		Single-Mood	Double-Mood	Walker-Lev Test 1	Walker-Lev Test 3
Mideast War and Oil Embargo					
Egypt:	CM	2.359*	0.280	9.343†	0.265
	IT	4.106†	0.694	9.360†	0.952
Syria:	CM	49.442†	1.732	-2.524	-61.121†
	IT	44.899†	1.727	0.776	-3.911
Israel:	CM	25.616†	2.220*	6.293*	9.943†
	IT	32.641†	2.275*	7.135*	10.958†
U.S.:	CM	-1.111	-0.668	0.674	0.775
	IT	-1.005	-0.220	1.292	0.158
U.S.S.R.:	CM	-1.921	-1.300	2.331	2.731
	IT	-2.152*	-1.932*	5.476*	5.765*
Mideast Disengagement					
Egypt:	CM	0.048	-0.013	1.838	0.017
	IT	-0.029	-0.080	1.254	0.035
Syria:	CM	-0.036	0.149	0.172	0.015
	IT	0.021	0.230	0.031	0.048
Israel:	CM	-0.224	-0.352	0.120	0.176
	IT	-0.297	-0.448	0.054	0.271
U.S.:	CM	0.122	0.493	0.025	0.362
	IT	-0.008	-0.166	0.153	0.026
U.S.S.R.:	CM	3.983†	1.962*	0.079	6.275*
	IT	3.313†	1.974*	0.230	7.020*
U.A.R.-U.S.S.R. Dispute					
Egypt:	CM	3.716†	1.852*	0.516	5.572*
	IT	4.456†	1.993*	0.798	6.756*
U.S.S.R.:	CM	2.891*	0.950	2.123	1.069
	IT	2.401*	1.180	2.810	1.584

Western Monetary Crisis					
Common Market:	CM	0.221	1.104	0.655	1.306
	IT	0.426	1.899*	1.795	4.753*
U.S.:	CM	-1.243	-0.973	0.188	2.691
	IT	-0.726	-0.839	0.269	1.629
Japan:	CM	1.305	1.660	0.002	4.170
	IT	1.442	1.753*	0.349	5.087*
Nixon's Peking Visit‡					
U.S.:	CM	-1.586	-0.420	0.000	1.182
	IT	-0.119	1.092	0.896	0.538
U.S.S.R.:	CM	1.080	0.284	0.435	0.740
	IT	1.376	0.667	-0.647	0.195
Japan:	CM	-1.520	0.443	0.189	0.076
	IT	-3.057	0.612	0.026	0.358
Nixon's Moscow Visit and SALT I Agreement‡					
U.S.:	CM	-1.142	-0.689	0.976	1.169
	IT	-1.101	-0.767	4.925*	0.049
U.S.S.R.:	CM	-0.327	0.182	0.973	0.699
	IT	-0.178	0.255	0.923	0.341
India's Initial Nuclear Test					
India:	CM	1.290	0.234	0.700	0.031
	IT	2.433*	0.720	0.822	0.507
U.S.-U.S.S.R. Resumption of Nuclear Tests					
U.S.:	CM	-0.080	1.296	5.153*	1.564
	IT	-0.404	1.024	3.612	0.923
U.S.S.R.:	CM	-0.610	0.350	3.168	0.289
	IT	-0.815	0.256	2.423	0.166

* Significant at 0.05 level.   † Significant at 0.01 level.

‡ Since this event took place within 150 days of the temporal bounds of our data coverage, we do not have ten data points for either the pre- or the posttest period. The findings reported for this event are based on all available data points over a thirty-four-month period, partitioned into the pre- and posttest periods according to the date of the test-event occurrence. Thus, unlike the other findings reported in this table, the data points for the pre- and posttest periods for this event are not comparable, and are not held constant to ten.

long-term change in the coverage of the Soviet Union and of the United States. If we use the Walker-Lev test 3 results as our measure, the treatment of the Soviet Union in the Chinese press underwent many more long-term changes than did that of the United States. Not only did the Nixon visits not produce relatively lasting change in coverage of the United States, neither did other events that could be reasonably strong candidates for the "qualitative change" category—such as the Western monetary crisis and the Mideast war, with the subsequent oil embargo. The only occasion on which we found any major sustained change for the United States was the bombing campaign against North Vietnam in October 1972. The impression of differences in stability of coverage of the two superpowers gleaned from our quasi-experimental analysis of responses to events is supported by results calculated from our whole *People's Daily* data series (table A-6, appendix A).

Only three of the eight candidate events for "qualitative change" in table 10-6 were examined in our previous analysis: the Mideast war, the Western monetary crisis, and the Indian nuclear test. The findings were similar in their implications.

Conclusions

With regard to our substantive expectations, many received strong support. We found that the concern with the "main contradiction" exercised a particularly powerful influence on Chinese media treatment of events, regardless of whether China was directly involved in these events. The *People's Daily* did exhibit tendencies to propagate developments that provided particularly "positive examples" of the advance of "progressive" forces, and to defer public discussion in situations of grave military threat to China. The latter tendency also applied to its treatment of regime changes with uncertain outcomes or implications for China. The results on possible "qualitative change" events were mixed. Policy responses to these events were for the most part delayed and ambiguous until long after the events took shape, unless the "main contradiction" enabled quick interpretation.

Expectations about the use of media to signal support for allies and warning against adversaries did not fare well. The results obtained from the various episodes related to the Vietnam war and Paracels case did not indicate such use of the *People's Daily*. Nor did we find strong evidence of attempts to bolster the morale of friendly third parties (for example, Pakistan, North Korea) or to embarrass or criticize unfriendly third parties (for example, India, the Soviet Union) in the cases examined. Consequently, our inferences about the use of official media by the Chinese for international signaling purposes were largely unsubstantiated. It is possible that our data on actor attention provide inadequate indication of signaling behavior.

More positively, there was a high degree of convergence between the results of our current and earlier attempts at quasi-experimental analysis, although they differed in the specifics of pre- and posttest data periods and other details.[10] We are more confident, then, that our results are not misleading because of problems of instability and maturation. The problem of "history" does remain and is particularly severe for those events that occurred close in time and for attention to major nations involved in many of the events we used.

10. The time series for the previous analysis had many gaps, which have been filled for this analysis.

CHAPTER 11

TREATMENTS OF NATIONS: TWO PATTERN ANALYSES

In the last chapter, we examined one set of ways in which Chinese belief and analytic structures may predict policy actions: response to events. In this chapter, we are concerned with the relationship between our inferences about Chinese doctrine regarding actors in international affairs and the ways in which the Chinese treat particular nations with respect to public classifications and interpretations. The Chinese beliefs about actors and policy analysis discussed in chapters 8 and 9 generate two sets of expectations about policy practice. The first concerns the sets of nations that will be grouped together as members of a type or class. The second concerns the treatment of particular nations that share reactionary characteristics from the Chinese perspective.

In presenting Chinese beliefs about actors and their relationships, we stressed the importance of assignments to a small number of roles. We also noted the Chinese emphasis on a "full systems analysis" and on the structuring role played by the primary and secondary contradictions. Our first analysis in this chapter examines whether the nations that are treated similarly in the public press are indeed those that ought to be so treated given more general Chinese precepts. Do they play a similar role from the perspective of Chinese policy premises? If the answer is yes, we have some basis for predicting what would have to happen for the Chinese to treat particular nations differently in terms of the policy instrumentality that we examine. If the answer is negative, the doctrinal precepts clearly have little implication for Peking's public classification of international relations actors, and we also have not progressed toward finding general rules that indicate the threshold conditions for changes in that policy behavior.

The beliefs discussed earlier in chapter 8 also stressed the importance of differentiating "friends" and "enemies" within the broad categories that are outside the main contradiction. For nations in other relationships to our Chinese protagonist, placement in the same category does not necessarily imply that they play identical roles in foreign affairs and should be treated identically for policy purposes. As with many other foreign policy elites (Finlay et al. 1967), Chinese maxims of statecraft attach special importance to understanding adversaries and potential adversaries. Because the Chinese assign the adversary role to "reactionary" national systems, they have developed rather detailed and complex conceptions of these systems, as reported in earlier chapters. Our second pattern analysis in this chapter examines the public portrayal of four "reactionary" nations, each of which has been involved in military conflict with the Chinese Communist Party. By clarifying the compatibility of these policy interpretations with the general conception of reactionary systems, we provide another empirical test of the extent to which the Chinese behave in ways their doctrine suggests. A positive answer implies that the general policy analytics do provide an important part of the cognitive context in which the Chinese make rather specific policy choices, and that they offer some basis for predicting these choices. To the extent that the images differ in ways suggested by the major Chinese beliefs presented earlier, we can understand better the implications of the complex relational constructs about the different contradictions featured in Chinese doctrine.

Chinese Classification Rules

Similar to the statements of other governments, Peking's pronouncements on foreign affairs issues are sometimes ambiguous and conflicting. More than one set of interpretive principles may apply to any particular foreign policy problem, and the terms in and implications of specific statements are often not specified for clear application. Two sorts of Chinese statements are relevant to the classification of participants in international affairs. The first, and most obvious, are explicit statements setting forth Chinese views on the political geography of the world. The second, and perhaps less obvious, source is composed of publicly stated guidelines for foreign policy analysis, such as those presented in part III. Both sources will be examined for their classificatory import. It is important to note that these Chinese cognitive frames of reference are not unusual. Political discourse in many cultures often contains a set of distinctions between actors of a more or less complete taxonomic nature *and* recommended rules for dealing with situations involving external parties. While the two may be distinguished analytically, in practice they operate simultaneously, and choice reflects their joint operation.

Political Geography. The outline of Chinese post–Cultural Revolution foreign policy was first delineated by Lin Piao in his keynote report to the Ninth Party Congress in April 1969. Although Lin was subsequently disgraced, this program, known as the Four-Point Program, seems to have continued as the basis for guiding Chinese policy in the early 1970s (Onate 1976). It calls for

1. The development of friendly and cooperative relations with the socialist countries on the principle of proletarian internationalism;
2. Support for the revolutionary struggles of all oppressed peoples and nations;

3. Peaceful coexistence with countries having different social systems on the basis of the Five Principles; and

4. Opposition to the policies of aggression and war on the part of the imperialists (Lin 1969: 31).

During the early 1970s, the groupings implicit in the Four-Point Program were formulated into an explicit mapping of world political geography, which identified four classes of countries (e.g., Shih 1972a, 1972b, 1972c, 1972d; Hua 1972). The first category consisted of "socialist countries." Andres Onate (1976) has suggested that the membership of this category consisted of North Korea, North Vietnam, Albania, Rumania, and China. The second category included the two "superpowers"—the United States and the Soviet Union. Between these two camps were the two intermediate zones, the first being the less-developed Asian, African, and Latin American countries and the second being all the industrialized, capitalist countries in Asia, Europe, and North America except the two superpowers. The basic texts cited previously also introduced a fifth category labeled "reactionary lackeys" and cited South Vietnam and Cambodia (under Lon Nol) as members. If this taxonomy is used in Chinese decision making, we may expect that media treatment of nations will cluster in ways that resembled these five categories.

Decision Analytics. As indicated in the introduction to chapter 10, the Chinese have developed certain guidelines regarding policy treatment in public forums. Like its public responses to events, Peking's media treatment of actors should vary in relation to the dimensions introduced earlier but now applied to actors:

1. The role of China's principal adversary (currently the Soviet Union) with regard to an actor;

2. The location of an actor toward opposite poles of a progressive-to-reactionary continuum in terms of its domestic characteristics;

3. The degree to which an actor is undergoing fundamental changes in its international role or internal capacity;

4. The degree to which an actor provides an example extremely supportive of or incompatible with stated Chinese policy lines; and

5. The degree to which an actor poses extremely sensitive or serious problems for China's territorial security.

With respect to these dimensions, it is important to note that they differ from Chinese statements on political geography in that they are not mutually exclusive choices. The rules allow, but do not require, the Chinese to plot nations on more than one dimension. It is also important to note that, in simultaneous operation, the two sets of rules present some incompatibilities. For example, the taxonomic mapping lumps the two superpowers together. The decision analytics do not because they allow for only one principal adversary at a time.

Events and Unpatterned Behavior.   In addition to the classification logics described above, Chinese treatment of international actors may possibly be related to events or it may be unpatterned. If patterns form around events that are pertinent to the two sets of classification logics, they indicate a special application of one or both of them. However, to the extent that the events upon which patterns are based are peripheral to these logics, this suggests that events per se rather than classification logics drive Chinese media behavior. The second alternative of unpatterned behavior supports the suggestion in chapter 1 that foreign policy choice does not involve consistently applied decision rules. In our data analyses, this alternative would be indicated by Chinese media behavior in which "anomalies" (that is, actor treatments unexplained by either of the two classification logics or by events) predominate.

Data and Procedures.   The data base for our analysis of Chinese treatment of international actors is coverage in the *People's Daily* from January 1972 to October 1974, drawn from the PAMIS data file whose characteristics and relative strengths and weaknesses have been described in the previous chapter. We limit our analysis to the sixty leading themes that appeared in the *People's Daily* during the 1972–1974 time period. Table 11-1 lists these leading themes, and table 11-2 provides their annual as well as cumulative frequencies. As the reader can see from the latter table, coverage for these themes is quite robust. Themes showing drastic annual frequency changes usually reflect the declining Vietnam war. Since attention to foreign actors in the *People's Daily* is characterized by a rather skewed distribution, we restrict our analysis to the forty leading countries in terms of the amount of news coverage they received. Table 11-3 identifies these countries and provides an annual breakdown of the number of news articles dealing with them. It also indicates the number of different themes used to describe these countries.[1]

The lists of leading actors and themes themselves have some interesting substantive and methodological implications for the subsequent mapping of international actors. The leading themes presented in table 11-1 clearly focus on foreign relations and internal political instability. Accordingly, it should be kept in mind that later mapping results deemphasize dimensions such as internal economic structure, which we know to be important in Chinese foreign policy choice. Further, with respect to many of the themes, it is clear that more is involved than Peking's media treatment of others' activities. References to themes involving diplomatic visits, for example, are often the

---

1. The reader should note that the frequencies used in this analysis are based on the number of times a country is associated with a selected theme as either an initiator or a target. For example, both North Vietnam (as a target) and the United States (as an initiator) can be associated with the theme *hegemony*. Differentiation according to initiator and target was not pursued, because it would lead to a substantial increase in the number of variables and a decrease in the coverage of these variables.

TABLE 11-1
THEME DESCRIPTIONS*

Code	Description	Code	Description
1032	Communism	1794	Hegemony: Military Penetration and Influence
1039	Imperialism, Colonialism, Racism, Militarism, Capitalism	1795	Foreign Policy: Political and Military Provocations
1051	Nationalism and Independence	1811	International Organizations: Participation and Membership
1052	National Unity		
1135	Government in Exile	1813	International Organizations: Complaints Against Other Countries
1151	Change of Chief of State		
1348	Insurgent or Illegal Political Groups: Activities	1830	International Functional Activities: Economic, Commercial, Financial
1349	Insurgent or Illegal Political Groups: Foreign Relations	1834	International Functional Activities: Religion, Sport, Women
1431	Political Instability: Defections, Riots, Demonstrations, Assassinations, Bombings, Insurrections, Coups d'Etat	2071	National Holidays and Celebrations
		2130	Foreign Cultural Relations: General
1573	Government Repression, Political Imprisonment	2132	Foreign Cultural Relations: Exchange of Persons, Exhibitions
1700	Foreign Policy	2741	Living Conditions: Cost of Living, Unemployment, Housing, Disasters
1710	Protocolary Activities		
1730	Visits: Foreign Delegations (General)	4132	International Fairs and Exhibitions
1731	Visits: Foreign Economic Delegations	4590	Labor Disputes and Strikes
1732	Visits: Foreign Military Delegations	7013	Armed Forces: Tradition, Ceremonies, Decorations
1733	Visits: Foreign Party Delegations		
1734	Visits: Foreign Labor and Industrial Delegations	7014	Armed Forces: Political Influence and Position
1735	Visits: Foreign Technical and Scientific Delegations	7173	Foreign Military Assistance: Material and Logistics
1736	Visits: Foreign Cultural Delegations	7180	Foreign Reaction to Military Policy or Actions
1737	Visits: Foreign Diplomatic Delegations		
1739	Visits: Foreign Distinguished Private Citizens	7202	Insurgent Armed Forces: Arms, Training, Domestic Relations
1740	Exchange of Greetings and Condolences: General	7204	Insurgent Armed Forces: Military Operations
1750	Exchange of Greetings: International Goodwill/Friendship Organizations	7225	Interception, Search, or Attack Aircraft or Ships
1751	Visits: International Goodwill/Friendship Organizations	7230	Military Operations Against Foreign Forces
1770	Foreign Relations	7232	Anti-Insurgent Operations
1771	Foreign Policy: Official Discussions and Negotiations	7236	Prisoners of War
		7237	War Crimes and Atrocities
1773	Foreign Policy: Unofficial Contacts and Negotiations	7251	Effects of War on Civilian Life
		7260	Cease-Fire, Truce, Armistice: General
1775	Recognition and Establishment of Diplomatic Relations	7261	Cease-Fire, Truce, Armistice: Overtures and Negotiations
1777	Territorial Disputes and Ambitions	7262	Cease-Fire, Truce, Armistice: Agreements
1790	Hegemony: Spheres of Influence (General)		
		7265	Violations of Cease-Fire, Truce Agreement, Military Treaties
1793	Hegemony: Economic Penetration and Influence	7275	Provisional Government

* China is not necessarily the implied initiator or target of events described by these themes. Moreover, each of the countries being examined in this analysis can be associated with the events described by these themes as either an initiator or a target.

TABLE 11-2
PEOPLE'S DAILY THEMATIC COVERAGE: SIXTY LEADING THEMES,
January 1972–October 1974 (*continued on following page*)

Theme	1972	1973	1974	Total
1032	115 (19)*	109 (25)	16 (8)	240 (29)
1039	104 (13)	41 (7)	53 (9)	198 (18)
1051	102 (16)	38 (15)	19 (11)	159 (23)
1052	23 (6)	57 (6)	56 (4)	136 (10)
1135	2 (2)	226 (12)	0 (0)	228 (12)
1151	47 (14)	42 (17)	22 (11)	111 (25)
1348	38 (6)	75 (5)	55 (5)	168 (8)
1349	44 (9)	422 (22)	423 (24)	989 (30)
1431	123 (21)	103 (22)	89 (18)	315 (30)
1573	28 (6)	46 (3)	85 (9)	159 (10)
1700	8 (6)	31 (15)	63 (23)	102 (29)
1710	958 (37)	1143 (37)	591 (33)	2692 (37)
1730	11 (7)	84 (23)	38 (13)	133 (28)
1731	247 (27)	202 (28)	106 (24)	555 (34)
1732	76 (13)	82 (11)	49 (12)	207 (19)
1733	377 (32)	341 (33)	223 (27)	941 (37)
1734	64 (13)	27 (10)	21 (11)	112 (19)
1735	162 (27)	182 (26)	46 (20)	390 (31)
1736	460 (34)	198 (22)	57 (20)	715 (35)
1737	130 (28)	131 (28)	37 (18)	298 (32)
1739	162 (24)	174 (22)	78 (18)	414 (33)
1740	219 (34)	153 (35)	54 (22)	426 (37)
1750	86 (20)	39 (15)	12 (6)	137 (23)
1751	67 (21)	65 (14)	5 (4)	137 (26)
1770	530 (35)	323 (35)	112 (23)	965 (40)
1771	224 (32)	147 (29)	46 (19)	417 (38)
1773	78 (12)	24 (4)	23 (5)	125 (14)
1775	48 (16)	108 (28)	27 (16)	231 (31)
1777	58 (9)	90 (12)	58 (13)	206 (18)
1790	73 (8)	89 (8)	84 (11)	246 (16)
1793	50 (10)	48 (10)	74 (10)	172 (16)
1794	133 (13)	157 (12)	115 (12)	405 (17)
1795	84 (11)	116 (15)	65 (13)	265 (21)
1811	65 (22)	87 (22)	25 (12)	177 (29)
1813	35 (11)	44 (8)	17 (9)	96 (16)
1830	14 (7)	32 (12)	45 (17)	91 (24)
1834	5 (3)	25 (12)	129 (9)	159 (17)
2071	115 (27)	84 (31)	66 (21)	265 (33)
2130	40 (15)	41 (16)	13 (8)	94 (23)
2132	37 (12)	407 (29)	292 (28)	736 (33)
2741	18 (13)	46 (15)	59 (20)	123 (27)
4132	52 (14)	41 (15)	36 (11)	129 (26)
4590	76 (13)	70 (13)	89 (14)	235 (17)
7013	39 (11)	37 (12)	24 (9)	100 (17)
7014	48 (10)	46 (10)	15 (4)	109 (17)
7173	41 (7)	45 (10)	20 (6)	106 (12)
7180	138 (26)	65 (16)	15 (4)	218 (31)
7202	12 (4)	65 (3)	21 (4)	98 (6)
7204	414 (12)	256 (7)	180 (7)	850 (12)
7225	133 (6)	25 (6)	2 (2)	160 (10)

TABLE 11-2 (*continued*)
PEOPLE'S DAILY THEMATIC COVERAGE: SIXTY LEADING THEMES,
January 1972–October 1974

Theme	1972	1973	1974	Total
7230	361 (18)	328 (9)	78 (12)	767 (19)
7232	23 (8)	62 (6)	31 (3)	116 (9)
7236	34 (4)	76 (8)	8 (5)	118 (9)
7237	101 (7)	8 (6)	8 (4)	117 (9)
7251	133 (4)	40 (7)	0 (0)	173 (7)
7260	55 (7)	88 (8)	0 (0)	143 (10)
7261	173 (5)	30 (7)	0 (0)	203 (7)
7262	6 (3)	90 (6)	7 (5)	103 (7)
7265	2 (2)	133 (9)	155 (7)	290 (12)
7275	5 (2)	170 (7)	54 (5)	230 (10)

* The figures without parentheses are the frequencies of news items for each theme. The figures within parentheses are the number of countries that each theme refers to. The latter figures have a numerical ceiling of 40, representing the number of countries being examined in this analysis. Data for December 1972 are the principal gap in the time series.

product of Peking's own policy—namely, invitations to leaders of other countries to visit China. In terms of the leading countries provided in table 11-3, one set of omissions from this list has important substantive implications. The only East European countries mentioned frequently enough to be included in this list are those that have displayed some opposition to Soviet leadership (that is, Yugoslavia, Rumania, and Albania). Countries such as East Germany, Poland, and Hungary are not given much attention despite significant diplomatic ties.

The analytic procedure we have employed is *O*-factor analysis. As exemplified by the work of Banks and Gregg (1965), this method allows us to determine the associations between countries on the basis of a set of variables about their characteristics. In contrast to the more familiar *R* technique, countries and variables are transposed so that countries are grouped rather than variables. In this analysis, the variables are the sixty leading themes in the *People's Daily*. Because different factor rotations may yield important differences in results, we examined results using three different types of orthogonal rotation (quartimax, varimax, and equimax) and oblique rotation. These niceties were in large measure uninformative, yielding very similar solutions, and we present only the equimax results.[2]

2. We used the quartimax rotation with its simplification of row entries (country scores) to expose the maximum power of the country-type taxonomy. We employed the varimax results with their simplification of column entries to expose the maximum power of the decision analytics. The equimax rotation represents a compromise that favors neither decision rule set. And the oblique rotation was intended to illuminate any distortion introduced by the factor-independence assumption in our other three manipulations. With two exceptions, the oblique rotation shows factor correlations to be consistently below the .05 level. The two exceptions involve correlations of .22 and .19. Parenthetically, the tendency for the equimax countries to have multiple loadings is to be expected, because the equimax method is a compromise between the varimax and quartimax methods. This greater complexity of data configuration is also congruent with our substantive concern, because it allows several frames of reference for policy treatment to operate simultaneously.

Results and Interpretation.   The results of the equimax rotation are presented in table 11-4. Before detailed analysis of their implications for our previous discussion, some general points should be made. We have omitted factor loadings less than .40 for ease of inspection and because of their modest contribution (especially in the light of the "noise" in our data set). In general,

TABLE 11-3

PEOPLE'S DAILY ATTENTION TO FOREIGN COUNTRIES:
SELECTED THEMES, January 1972–October 1974

Overall Rank	Country	1972	1973	1974	Total
1	United States	1505 (46)*	829 (48)	271 (36)	2605 (53)
2	Japan	642 (37)	736 (35)	410 (32)	1788 (41)
3	Cambodia	592 (44)	722 (32)	374 (17)	1688 (48)
4	North Vietnam	834 (39)	522 (45)	181 (25)	1537 (49)
5	North Korea	522 (34)	549 (38)	369 (34)	1440 (42)
6	South Vietnam	373 (35)	463 (37)	303 (22)	1139 (46)
7	Albania	361 (30)	232 (27)	110 (18)	703 (35)
8	Laos	207 (31)	231 (25)	147 (24)	585 (44)
9	Soviet Union	110 (20)	243 (22)	230 (24)	583 (31)
10	Rumania	202 (24)	231 (26)	148 (25)	581 (32)
11	Israel	113 (16)	288 (26)	113 (16)	514 (32)
12	Pakistan	146 (29)	170 (28)	101 (21)	417 (39)
13	South Korea	87 (18)	164 (20)	158 (19)	409 (29)
14	France	103 (20)	178 (26)	64 (18)	345 (32)
15	United Kingdom	139 (30)	127 (25)	77 (20)	343 (39)
16	Egypt	110 (24)	132 (30)	51 (20)	293 (43)
17	Iran	69 (14)	103 (22)	117 (16)	289 (27)
18	Mexico	73 (18)	136 (28)	68 (19)	277 (31)
19	Canada	107 (15)	111 (21)	46 (15)	264 (27)
20	Tanzania	85 (22)	70 (25)	103 (21)	258 (35)
21	Australia	44 (15)	108 (18)	62 (18)	214 (28)
22	India	65 (21)	57 (16)	91 (19)	213 (32)
23	Algeria	88 (22)	52 (19)	62 (16)	202 (30)
24	Syria	68 (16)	70 (18)	63 (21)	201 (34)
25	Nepal	77 (15)	82 (17)	36 (14)	195 (24)
26	Chile	104 (24)	83 (23)	5 (5)	192 (31)
27	Sweden	86 (21)	74 (22)	27 (14)	187 (32)
28	Yugoslavia	75 (15)	78 (17)	34 (11)	187 (25)
29	Italy	68 (15)	70 (23)	33 (15)	171 (26)
30	Peru	83 (21)	56 (18)	28 (12)	167 (29)
31	West Germany	37 (10)	78 (19)	51 (20)	166 (25)
32	Ceylon	80 (22)	40 (10)	35 (12)	155 (26)
33	Zambia	11 (5)	77 (19)	61 (16)	149 (24)
34	Switzerland	48 (11)	54 (15)	32 (10)	134 (22)
35	Congo, Brazzaville	30 (14)	70 (14)	24 (10)	124 (28)
36	Thailand	58 (16)	33 (9)	32 (11)	123 (22)
37	Argentina	19 (10)	63 (17)	32 (13)	114 (22)
38	Ethiopia	34 (12)	60 (16)	7 (5)	101 (22)
39	Rhodesia	31 (11)	41 (8)	20 (7)	92 (14)
40	Taiwan	28 (7)	29 (9)	7 (3)	64 (12)

* The figures without parentheses are the frequencies of news items referring to each of the forty countries as either an initiator or a target of those selected themes. The figures within parentheses are the number of themes pertinent to each country. The latter figures have a numerical ceiling of 60, representing the number of leading themes being examined in this analysis. Data for December 1972 are the principal gap in the time series.

TABLE 11-4

EQUIMAX ROTATED FACTOR MATRIX: 1972–1974

Country	F1	F2	F3	F4	F5	h^2
Algeria	.84					.91
Zambia	.81					.87
Congo, Brazzaville	.80					.90
Nepal	.76			.49		.93
Tanzania	.73			.51		.91
Ceylon	.72			.56		.95
North Korea	.71			.51		.86
Rumania	.68			.56		.90
Pakistan	.67			.48		.79
Yugoslavia	.60			.58		.81
Iran	.47					.39
United States		.90				.87
North Vietnam		.89				.85
Syria		.87				.79
Israel		.77				.87
Egypt	.62	.66				.90
Cambodia			.90			.86
Laos			.89			.83
South Vietnam			.87			.78
Rhodesia			.70			.64
Thailand			.65	.57		.84
Italy				.82		.74
United Kingdom	.44			.79		.88
Canada	.49			.77		.95
Australia	.56			.72		.92
Japan	.56			.71		.92
Chile	.49			.70		.79
Mexico	.59			.69		.93
Sweden	.57			.69		.90
Ethiopia	.52			.68		.83
Argentina	.52			.66		.80
Peru	.55			.66		.83
West Germany	.56			.63		.81
Albania	.55			.62		.81
France	.62			.62		.85
Switzerland	.56			.61		.79
Soviet Union					−.74	.56
India					−.70	.61
Taiwan					−.57	.37
South Korea					−.44	.20
% Variance	54.7	10.1	6.3	5.2	3.5	79.8

one can see that the factor matrix is quite robust. The five dimensions jointly explain 79.8 percent of the data variance, and factor 1 contributes more than half of the total variance (54.7 percent). The communality (h^2) scores exceed 60 percent of the variance for all but four of the forty countries with a substantial volume of coverage. The weak exceptions (Iran, the Soviet Union, Taiwan, and South Korea) will be discussed later.

As a preliminary test, the factor matrix suggests that the Chinese do consistently apply decision rules in the treatment of actors. There is not a large amount of unaccounted variance either for the scores as a whole or for many countries. Appraisal of the factor structure and country scores in more detail will, however, provide a stronger test: do the patterns in table 11-4 make sense in terms of the taxonomic categories and decision analytics put forward by the Chinese?

The countries whose highest coefficients are on factor 1 are those that fall into the "socialist" or "first intermediate zone" categories. With respect to the decision analytics, these countries tend to be characterized by an independent posture toward the Soviet Union (China's principal adversary), by their "progressive" regime from the Chinese perspective, and by actions that provide positive examples for Peking's foreign policy program. It is interesting to note that fifteen other countries have substantial scores on this factor even though they score more highly on factor 4. These split-image nations tend to belong to another of the taxonomic categories—the "second intermediate zone," consisting primarily of Western, industrialized states. They resemble the high-scoring nations in their independence vis-à-vis the Soviet Union. With respect to the Chinese Four-Point Program, the countries that have substantial scores on factor 1 are those for whom the enjoinders "develop friendly relations with socialist countries" and "strive for peaceful coexistence with countries having different social systems" are most applicable. Not surprisingly, these nations are most frequently mentioned in terms of diplomatic-protocol themes, which indicate positive state-to-state relations.

Two apparent anomalies to the above interpretation merit mention. One is Albania, which, although a close Chinese ally during the time period under analysis, scores more highly on factor 4 than on factor 1. While this finding is surprising at first glance, we now know that the deterioration of relations between Tirana and Peking had already started in 1972 when Nixon was invited to visit Peking and was further exacerbated by the later purge of "radical Chinese leaders favored by the Albanians" and the development of "warm relations with Yugoslavia, an old Albanian foe" (*International Herald Tribune*, July 15–16, 1978: 2). Iran, the second apparent anomaly, is also less puzzling upon closer inspection. As Iran's low communality score indicates, Chinese treatment of that nation was not captured well by our factor matrix. Iran's ambiguous status may be accounted for by its independence vis-à-vis the Soviet Union and its role as a positive example for Peking's foreign policy due to its support for Pakistan vis-à-vis India (Entessar 1978), while having a "reactionary" regime in terms of its domestic characteristics.

The countries whose highest scores are on factor 2 are the major direct participants in the two major "hot" wars of this period: Vietnam and the 1973 Middle East conflict. At first inspection, this dimension seems to constitute an ad hoc construction in response to events. The countries are not similar in terms of taxonomic category or in terms of relations with the principal adversary, regime character, or propaganda value. Nevertheless, this dimension seems to us less an illustration of "ad-hocery" than a derivation from the policy program and decision analytics introduced earlier.[3] With respect to the policy program, both the Vietnam and Middle East situations related to the injunctions to "oppose imperialist aggression" and "support the national liberation of all oppressed peoples and nations." Unlike other nations that might invoke similar policy imperatives, the relations among the parties loading heavily on factor 2 directly involve the decision rule calling for special attention to situations with a potential for yielding a qualitative change in power relationships, at least regionally and perhaps more broadly. Of equal imortance, and very much in line with the decision rule to concentrate on event implications for the main contradiction, both situations involved countries (especially North Vietnam and Syria) very strongly backed by the Soviet Union. Factor 2 seems to be reserved for nations that were the focus of several Chinese rules whose implications for preferred outcomes were in at least partial oppostion. The regimes the Chinese felt compelled to support were also those for whom an overwhelming victory would redound to the benefit of the Soviet Union. Concomitantly, the governments the Chinese felt compelled to oppose were also those for whom an overwhelming defeat would redound to the benefit of the Soviet Union. Singling out such nations for special treatment seems to argue less for an "event" interpretation than for one which gives importance to the decision analytics we have imputed to the Chinese. Parenthetically, the split image of Egypt, which also loads substantially on factor 1, seems compatible with this interpretation. Unlike the other high scorers on factor 2, Egypt tended during our period to have, from the Chinese perspective, many of the characteristics of the "first intermediate zone" nations. Finally, none of the countries loading on this factor can reasonably be considered to be "puppet" regimes in the Chinese view. In contrast, those loading on the next factor, factor 3, tend to fall under this designation.

For our period, the nations whose highest scores are on factor 3 clearly fall into the "lackey" category and lie at the "reactionary" and "negative example" extremes of the Chinese encoding continua posited earlier. Of the five heavy loaders (Cambodia, Laos, South Vietnam, Rhodesia, and Thailand), only Thailand has a split image in the sense of a substantial score on another dimension (factor 4). This split is compatible with the developments unique to Thailand during our period—namely, a change of regime (the overthrow of Kittikachorn in October 1973) followed by attempts to establish closer relations with Peking. The clustering on our third dimension is interpretable in terms of the policy injunction to "support the national liberation of all

---

3. This grouping is also facilitated by the insensitivities in the PAMIS coding scheme that were discussed previously.

oppressed peoples and nations," operating without the relevance of the qualitative change and principal adversary complications that applied to the heavy loaders on factor 2.

The nations that scored most heavily on factor 4 were primarily the Western, industrialized nations belonging to the "second intermediate zone." As noted earlier, the grouping is interpretable and expected given their independence from the Soviet Union, the policy program recommendation to "strive for peaceful coexistence with countries having different social systems," and the rather unprogressive character of these regimes in Chinese terms. Strong support for this interpretation is provided by the fact that the countries loading highly on factor 4 are distinguished by thematic emphasis on domestic problems *(political instability* # 1431, *living conditions* #2741, *labor disputes and strikes* #4590), economic transactions (*international fairs and exhibitions* #4132), and "people's diplomacy" (*foreign cultural relations* #2132) rather than state-to-state relations.

Just as the highest scorers on factor 1 have substantial scores on factor 4, the highest scorers on factor 4 also have substantial loadings on factor 1. This is unsurprising given their similarity in independence vis-à-vis the Soviet Union and the appropriateness of some of the same forms of positive relations (for example, visits of leaders) with "socialist" and "first intermediate zone" nations as with the members of the "second intermediate zone."

The countries whose highest scores are on our last dimension, factor 5, are Peking's "enemies": the Soviet Union, India, Taiwan, and South Korea. They have in common the significant probability that their actions pose national security problems for China. Additionally, they all provide negative examples for Chinese leaders. The thematic emphases for the Soviet Union and India on *imperialism* (# 1039) and *hegemony and spheres of influence* (# 1790) fit with this interpretation. It is also the case that the nations featured on factor 5 are characterized by weak communality scores. The low communality scores can be explained in two ways. First, the grave implications of the policy of these nations for the People's Republic may lead to their being treated by an additional and much more refined set of decision rules. Second, the Chinese have no consistent rules for the treatment of actors of this sort. Our later analysis of Chinese images of adversaries will shed some light on this possibility.

Concluding Observations.   Our results are by and large consonant with the groupings one would expect from the simultaneous operation of the several sets of rules that we attribute to the Chinese government. The absence of apparently random combinations across several years and numerous nations and themes is contrary to the proposition that the Chinese do not use consistent decision rules in their treatment of actors. While all the decision analytics seem to apply with considerable power, it is clear that the taxonomic categories vary substantially in their capacity to distinguish clusters of nations. The hostile categories seem to operate with much more exclusiveness—witness the "lackeys" clustered on factor 3 and the "enemies" on factor 5—than the neutral and positive categories whose occupants have split images between factors 1 and 4. The discrimination between members respectively of the "socialist," "first intermediate," and "second intermediate" zones seems weak, perhaps because many dimensions of Chinese policy toward them are appropriate whichever of those three bins a nation occupies.

Beyond the specific findings, the analysis supports the value of basic nation taxonomies and the decision analytics to map countries into organized clusters. The nation taxonomies provided by Lin's formulation proved to be useful for understanding Chinese media treatment of international actors even after his purge in 1971. Similarly, the decision analytics—which we inferred from documents spanning more than two decades of the Chinese regime—were also shown to be informative for understanding this treatment. Thus, our findings for the 1972–1974 period encourage confidence in, although they do not validate, their utility for research on other periods of Chinese foreign policy.

However, it is important to recognize that we are unlikely to achieve a simple and direct correspondence between nation taxonomies and decision analytics on the one hand and public media treatment on the other. As we pointed out earlier with respect to the East European countries, patterned omission in the latter can be both important and informative in a policy sense. What is significant is that the map does not give any particular nation an inherently static location. The latent structure of the map can be clear and apparently stable and yet allow for national locations (that is, factor scores) to vary with changes in their internal politics and external relations. Indeed, the latent structure we have developed for the 1972–1974 period suggests that an analysis of comparable date for more recent years—for example, 1976–1978—will show particular locational changes. With regard to the nations of Southeast Asia, for example, Laos should shift to factor 1, Cambodia to either factor 1 or factor 2, and Vietnam possibly to factor 5. If the map has this rather predictable adaptability, our line of argument suggests that changes in the treatment of nations by China need not require explanations that emphasize the stochastic character of foreign policy processes.

Images of Adversaries

As has been described in detail in parts II and III, the Chinese in their public statements prescribe the existence of only one major enemy at any particular time. Historically, the identity of this "main enemy" has shifted a number of times, changing from the Kuomintang, to Japan, to the United States, and now to the Soviet Union. Shifts in the identification of the "main enemy" have important policy implications for the Chinese. Any light we can shed on the basis for this decision will contribute significantly to our understanding of Chinese foreign policy decision making.

While, on the surface, the determination of which actor constitutes the main enemy seems straightforward, two questions arise in relation to understanding this decision. First, what criteria do the Chinese employ in assigning specific actors to the "main enemy" role? In parts II and III, the Marxist-Leninist basis of Chinese analysis of international affairs is apparent. Does this framework, in particular the Leninist analysis of imperialism, provide the basis for this "main enemy" determination? If alternate criteria are employed, how do they affect Chinese policy dialogue on this issue? Second, how do the Chinese regard "nonfriendly" actors who are not assigned to the "main enemy" role? In light of their views on the importance of coalition politics in international affairs, we expect that the Chinese assign considerable significance to nations that have a history of conflict with China and are "reactionary" in domestic terms but have some capacity to do China either substantial ill or good. Are such actors accorded different status and, if so, on what basis?

With regard to these two questions, the structure of Chinese treatment of actors previously revealed in table 11-4 is both suggestive and limiting. On the suggestive side, China's present and historical adversaries are not in any sense treated as a monolithic group. Japan, with its "split image," is regarded as at least a potential friend, while the Soviet Union and India are clearly designated as adversaries. Regarding past and present adversaries as "unprogressive" in domestic terms does not mean that they are treated identically. With reference to the earlier discussion about decidability and flexibility, the images of the Soviet Union and India are more conducive to the former; that of Japan to the latter. In terms of limitations, the structure obscures rather than clarifies Chinese understanding of the internal characteristics of adversaries. The treatment of the United States as a conflict participant reveals little of Peking's understanding of its internal dynamics. Similarly, the clustering of "enemies" evident in the structure (the Soviet Union, India, Taiwan, and South Korea) fails to capture substantial differences in both internal characteristics and the capacity to pose a threat to China. Because the previous data analysis focused largely on foreign policy themes, internal characteristics were not emphasized.

To pursue these concerns, we explore three questions. First, what are the hallmarks of the "main enemy," currently the Soviet Union? Second, how do countries whose image facilitates decidability in Chinese policy interpretations and selections differ from those whose image does not (as suggested by unified or split images in our factor analysis)? Third, to what extent do the images of reactionary adversaries conform to or deviate from the basically Marxist-Leninist formulation of imperialism presented in chapter 6? In other words, does this model of reactionary behavior have import for the public treatment of actual or potential adversaries, or is it merely an orthodox relic that has little to do with actual policy practice? As we shall see, the extent to which different country images fit this standard Marxist-Leninist conception has important cognitive and political implications for Chinese foreign policy decision making.

To answer the above questions, we examine thematic patterns in the *People's Daily* treatment of the four candidate Chinese enemies—the Soviet Union, Japan, the United States, and India. The data cover the same time period as our previous analysis, January 1972–October 1974. Any theme that received an aggregate coverage of more than 1,000 square centimeters for one of these countries appears in table 11-5. As before, no distinction has been made as to the initiator or recipient status of a country in any particular news report. We group these themes under broad substantive headings for ease of inspection. To control for the effects of different volumes of coverage for these countries, we discuss the relative importance of themes in terms of their percentage contribution to the total coverage of a country.[4]

Table 11-5 shows quite clearly that current involvement in international conflicts is not an important criterion for determining China's "main enemy." Because of their participation in the Indochina and Bangladesh wars, the United States (38.73 percent) and India (18.55 percent) received considerable attention on this score. On the other hand, the Soviet Union—China's defined "main enemy"—did not directly engage in overt conflict on a massive scale during the time period under examination; only 11.36 percent of the *People's Daily* coverage of that country was devoted to international conflict.

What distinguishes the Chinese image of the Soviet Union from that of other enemies or quasi enemies is attention to activities that potentially can lead to international conflict. The Chinese clearly laid heavy emphasis on Soviet expansionist policies that fell short of direct, massive conflict involvement by Moscow and on Soviet military preparations that might be used in such involvement. We find that 30.77 and 16.83 percent of the coverage of the Soviet Union was devoted to subjects under the headings of foreign expansion and armament respectively. The comparable figures are 7.80 and 9.58 percent for the United States. This data pattern reflects Chinese concern with the diminishing strategic gap between the two superpowers and the concomitant danger of conflict occurrence mentioned in chapter 7. Parenthetically, with regard to foreign expansion, India also received a great deal of Chinese attention (23.12 percent), thus partially accounting for the similarities of India and the Soviet Union in the factor-analytic scores presented earlier.

According to table 11-5, Japan is clearly the least threatening country from Peking's perspective. References to Japan in the context of "international conflict," "foreign expansion," or "armament" discussions were uniformly

---

4. The reader should keep in mind that the percentage figures for India are based on a significantly smaller *N* than those for the other nations.

TABLE 11-5

THEMATIC ATTENTION TO POSSIBLE ADVERSARIES,

January 1972–October 1974* *(continued on following page)*

Code	Themes	U.S.A.	U.S.S.R.	Japan	India
	Ideology	**.95**	**1.01**	**.95**	**1.54**
1000	History and ideology	.00	.61	.00	.00
1032	Communism	.08	.40	.50	.55
1051	Nationalism and independence	.87	.00	.00	.99
1052	National unity	.00	.00	.45	.00
	Domestic Politics	**6.19**	**3.62**	**4.18**	**6.96**
1151	Change of chief of state	.45	.00	.13	.15
1152	Change of head of government	.00	.00	.45	.00
1348	Activities of illegal groups	.72	.24	.21	.00
1398	Political clubs	.18	.00	1.59	.00
1431	Political instability	1.41	.34	1.81	5.74
1630	Propaganda	.21	.89	.00	.18
2554	Immigration and emigration	.00	2.07	.00	.17
7251	Effects of war on civilians	2.78	.00	.00	.73
7440	Civilian exploitation and utilization	.43	.07	.00	.00
	Economic Problems and Policies	**8.50**	**11.43**	**7.03**	**15.21**
1731	Economic missions and delegations	.13	.18	2.90	.00
1734	Labor and industrial missions and delegations	.10	.00	.58	.00
1793	Economic penetration and influence	2.02	7.88	.75	2.35
2741	Living conditions	.79	.14	.47	3.79
4016	Nationalization of enterprises	.58	.00	.00	.00
4590	Labor disputes and strikes	1.70	.00	1.63	5.79
4750	Government finance and monetary policies	.47	.00	.15	.00
4752	Government budget	.25	.00	.00	.00
4850	Foreign trade	.17	1.29	.29	1.02
4891	Foreign exchange and gold	.75	.21	.04	.00
4892	Balance of payment	.47	.18	.02	.00
4910	Economic warfare	.95	.00	.19	.00
4931	Foreign economic aid	.08	.76	.00	2.26
4932	Loans to foreign countries	.04	.80	.00	.00
	External Relations	**20.16**	**12.73**	**62.55**	**11.42**
1700	Foreign policy	.69	1.16	.42	.23
1710	Protocolary activities	4.17	.24	22.85	2.01
1733	Party missions and delegations	.71	.53	2.93	6.10
1735	Technical and scientific missions and delegations	1.32	.00	1.12	.00
1736	Cultural missions and delegations	1.02	.00	6.59	.17
1739	Visits of distinguished private citizens	1.41	.00	4.47	.22
1740	Exchange of greetings and condolences	.18	.26	1.44	.19
1750	International goodwill organizations	.30	.00	1.82	.00
1751	Visits of international goodwill organizations	.12	.00	.63	.00
1770	Foreign relations	5.78	7.87	6.63	2.26
1771	Official discussions and negotiations	2.73	.62	2.29	.00
1773	Unofficial contacts and negotiations	.18	.18	1.32	.00
1811	Participation in international organizations	.29	1.68	.16	.26
1834	International functional activities	.01	.00	3.21	.00
2130	Foreign cultural relations	.08	.12	2.09	.00
2132	Exchange of persons and exhibitions	1.18	.08	4.57	.00

TABLE 11-5 (*continued*)
THEMATIC ATTENTION TO POSSIBLE ADVERSARIES,
January 1972–October 1974*

Code	Themes	U.S.A.	U.S.S.R.	Japan	India
	Foreign Expansion	**7.80**	**30.77**	**2.05**	**23.12**
1039	Imperialism	2.64	8.06	1.16	10.70
1590	Intelligence and espionage	.07	3.63	.21	.00
1790	Hegemony and spheres of influence	2.34	15.68	.51	6.27
1791	Political penetration and influence	.57	.24	.14	4.00
7160	Collective security	.30	1.85	.03	.00
7170	Foreign military assistance	.54	.22	.00	.30
7173	Foreign military assistance (matériel/logistics)	1.33	1.09	.00	1.84
	Armament	**9.58**	**16.83**	**.90**	**3.41**
1794	Military penetration and influence	5.73	7.29	.64	3.18
7071	Military readiness	.27	.13	.00	.00
7100	Rearmament	.21	3.11	.02	.00
7110	Disarmament	.19	3.76	.00	.00
7130	Military research and development	.22	1.33	.00	.00
7180	Foreign reaction to military policy	2.95	.40	.18	.23
7370	Navy	.00	.80	.05	.00
	International Conflict	**38.73**	**11.36**	**4.50**	**18.55**
1025	Struggle against foreign dominance	.29	.16	.18	.00
1777	Territorial disputes and ambitions	1.37	5.64	3.98	.59
1795	Political and military provocations	2.39	1.52	.28	.71
1813	Complaints against other countries	.58	3.89	.00	.68
7204	Military operations of insurgent movements	2.15	.00	.00	.00
7225	Interception, search, or attack aircraft or ships	1.76	.00	.00	.00
7230	Military operations against foreign forces	15.41	.14	.06	1.19
7232	Anti-insurgent operations	.41	.00	.00	.00
7236	Prisoners of war	.60	.00	.00	10.03
7237	War crimes	1.95	.00	.00	1.72
7260	Cease-fire: general	1.70	.00	.00	3.36
7261	Cease-fire: overtures and negotiations	4.43	.00	.00	.00
7262	Cease-fire: agreements	3.15	.00	.00	.00
7265	Cease-fire: violations	2.56	.00	.00	.26
	Culture and Society	**.01**	**.00**	**1.61**	**.00**
2040	National characteristics	.00	.00	.34	.00
2077	Recreation and entertainment	.00	.00	.66	.00
2394	Theater and cinema	.01	.00	.61	.00
	Total coverage in centimeters	471170	169169	292648	43084
	% of selected themes of total coverage	91.92	87.75	83.77	80.21

* The figures are percentages of total country coverage captured by each individual theme. No distinction was made between countries as action initiator or target. Nor were favorable, neutral, or unfavorable comments by the *People's Daily* differentiated. Data for the month of December 1972 constitute the biggest gap in the time series.

low in comparison with the other three countries. Moreover, these references more often than not indicated that Japan was the victim rather than the perpetrator of these acts, particularly with regard to its border negotiations with the Soviet Union (*territorial disputes and ambitions* constituted 3.98 percent of references to Japan).

The image of a relatively friendly Japan is bolstered by extensive coverage of governmental and nongovernmental interactions between Peking and Tokyo. In this respect, Japan received the same kind of policy treatment by Peking as other countries belonging to the first or second intermediate zones. Friendly interactions under the heading "external relations" constituted 62.55 percent of the *People's Daily* coverage of that country. The United States was a distant second (20.16 percent) but was still far ahead of the Soviet Union (12.73 percent) and India (11.42 percent). It should also be pointed out that much of the coverage of the Soviet Union and India under the heading of external relations was related to the topic of *foreign relations*, which does not necessarily imply favorable Chinese treatment. On the other hand, themes indicating positive Chinese behavior, such as *protocolary activities, cultural missions and delegations, visits of distinguished private citizens* and *official discussions and negotiations*, received much more prominent coverage in the case of Japan and, to a lesser extent, the United States. This does not imply that Peking's images of Japan and the United States were overwhelmingly favorable. We have already commented on a very substantial portion (38.73 percent) of the Chinese coverage of the latter being devoted to discussion of its involvement in the Indochina war.

With regard to the Marxist-Leninist model of imperialism, we find modest but not overwhelming support in the entries in table 11-5. A considerable amount of attention was directed to the domestic political difficulties of the Japanese, American, and Indian governments and slightly less to those of Moscow. Nevertheless, the percentages are quite modest. Coverage of economic problems and policies was also modest if noticeable in amount. What does emerge is that the substance of the economic matters presented for the United States, Japan, and India is primarily domestic in nature—for example, the emphasis on *living conditions* and *labor disputes and strikes*. For the Soviet Union, the economic themes are primarily foreign in nature. In the most primitive interpretation, the Marxist-Leninist conception of imperialism would imply that attention to the domestic political economy of adversaries would be high proportional to international relations and conflicts of a less narrowly economic character. Clearly that did not happen. Whether the Chinese public presentations of adversaries give more emphasis to domestic political economy matters relative to the analogous behavior of the policy elites of other countries surely merits exploration but cannot be answered here.

The Chinese characterizations of the United States and India come closest to presenting the properties of reactionary systems as posited in Chinese doctrine. In the case of the United States, this is not particularly surprising, inasmuch as the period under analysis involved the sorts of events associated in Marxism-Leninism with reactionary imperialism—for example, military involvement in Indochina, the raw material strain associated with the O.P.E.C.

oil-pricing decisions, the Watergate affair, and economic inflation and recession at home. The image of India seems curious at first, given that country's underdeveloped economic sectors and avowedly nonaggressive philosophy about the conduct of international affairs. However, it does gain rationale in the light of India's advanced industrial sectors and weapons programs, actions toward Bangladesh and Pakistan, and web of ties with the Soviet Union. Japan quite clearly is the most deviant case in terms of the classic formulation of reactionary actors.

It is with regard to the Soviets that our findings are most interesting and suggestive. Here we have a nation placed in the key reactionary role—that of the main enemy—without the media portrayal that reactionaries supposedly warrant. Note the relative paucity of Chinese attention to direct Soviet involvement in international conflicts and to Soviet domestic economic and political affairs. Despite Chinese attempts to fit the Soviet Union into their traditional framework for policy analysis through such formulations as "state capitalism" and "social imperialism," they had not managed to do so during the time period we examined.

From cognitive-perceptual research (de Rivera 1968), we note that recognition of and adjustment to an unprecedented phenomenon that is not easily accommodated by existing categories tend to be slow and erratic processes. In the Chinese case, the Soviet Union clearly does not fit with the conceptions of reactionary adversaries developed in the revolutionary years or the first decade of power of the Peking leadership, or with the received wisdom of Marxism-Leninism-Stalinism. In that sense, concern about the Soviet Union is relatively recent, albeit signs of concern and policy reexamination were visible at least a decade before the period covered by our data (Bobrow 1966; Zagoria 1962). The need for explicit public interpretation only became overriding with the Soviet invasion of Czechoslovakia in 1968 and the Sino-Soviet border clashes of 1969 (Dillon et al. 1977). Accordingly, Peking's decision logics to explain and interpret Soviet domestic and foreign policies are not likely to be as well developed in the sense of coherence and persuasiveness as those for Western capitalist systems.

This point has several important implications. First, in the absence of a well-developed category for the Soviet Union, Chinese decision makers are more likely to disagree about the extent to which the prevailing policy-analytic paradigm is relevant and applicable, and about the significance and implications of Soviet behavior. Peking's recurrent policy "debates" have focused precisely on the issue of whether the United States or the Soviet Union is China's "main enemy" and the policy implications of this conceptual definition (e.g., Gottlieb 1977; Zagoria 1967). Second, the absence of a well-established conceptual framework that accounts for Soviet behavior has the additional implication that Peking's policies are less likely to be "constrained" by generally accepted policy logics than in the case of Western capitalist systems. Consequently, idiosyncratic factors may play a more important role in determining these policies, an inference that is consistent with the previous observation that these policies are likely to be more controversial. Finally, to the extent that these policies are not based on a firm conceptual framework shared by Peking's decision makers, they are more vulnerable to changes and reversals. Given the obvious pressures to maintain traditional categories of analysis, the determination that the Soviet Union is China's "main enemy" seems particularly susceptible to a "reversal of verdicts."

PART V

Conclusion

CHAPTER 12

ASSESSMENT AND IMPLICATIONS

In our introductory chapter, we put forth a number of questions central to this work. It is now time to see if the incremental progress we hoped to achieve in answering them has been made. The questions were as follow:

1. Does foreign policy exhibit the strong patterns that the use of consistent decision rules implies?
2. Do different regimes use generically different decision logics and information-processing rules for foreign policy decision making?
3. Are propositions about those logics and rules confirmed by the use of several diverse data sources and methods?
4. Do these rules and logics have significant implications for foreign policy actions and yield predictions that can be disconfirmed?
5. Can we identify at least a partial structuring of decision logics and information-processing rules?
6. Does our approach contribute to the substantive understanding of Chinese foreign policy?

Like Chinese officials engaged in post hoc policy evaluations, we take the view that "to affirm everything or to deny everything is partial" (Mao quoted in Worker-Peasant-Soldier Team 197*b*: 12). Our hopes have been for progress vis-à-vis our questions rather than for complete, dramatic answers, as if our methods offer some sort of magic. Indeed, operational-code approaches do not stake their success on the sort of MAGIC that provides direct, almost automatic access to others' foreign policy thinking (Wohlstetter 1962). They necessarily work with peripheral information, and are more concerned with explanation and prediction than with descriptive confirmation and warning.

As the reader will recall, the "garbage can" view of policy processes essentially argues that an emphasis on the decisional aspects of foreign policy making may not be of much help in explaining and predicting policy actions. Foreign policy decision processes allegedly have a significant stochastic element as a result of the matching or mismatching of goals, problems, and participants. The analyses presented in the previous chapters do not claim to offer an exact assessment of the importance of nondecisional considerations, but they do establish a reasonable case that the behavior of the Chinese decision system is basically nonrandom. And the policy doctrine of the Peking elite has been shown to provide reasonable explanations of and predictions about Chinese policy behavior.

We have also built a prima facie case that there are substantial differences in the views and logics employed by different national decision makers to conduct and analyze foreign policy. To be sure, our cross-national comparison has been largely restricted to the United States. Success in demonstrating major differences in Chinese and U.S. decision logics does not in itself assure discovery of differences of similar magnitude between other national elites. Yet if decision makers from countries with national experience and culture as different as these two did not show significantly divergent views and logics, our argument about cross-national heterogeneity would be deservedly suspect. Conversely, a cognitive approach to foreign policy analysis need not be less useful for countries more similar in cultural or political characteristics. The Chinese emphasis on the development and propagation of relatively explicit policy rationales has facilitated our research task, but problems of access to information have constrained our analyses in other important ways. Research on other regimes often will not confront such severe data limitations. Accordingly, other cases should provide better opportunities to generate cognitively based foreign policy findings that our broad-stroke analyses of the Chinese case were unable to reveal or establish firmly. Examples include the relevance of elite doctrine for structuring bureaucratic politics debates, the distribution of belief precepts and decision logics across institutions and groups of specialists, and the thinking of individual decision makers on particular occasions. Obviously, more abundant and diverse data about policy behavior would also allow for the testing of a much larger portion of the substantive expectations derived from qualitative content analysis of doctrine than was possible for the Chinese case.

In spite of the obvious data problems, we have been relatively successful in making progress toward answering questions about Chinese foreign policy decision making. First, we were able to produce a rather extensive codification of Chinese policy analytics. This progress did not stop with a simple compilation but went on to provide some structure in terms of the general relationships between them and their relative clarity and importance for practical applications. That is, our work does differentiate between beliefs with clear and central decision import for Chinese foreign policy and beliefs whose status and implications are more peripheral and contingent. Second, we found it possible to derive specific hypotheses about policy behavior from research on the operational codes of elites, and to test these hypotheses empirically. While the test results do not uniformly support our hypotheses, disconfirmation is as important as confirmation. Our evidence enables us at least to discriminate areas where the implications of key beliefs and decision rules are relatively strong from areas where they are weak and elusive. Third, the analyses provide encouragement about the payoffs from a multimethod research strategy for studying inaccessible decision systems in general. While our individual methods and data sets all have important limitations, their combined contribution has the effect of heightening confidence in the research results, which we would otherwise lack.

In our view, chapters 4 through 11 do enhance understanding of Chinese foreign policy. Of course, the propositions advanced are not entirely novel, comprehensive, or applicable to all decision situations. Important enigmas remain in our understanding of Chinese decision making, and further refinement and testing are obviously desirable. What we have done is to identify general tendencies in Peking's foreign policy decision process and to subject these tendencies to some systematic tests. Our quantitative analyses have had to focus largely on one stream of policy behavior—namely, Chinese media treatment of events and actors. The general support provided by this evidence for our qualitative content-analytic inferences does not, of course, assure the utility of these inferences for other kinds of Chinese policy behavior. Nor is it certain that all the beliefs we attribute to Chinese decision makers will be maintained through present and future leadership changes. However, the framework we have developed makes it possible to test the understanding gained from our analyses for other forms of policy behavior and for future contexts.

Three areas of remaining work stand out. First, we clearly need to improve our understanding of areas that lack decidability for the Chinese, particularly with respect to the bimodal orientations we have noted. What kinds of situational factors induce Chinese analysts to stress one rather than the other member of these injunctions? What rules are applied to decide their relative stress or to adopt a course of the "middle road"? Second, our understanding of the rules for updating and adapting policy lines is relatively weak. While we know, for example, that the definition of the main contradiction, the determination of the impending or actual occurrence of a qualitative change, and the assessment of the class stand of actors are especially important for influencing Chinese foreign policy responses, we have a weak grasp of the rationale and indicators that the Chinese use to make these judgments. There is the possibility that there are no clearly valid indicators or consistent rules for applying them, so that judgments on these matters follow from ad hoc consideration of particular situations or post hoc rationalization of previously taken decisions or actions. Clear evidence to that effect would clarify the limits of the cognitive approach to foreign policy analysis.

Third, realizing the full analytic potential of research on elite operational codes depends on systematizing the cognitive process of decision making. In our analysis of Chinese treatment of critical international events in chapter 10, we report one effort in this direction that relates logics and beliefs about the encoding of external developments, the instrumental values of a particular policy tool (media treatment), and the assessment of possible external reactions to Chinese policy treatment. We found policy response to be a largely predictable joint product of these multiple considerations operating sequentially. The analysis of the treatment of nations in chapter 11 illustrates complex reasoning that takes the form of the simultaneous operation of several sets of rules on a common problem. As a further and somewhat more formal illustration, we now introduce a set of ordered decision rules for Chinese policy making with regard to intervention in second-order crises—that is, critical incidents in which Peking is not directly involved initially. These rules stem from our qualitative content analysis, historical case studies, and quasi-experimental exercises. The rules, expressed in flow-chart form in figure 12-1, indicate the necessary conditions for a crisis-intervention decision. Each one provides a "gate" for the next step in the decision-making analysis. The ordered rules themselves (Bobrow et al. 1977: 206–9) are as follow:

Rule 1: Identify China's main enemy.

Rule 2: Assess the level of involvement (e.g., high, low) of China's main enemy in the crisis.

Rule 3: (a) To the extent that China's main enemy is not heavily involved in the crisis, Chinese policies should have a higher threshold for direct involvement in the crisis.

(b) To the extent that China's main enemy is heavily involved in the crisis, Chinese policies should be designed to maximize its loss or vulnerability or conversely, to minimize its gains.

Rule 4: Identify the major third-party actors (i.e., those who are not directly involved in the crisis), including China's allies and secondary enemies.

Rule 5: Assess the prevailing current of international relations; that is, the level of opposition of these intermediate actors to the policies of China's main enemy.

Rule 6: (a) To the extent that the prevailing current is unfavorable (i.e., to the extent that the major third-party actors are badly divided or are supportive of China's main enemy), China should abstain from direct involvement in the crisis.

(b) To the extent that the prevailing current is favorable (i.e., to the extent that the major third-party actors are strongly opposed to the policies of China's main enemy), China should adopt a more active policy posture. China should not, however, initiate unilateral intervention, but should instead stress approaches such as "divide and rule," "conflict through proxies," and "united front" (including "parallel tracking" policies of mutual support with secondary enemies in the absence of formal mechanisms of consultation and coordination).

Rule 7: Assess the political reliability of major third-party actors.

Rule 8: (a) To the extent that a third-party actor is characterized by domestic instability or dubious ideological outlook, China should not expect constancy in its foreign policies. In particular, China should discount its reliability as a potential ally, and raise the threshold for direct involvement in a crisis.

(b) To the extent that a third-party actor is characterized by domestic stability and "correct" ideological outlook, confidence in its reliability as a potential ally is enhanced, and China should therefore consider joint actions to crisis intervention.

Rule   9: Identify the direct conflict participants in the crisis.

Rule 10: Assess the nature of relations (e.g., friendly, hostile) between the direct conflict participants and China's main enemy.

Rule 11: (a) To the extent that all of the direct conflict participants are friendly towards China's main enemy (i.e., to the extent that they represent "reactionary" forces), China should raise its threshold for direct involvement in the crisis. Instead, China should exploit the effects of their dispute on their relations with China's main enemy, thereby reducing the latter's influence and credibility.

(b) To the extent that at least one of the direct conflict participants is hostile to China's main enemy (i.e., to the extent that it represents "progressive" forces), China should consider supporting it in the crisis.

Rule 12: Assess the internal characteristics of the direct conflict participants.

Rule 13: (a) To the extent that the conflict participant representing the "reactionary" forces is strong, stable, and united, or to the extent that the conflict participant representing the "progressive" forces is weak, unstable, and disunited, China should raise its threshold for direct involvement in the crisis.

(b) To the extent that the conflict participant representing the "reactionary" forces is weak, unstable, and disunited, or to the extent that the conflict participant representing the "progressive" forces is strong, stable, and united, China should lower its threshold for direct involvement in the crisis.

Impressionistically, this representation of Chinese decision logics seems to match Peking's behavior in such pertinent recent episodes as Zaïre, Angola, Ethiopia, and Bangladesh. As work proceeds along the three lines just discussed, we can move beyond such schemata as that in figure 12-1 toward dynamic predictive tools such as those provided by the production rules of an artificial-intelligence model.

More generally, if the reader shares our self-assessment of modest success, the case for the foreign policy and conflict research strategy we proposed in chapter 1 is strengthened. It seems capable of producing verifiable findings of foreign affairs importance and of laying a basis for the analysis of national elites that would retain its applicability over substantial periods of time and across geographic arenas. As a result, application of our basic perspective and research strategy to other cases appears both more feasible and promising. Efforts to do so are our principal recommendation for research policy. As for public policy, systematic work on the cognitions of different national elites seems capable of producing policy-relevant conclusions. This demonstration suggests that there is no sound technical reason to content ourselves with the

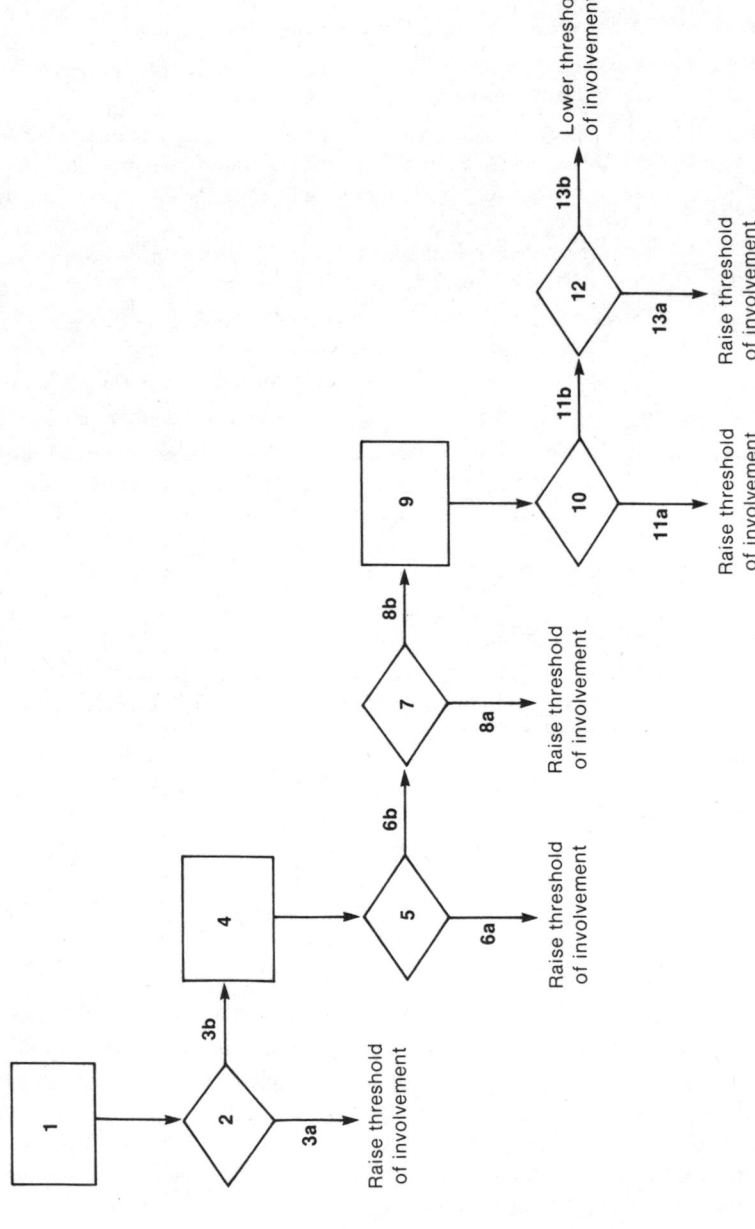

FIGURE 12-1
INVOLVEMENT IN SECOND-ORDER CRISES

present basis on which national elites assess the behavior of their counterparts, select signals to send to them, or engage in complex policies to shape their perceptions. We already know that a more tranquil and acceptable pattern of international affairs cannot be produced by unilateral actions on the part of the United States or anyone else. And we believe that the number and cultural diversity of the relevant parties to enduring mutual accommodation and cooperative action will continue to increase. The elucidation of cognitive-analytic precedents, precepts, and decision rules is a modest, but potentially helpful, measure to deal with these realities. Failure to use this instrument amounts to acceptance of the existing rate of misperception and ineffective communication in international affairs, and the vastly more serious costs such policy failures will entail in the world of the late twentieth century.

MEDIA ANALYSIS AND CHINA'S FOREIGN POLICY

Research on China's foreign policy has relied heavily on statements in Peking's media. Whether conducted qualitatively or quantitatively, it shares certain assumptions about the relationship between public statements and Chinese policy. Most important, media attention is held to reflect policy attention. That is, media statements are taken to be a purposeful policy treatment by the elite and thus are used to infer its concerns and intentions. For example, Dillon et al. (1977: 457) argue that *Peking Review* is "an accurate and reliable indicator of official Chinese foreign policy perceptions." Researchers frequently assume that open media statements present a consistent policy rationale that represents the views of a homogeneous leadership. They often ignore such factors as the institutional sponsorship and the intended audience of the media in terms of their possible influence on news treatment.

These assumptions are worth checking. While it is clear that in the People's Republic of China the views expressed in official media sources bear some relationship to the policy agenda of the elite, it is less clear that this linkage is either simple or direct. Since there are multiple official media sources as well as a number of "restricted access" means of communication in China, we can enhance our understanding of the relationship between public communication and Chinese policy through a systematic analysis of several media sources.

Three issues are particularly pertinent. First, to what degree do "official" Chinese statements vary across media sources? Even a casual examination of different Chinese publications (for example, *Red Flag, People's Daily, Peking Review*) suggests substantial differences in thematic content. Systematic identification of the degree and type of variation across sources helps scholars to select sources and deepens our understanding of what "official" news treatment means. Comparison across sources does not directly test the validity of particular sources as indicators of elite policy attention. It can show how "representative" different sources are of Chinese media coverage in general. If particular sources are deviant in their content, inferences from them should be made only with especially great caution.

Second, to what extent does a particular media source change over time? Content analyses of the Chinese media, particularly those of a quantitative sort

(Dillon et al. 1977; Tretiak 1971), often assess what constitutes a "significant" change in attention. Meaningful answers to questions of this sort require a sound understanding of the parameters of attention in a particular source in order to discriminate significant deviations from stochastic fluctuations. The identification of the stability of these parameters may have important substantive implications as well, as we have shown in chapter 10.

Finally, given the existence of various "restricted access" means of communication in the People's Republic of China, to what extent does the regime apply different "filters" to different public media sources? We know that information presented for public consumption represents only a small subset of the information that Chinese decision makers have available to them through these various "restricted access" sources (Liu 1974; Schwarz 1966). Although Schwarz's analysis of six issues of the *Reference News* indicated that the "biases" evident in selection were substantially similar to those operating with respect to the *People's Daily,* the existence of several "restricted access" information channels and the small size of his data base caution against generalizing his finding. Accordingly, further analysis is needed to identify the "filters" applied to the public treatment of news. To the extent that systematic discrepancies exist between the content of "restricted" and public sources, caution is warranted in extrapolating from views presented in the latter to the elite's knowledge of foreign affairs. Such discrepancies may also be substantively informative for revealing the elite's logics for presenting events in public forums.

Data Sources and Constraints

We pursue these issues using two data sets. As in our previous analyses in chapters 10 and 11, the data on open media sources used in this analysis are from the PAMIS project and cover the following Chinese sources: *People's Daily, Peking Review, Red Flag, China Pictorial, China Reconstructs,* and the domestic (the news reviews broadcast at 12.00 and 22.30 G.M.T.) and foreign (one-hour news review in English) services of Peking Radio (Katz et al. 1973; Katz 1972). Altogether, we have data on seven public sources, differentiated in terms of their intended audience (domestic versus foreign), institutional sponsorship (party versus government), and types of media (print versus audio; daily newspaper versus weekly or monthly journals). Except where noted otherwise, these data cover the period January 1973 to April 1974.

On the positive side, the relatively large size of the PAMIS data set allows for aggregate analysis of general patterns. The large number of news items for each media source makes it less likely that these patterns are part of purposeful attempts to deceive external analysts.[1] The relatively extended time period

1. The number of news items for the periodicals is naturally fewer than that for sources providing daily coverage.

covered by these data also reduces the distorting effects of transient events. On the negative side, some data are missing. The data set for the *People's Daily* contains the greatest amount of missing data (sixteen days); missing data for the other sources are negligible. As mentioned earlier, the coding scheme employed by the PAMIS developers is not very sensitive in that it uses news items rather than paragraphs, sentences, or words as units of analysis. It also does not allow multiple actors or themes to be assigned to a single news item. Consequently, these data provide only a rough description of the thematic content of Chinese media.

Since materials with "restricted access" in China are seldom available for scholarly analysis, the data base from such sources is very limited. We have applied the PAMIS coding scheme to a publication entitled "News from Foreign Agencies & Press" (NFFAP) for the period of April 16 to May 13, 1973.[2] This English-language publication is distributed within China to journalists and other foreign visitors to keep them informed of international developments. As the title indicates, it is a compendium of selections from various world news agencies and foreign newspapers; they are reproduced without editorial comment. While it is impossible to know the precise relationship between this publication and such important "restricted access" publications as the *Reference News* and the *Reference Materials,* the NFFAP coverage provides some indication of the range and types of information that Chinese decision makers are exposed to outside the known set of public sources.

Source Comparison of Open Media

We find that attention to foreign countries depends heavily on the source used. In terms of total coverage, *Red Flag* and *China Reconstructs* display very little concern with events unrelated to China (2 and 3 percent respectively), while *Peking Review* (47 percent) and Peking Radio Foreign Services (46 percent) give the most attention to foreign actors. The other media sources reflect intermediate degrees of attention to other countries (Peking Radio Domestic Service, 36 percent; *People's Daily,* 35 percent; and *China Pictorial,* 12 percent). Thus, assessments of the level of attention given by the Chinese leadership to foreign countries are likely to vary with the media source selected, although the *Peking Review,* the *People's Daily,* and the two radio broadcasts are roughly comparable in their levels of concern with other nations.

2. We thank Professor Daniel Tretiak for providing us with this set of materials. The size of this data set cautions against unwarranted extrapolation of the results. Also, the data for April 17, 22, 24, 29, and May 10, 1973, are missing. Yet it should be kept in mind that the number of issues analyzed is large relative to previous examinations of "restricted access" materials.

With respect to attention to particular international actors, our comparisons reveal considerable similarity, as indicated by the high correlation coefficients in table A-1. In particular, the coefficients summarizing the relationships between *People's Daily, Peking Review,* and the domestic and foreign news services of Peking Radio are all above .80. The figures for *Red Flag, China Pictorial,* and *China Reconstructs* are somewhat lower, no doubt reflecting their more infrequent coverage of foreign affairs. Table A-2 lists the international actors most frequently referred to in *People's Daily, Peking Review,* and the radio broadcasts. Predictably, all these sources show an overwhelming concern with the major powers (for example, the Soviet Union and the United States) and with China's Asian neighbors. Additionally, nations such as Rumania, Albania, and Egypt receive considerable attention, probably as a function of their roles vis-à-vis the Soviet Union. In terms of regional orientation, Indochina and the Middle East are predominant while Latin America and Africa are less salient. Attention to Indochina and the Middle East reflects their status as centers of military conflict during this time period.

Moving beyond attention patterns, research on Chinese foreign policy frequently attempts to attribute images of specific nations based on Chinese public media. Comparison of the thematic content of the different sources reported in table A-3 demonstrates, as we expected, substantial differences. *Peking Review, People's Daily,* and the Peking Radio broadcasts give greater emphasis to foreign relations. *Red Flag* is primarily devoted to domestic politics and ideology; and *China Pictorial* and *China Reconstructs* are largely concerned with social and cultural activities. Thus, the institutional mission and audience of particular sources obviously play an important role in determining the thematic focus of their reports.

To explore the implications of source differences for perceptions of particular nations, we turn to the images of the United States, the Soviet Union, and Japan in the four sources most concerned with foreign affairs—*Peking Review, People's Daily,* and the foreign and domestic radio broadcasts. The correlation coefficients in table A-4 indicate the degree of correspondence between the media perceptions of the three nations examined. Table A-5 presents the top ten themes for each country by media source. Of the four sources compared, the *Peking Review* coverage tends to be the most deviant. The lower coefficients associated with it in table A-4 raise questions about using *Peking Review* to explore images of particular nations. Additionally, table A-4 demonstrates a much higher degree of source convergence for the Soviet Union than for the United States or Japan. This greater cross-source consistency may well be the consequence of the position of the Soviet Union as China's "main enemy." As table A-5 shows, all four sources emphasize Soviet "expansionist activity." The media images of the three countries in table A-5 differ substantially. Media attention to the Soviet Union stresses the general dangers of social imperialism. Coverage of the United States focuses

TABLE A-1
CORRESPONDENCE BETWEEN SOURCES: ACTOR ATTENTION
(Excluding China),* January 1973–April 1974

	Peking Review	Red Flag	China Pictorial	China Reconstructs	Peking Radio: Domestic Service	Peking Radio: Foreign Service
People's Daily	.82 (.001)	.32 (.001)	.75 (.001)	.42 (.001)	.92 (.001)	.91 (.001)
Peking Review		.59 (.001)	.60 (.001)	.56 (.001)	.87 (.001)	.93 (.001)
Red Flag			.33 (.001)	.66 (.001)	.44 (.001)	.44 (.001)
China Pictorial				.48 (.001)	.58 (.001)	.61 (.001)
China Reconstructs					.44 (.001)	.49 (.001)
Peking Radio: Domestic Service						.96 (.001)

* The cases (N = 219) are countries, and the data values are the percentages of total coverage (in terms of item frequency) of each source captured by the countries (both as initiator and as target). The figures without parentheses are the Pearson correlation coefficients, while the figures within parentheses are the significance levels. Since attention to China itself would bias these coefficients substantially, it is excluded from this analysis.

TABLE A - 2

CHINESE MEDIA COVERAGE OF INTERNATIONAL ACTORS, January 1973–April 1974*

People's Daily			Peking Review			Peking Radio: Domestic Service			Peking Radio: Foreign Service		
Actor	N	%	Actor	N	%	Actor	N	%	Actor	N	%
China	31,865	64.5	China	1,988	53.2	China	15,687	64.1	China	8,464	53.8
United States	1,157	2.3	United States	165	4.4	Cambodia	863	3.5	United States	723	4.6
Cambodia	1,059	2.1	U.S.S.R.	140	3.7	U.S.S.R.	650	2.7	Cambodia	594	3.8
Japan	1,044	2.1	Cambodia	93	2.5	United States	616	2.5	U.S.S.R.	470	3.0
N. Korea	937	1.9	Worldwide	91	2.4	N. Vietnam	523	2.1	S. Vietnam	350	2.2
N. Vietnam	811	1.6	Japan	53	1.4	S. Vietnam	413	1.7	N. Vietnam	332	2.2
S. Vietnam	759	1.5	Third World	53	1.4	N. Korea	396	1.6	Worldwide	299	1.9
U.S.S.R.	528	1.1	Superpowers	49	1.3	Third World	395	1.6	Israel	274	1.7
Third World	513	1.0	N. Vietnam	44	1.2	Israel	290	1.2	N. Korea	219	1.4
Worldwide	491	1.0	S. Vietnam	37	1.0	Worldwide	274	1.1	Japan	202	1.3
Laos	450	0.9	N. Korea	34	0.9	Japan	272	1.1	Third World	186	1.2
Albania	412	0.8	Pakistan	32	0.9	Laos	227	0.9	Laos	175	1.1
Israel	385	0.8	U.K.	32	0.9	Superpowers	218	0.9	Mideast	171	1.1
Rumania	337	0.7	Mideast	32	0.9	Albania	206	0.8	U.K.	149	0.9
S. Korea	302	0.6	Israel	28	0.7	Mideast	194	0.8	Arab countries	127	0.8
Arab countries	261	0.5	Africa	27	0.7	Arab countries	191	0.8	Superpowers	119	0.8
France	252	0.5	Arab countries	26	0.7	S. Korea	136	0.6	Albania	118	0.7
Pakistan	224	0.5	Laos	24	0.6	Rumania	132	0.5	S. Korea	105	0.7
Mideast	223	0.5	Latin America	23	0.6	France	125	0.5	France	100	0.6
Africa	202	0.4	France	22	0.6	Algeria	101	0.4	Rumania	98	0.6
Superpowers	195	0.4	India	22	0.6	Egypt	101	0.4	Africa	96	0.6
U.K.	187	0.4	West Germany	21	0.6	Pakistan	89	0.4	West Europe	90	0.6
Mexico	181	0.4	Australia	19	0.5	Portugal	81	0.3	Pakistan	79	0.5
Tanzania	161	0.3	Mexico	19	0.5	Taiwan	80	0.3	Portugal	79	0.5
Egypt	160	0.3	Nepal	19	0.5	Asia	80	0.3	Egypt	69	0.4
% of 25 major actors		87.1			82.7			91.2			86.9
Total N	49,390			3,740			24,486			15,742	

* The news-item frequencies presented in this table include references to an actor as either initiator or target.

TABLE A - 3

DISTRIBUTION OF THEMATIC ATTENTION ACROSS MEDIA SOURCES: NEWS ITEM PERCENTAGES

Thematic Groups	People's Daily	Peking Review	Red Flag	China Pictorial	China Reconstructs	Peking Radio: Domestic Service	Peking Radio: Foreign Service
History and ideology	9%	8%	34%	6%	13%	6%	10%
Government and politics	20	10	36	5	3	25	11
Foreign policy and relations	23	29	8	19	2	22	24
International and regional organizations	3	5	0	0	2	4	4
Social and cultural activities	13	13	9	29	30	9	10
Science and technology	2	3	2	9	13	2	2
Commerce, industry, and finance	11	11	11	12	14	9	9
Transportation and communication	1	2	0	1	3	1	1
Resources and production	5	7	5	13	9	6	5
Military forces	10	8	3	5	1	13	17
Miscellaneous (e.g., commercials, weather)	3	4	0	1	11	2	7

TABLE A - 4
CORRESPONDENCE BETWEEN CHINESE MEDIA SOURCES:
THEMATIC ATTENTION*

	Peking Review	Peking Radio: Domestic Service	Peking Radio: Foreign Service
UNITED STATES			
People's Daily	.08 (.358)	.68 (.001)	.37 (.035)
Peking Review		−.08 (.352)	.33 (.054)
Peking Radio: Domestic Service			.39 (.027)
SOVIET UNION			
People's Daily	.84 (.001)	.90 (.001)	.88 (.001)
Peking Review		.66 (.001)	.87 (.001)
Peking Radio: Domestic Service			.72 (.001)
JAPAN			
People's Daily	−.04 (.418)	.76 (.001)	.36 (.040)
Peking Review		.22 (.145)	.61 (.001)
Peking Radio: Domestic Service			.62 (.001)

* The computation of these coefficients was based on percentage values for the twenty-five themes that appear most frequently in the *People's Daily* for each country. These twenty-five themes account for a substantial portion (56 to 90 percent) of the total coverage of these countries. The figures without parentheses are the Pearson correlation coefficients, and the figures within parentheses are the significance levels.

on U.S. involvement in the war in Indochina, while reporting on Japan concentrates on diplomatic and nondiplomatic relations with China.

Overtime Stability in Attention

Inferences about changes in Chinese policy attention from changes in press coverage patterns require us to determine whether or not an observed change represents a significant departure from an existing trend. While different methods such as descriptive trend analysis, serial correlation, and quasi-experimental analysis have been used to make such inferences, all try to assess the magnitude and durability of changes in behavior (Bobrow et al. 1976; Tretiak 1971; Smoker 1969). If past attention to a nation has been volatile, changes seem less likely to have policy significance. Shifts may only reflect Peking's heightened attention to particular episodes (for instance, visits by foreign

Table A - 5(a)

CONTENT OF THEMATIC COVERAGE OF THE UNITED STATES: TOP TEN THEMES*

People's Daily	%	Peking Review	%	Peking Radio: Domestic Service	%	Peking Radio: Foreign Service	%
1. Foreign military operations	10.4	1. Foreign visits by private citizens	4.8	1. Foreign policy	9.3	1. Foreign reaction to military policy	9.1
2. Protocolary activities	7.9	2. Economic penetration and influence	4.2	2. Military penetration and influence	8.9	2. Foreign military operations	6.4
3. Military penetration and influence	6.1	3. Treaties, agreements	4.2	3. Truce agreements	8.1	3. Truce agreements	6.1
4. Truce violations	6.1	4. Foreign reaction to military policy	4.2	4. Protocolary activities	7.3	4. Truce violations	4.7
5. Truce agreements	4.8	5. Labor disputes	3.6	5. Foreign military operations	5.7	5. Hegemony	4.6
6. Foreign visits by private citizens	3.4	6. Negotiation	3.6	6. Hegemony	5.5	6. Military penetration and influence	3.7
7. Foreign policy	3.4	7. Imperialism	3.0	7. Truce violations	4.9	7. Foreign policy	3.3
8. Truce: general	2.6	8. Territorial disputes, ambitions	3.0	8. Foreign visits by political parties	4.4	8. Imperialism	2.8
9. Hegemony	2.5	9. Armed insurgency	3.0	9. Political insurgency	3.4	9. Truce: general	2.6
10. Provocation	2.3	10. Military penetration and influence	2.4	10. Military research and development	3.1	10. Negotiation	2.5
Cumulative	49.4		36.4		60.6		45.8

* The figures in this table are percentages of total media coverage by each source as captured by the ten most frequently mentioned themes. Note that the United States is related to the themes as either initiator or target in the news story. China is not necessarily the implied initiator or target.

TABLE A - 5 (b)
CONTENT OF THEMATIC COVERAGE OF THE SOVIET UNION: TOP TEN THEMES*

People's Daily	%	Peking Review	%	Peking Radio: Domestic Service	%	Peking Radio: Foreign Service	%
1. Hegemony	13.4	1. Hegemony	13.1	1. Foreign policy	15.1	1. Hegemony	13.4
2. Military penetration and influence	10.0	2. Economic penetration and influence	10.2	2. Military penetration and influence	13.1	2. Military penetration and influence	8.5
3. Foreign policy	7.8	3. Military penetration and influence	8.0	3. Hegemony	10.3	3. Immigration and emigration	6.0
4. Territorial disputes, ambitions	6.1	4. Imperialism	8.0	4. Imperialism	5.8	4. Economic penetration and influence	5.5
5. Intelligence and espionage	5.9	5. Intelligence and espionage	5.8	5. Territorial disputes, ambitions	5.5	5. Territorial disputes, ambitions	5.5
6. Economic penetration and influence	5.7	6. Territorial disputes, ambitions	5.1	6. Intelligence and espionage	5.2	6. Intelligence and espionage	4.5
7. Imperialism	4.7	7. Disarmament	4.4	7. Economic penetration and influence	5.1	7. Foreign reaction to military policy	4.5
8. Armament	4.2	8. Communist party: shortcomings	4.4	8. Immigration and emigration	4.2	8. Imperialism	4.3
9. Immigration and emigration	3.8	9. Mutual security agreements	3.6	9. Military research and development	4.2	9. Foreign policy	4.0
10. Military research and development	3.0	10. International organizations: activities	3.6	10. Foreign relations	3.1	10. Mutual security agreements	2.8
Cumulative	64.6		66.4		71.5		59.0

* The figures in this table are percentages of total media coverage by each source as captured by the ten most frequently mentioned themes. Note that the Soviet Union is related to the themes as either initiator or target in the news story. China is not necessarily the implied initiator or target.

Table A - 5 (c)

CONTENT OF THEMATIC COVERAGE OF JAPAN: TOP TEN THEMES*

People's Daily	%	Peking Review	%	Peking Radio: Domestic Service	%	Peking Radio: Foreign Service	%
1. Protocolary activities	30.5	1. Territorial disputes, ambitions	7.5	1. Protocolary activities	24.6	1. Territorial disputes, ambitions	11.9
2. Foreign cultural relations	7.6	2. Labor disputes	7.5	2. Territorial disputes, ambitions	11.8	2. Protocolary activities	8.9
3. Foreign visits by private citizens	5.7	3. Visits by goodwill organizations	7.5	3. Foreign policy	8.8	3. Foreign visits by private citizens	5.9
4. Foreign visits by military groups	5.0	4. Foreign cultural relations	5.7	4. Cultural activities	7.4	4. Foreign visits by diplomatic groups	5.4
5. Foreign visits by cultural groups	4.8	5. Foreign visits by diplomatic groups	5.7	5. Foreign visits by private citizens	6.3	5. Foreign cultural relations	5.4
6. Foreign visits by scientific groups	4.6	6. International fairs and exhibition	5.7	6. International civil aviation	3.7	6. Labor disputes	5.0
7. Cultural activities	3.1	7. Political clubs	3.8	7. Labor disputes	2.9	7. Domestic political instability	5.0
8. Territorial disputes, ambitions	2.9	8. Foreign visits by economic groups	3.8	8. Provocation	2.9	8. Foreign visits by economic groups	5.0
9. Foreign policy	2.6	9. Negotiation	3.8	9. Political clubs	2.9	9. Foreign visits by cultural groups	4.6
10. Foreign visits by political parties	2.1	10. Foreign visits by private citizens	3.8	10. Greetings and condolences	2.9	10. Visits by goodwill organizations	3.5
Cumulative	68.8		54.7		74.3		60.4

* The figures in this table are percentages of total media coverage by each source as captured by the ten most frequently mentioned themes. Note that Japan is related to the themes as either initiator or target in the news story. China is not necessarily the implied initiator or target.

leaders, crisis developments).[3] If past attention patterns have been stable, shifts in attention seem more likely to have policy significance.

Table A-6 presents data on the degree of autocorrelation in *People's Daily* coverage of thirteen countries (including China); the coefficients indicate the stability of press attention to these countries, measured in terms of fifteen-day aggregations. The level of stability in attention varies widely across countries. As reflected in their relatively high autocorrelations, the United States and the Soviet Union receive a fairly constant level of attention. In contrast, attention to North Korea, Pakistan, and the United Kingdom is very ephemeral. The autocorrelations for these three countries approach zero, indicating that the amount of coverage at one point in time provides a poor basis for predicting the amount of coverage later. While most analysts use the amount of press coverage as a measure of a nation's importance to the Peking elite, measurement of stability in attention to particular countries offers an interesting alternative. The stability of coverage may indicate the degree to which a nation is considered sufficiently important to warrant a consistent level of press monitoring. Along this line, there is no obvious relationship in table A-6 between gross attention levels and stability of attention.

Table A-6 also informs us about how the Chinese media treat China. The correlations of attention in terms of news items and news space indicate that generally these two measures are highly related. The only exception is attention to China itself; the relationship between space and item measures for China is a moderate .72. When measured in terms of item frequency, attention to China is relatively stable; when measured in terms of item space, it is highly unstable. This finding may simply mean that the amount of *People's Daily* coverage of China's domestic as well as foreign activities is frequently squeezed out by events relating to other countries and vice versa.

Comparison of Open and "Restricted" Sources

How do the attention patterns displayed by open media sources such as the *People's Daily* compare with those revealed by "restricted access" sources? We examine the *People's Daily* and the "News from Foreign Agencies & Press" (NFFAP) for a comparable period (April 16 to May 13, 1973) in terms of attention to actors, regions, and themes.[4]

---

3. Since there is only a finite amount of media coverage, increased attention to one actor results in decreased attention to another. Consequently, decreases in attention levels may only reflect preoccupation with important events elsewhere.

4. Pattern stability does not seem to be a major problem for the *People's Daily* data; comparison of results from this restricted period with those covering a more extended period reveals little difference. For example, the positions of the leading countries in its coverage are roughly comparable in tables A-2 and A-7. The stability of data patterns in the NFFAP is unknown, since these are the only data available.

TABLE A - 6

OVERTIME STABILITY OF ACTOR ATTENTION: THE *PEOPLE'S DAILY*

Country	Freq. of Items* as % of Total Coverage	Autocorrelation Item *N*†	Autocorrelation Space†	Correlation Item *N* with Space†
China	64.5%	.45 (.002)	.09 (.286)	.72 (.001)
United States	2.3	.70 (.001)	.65 (.001)	.91 (.001)
Japan	2.1	.30 (.030)	.38 (.007)	.89 (.001)
N. Korea	1.9	-.02 (.451)	-.12 (.237)	.94 (.001)
N. Vietnam	1.6	.37 (.009)	.21 (.092)	.95 (.001)
S. Vietnam	1.5	.23 (.074)	.22 (.088)	.92 (.001)
U.S.S.R.	1.1	.54 (.001)	.58 (.001)	.92 (.001)
Israel	0.8	.32 (.021)	.25 (.058)	.99 (.001)
S. Korea	0.6	.27 (.046)	.19 (.116)	.96 (.001)
Pakistan	0.5	-.02 (.460)	-.03 (.419)	.95 (.001)
U.K.	0.4	.09 (.298)	-.05 (.382)	.93 (.001)
Egypt	0.3	.49 (.001)	.55 (.001)	.97 (.001)
India	0.2	.29 (.036)	.39 (.006)	.95 (.001)

* Item frequency includes references to initiators as well as targets.
† The figures without parentheses are the Pearson correlation coefficients, and the figures within parentheses are the significance levels. The coefficients are computed with fifteen-day aggregations of the data, covering the period January 1973–October 1974.

TABLE A - 7

SOURCE COMPARISON OF THE *PEOPLE'S DAILY* AND THE NFFAP: ACTOR ATTENTION*

People's Daily				NFFAP		
Actor	Item *N*	%		Actor	Item *N*	%
China	1792	63		United States	299	19
Japan	107	4		U.S.S.R.	131	8
Cambodia	84	3		Cambodia	112	7
United States	70	2		Japan	69	4
N. Korea	67	2		Lebanon	64	4
Mexico	54	2		P.L.O.	48	3
N. Vietnam	52	2		N. Vietnam	40	3
S. Vietnam	39	1		Egypt	39	2
Worldwide	33	1		W. Germany	38	2
Albania	27	1		E.E.C.	34	2
Laos	27	1		Israel	33	2
Rumania	24	1		China	30	2
France	17	1		France	28	2
U.S.S.R.	16	1		Pakistan	28	2
Third World	16	1		U.N.	25	2
Subtotal	2425	85			1018	65
Total	2856	100			1564	100

* The figures include references to both initiators and targets of events. Data on April 17, 22, 24, and 29, and May 10, 1973, are missing for the NFFAP.

Table A-7 lists the fifteen nations most frequently mentioned in these two sources. There are a number of discrepancies in patterns of attention to particular actors, beginning with attention to China (63 percent for the *People's Daily;* 2 percent for the NFFAP). Conversely, the NFFAP provides greater attention to the major Western powers, with the preeminent status of the United States being particularly striking The NFFAP coverage also focuses more on countries in the Middle East. In contrast, *People's Daily* reporting is more oriented toward China's Asian neighbors and, to a lesser extent, the two "friendly" East European countries of Albania and Rumania. Aggregation of attention to specific actors into regional groupings produces the same patterns more visibly, as shown in table A-8. The *People's Daily* is much more concerned with Asian affairs, even with China excluded, and the NFFAP with the Middle East and North America. While Asian nations are frequently singled out for public media treatment, sources such as the NFFAP—relying as they do on Western press agencies—are more oriented toward the major global powers and the regional arenas where they compete most intensely.

Finally, there are some important differences in thematic attention. As shown in table A-9, the NFFAP provides greater coverage of military and, to a lesser extent, foreign affairs; the *People's Daily,* of cultural and social policy matters. These discrepancies exist even when reports on China in the *People's Daily* are excluded. These findings strengthen our warnings not to infer Chinese elite knowledge and concern about military and foreign affairs simply from the thematic emphases in open media sources. They also reinforce the common view that social and cultural matters are significant issues for Chinese policy and mass politics.

Conclusions

The relationship between public media treatments and the policy concerns of the Chinese leadership is complex rather than straightforward. For example, Chinese media treatments of particular international actors clearly vary across sources. Our findings leave us with questions about whether such discrepancies reflect substantive policy differences on the part of the sponsoring institutions or only nonpolicy adaptations to particular audiences.

However, we also find that simple measurement assumptions are sometimes appropriate. Attention to international actors is constant across a number of Chinese media sources. Space and frequency attention measures are highly related.

As a whole, this set of results argues that inferences from the Chinese media need to take into account the complexities of Chinese beliefs about the four elements in our cybernetic perspective, introduced in chapter 1, including beliefs about the use of public and restricted circulation media, as discussed in chapter 10. We are wary about the value of conclusions drawn solely from Chinese media sources.

TABLE A - 8

SOURCE COMPARISON OF THE *PEOPLE'S DAILY* AND THE NFFAP:
REGIONAL ATTENTION

	People's Daily (with China)	People's Daily (without China)	NFFAP (with China)
Asia	2254 (79%)*	462 (43%)	429 (27%)
Mideast	69 (2)	69 (6)	298 (19)
North America	81 (3)	81 (8)	303 (19)
Communist Europe	88 (3)	88 (8)	183 (12)
Noncommunist Europe	131 (5)	131 (12)	161 (10)
Latin America	91 (3)	91 (9)	56 (4)
Oceania	10 (0)	10 (1)	15 (1)
Sub-Sahara Africa	79 (3)	79 (7)	57 (4)
Other	53 (2)	53 (5)	62 (4)
	N = 2856 (100)	1064 (100)	1564 (100)

* The figures without parentheses are the item frequencies for countries as both initiators and targets of events, while the figures within parentheses are the percentages. Data on April 17, 22, 24, and 29, and May 10, 1973, are missing for the NFFAP.

TABLE A - 9

SOURCE COMPARISON OF THE *PEOPLE'S DAILY* AND THE NFFAP:
THEMATIC ATTENTION

	People's Daily (with China)	People's Daily (without China)	NFFAP (with China)
History and ideology	128 (9%)*	40 (6%)	5 (11%)
Government and politics	222 (16)	90 (13)	133 (17)
Foreign policy and relations	442 (31)	301 (45)	364 (47)
International and regional organizations	36 (3)	20 (3)	24 (3)
Social and cultural activities	182 (13)	53 (8)	0 (0)
Science and technology	24 (2)	5 (1)	0 (0)
Commerce, industry, and finance	145 (10)	36 (5)	27 (3)
Transportation and communication	11 (1)	4 (1)	9 (1)
Resources and production	61 (4)	9 (1)	12 (2)
Military forces	137 (10)	113 (17)	200 (26)
Miscellaneous (e.g., commercials, weather)	40 (3)	2 (0)	8 (1)
	N = 1428 (100)	676 (100)	782 (100)

* The figures without parentheses are the item frequencies, while the figures within parentheses are the percentages. Data on April 17, 22, 24, and 29, and May 10, 1973, are missing for the NFFAP.

MAJOR EVENTS IN THE HISTORY OF IMPERIALIST WARS: A CHINESE PRECEDENT SET

Translated from Writing Team 1974: 161–69.

The American-Spanish war of 1898, the British-Boer war of 1899, and the Russo-Japanese war of 1904 are major indicators of the formation of imperialism; since that time, wars launched by the various imperialist powers continue to take place and have never ceased. From a simple survey of history since the birth of imperialism, one will recognize that the history of imperialism is a history of aggression, a history of wars.

Apr. 1898   American imperialism launched war against Spain because it wanted to seize the Spanish colonies of the Philippines, Cuba, and Puerto Rico. The American-Spanish war was the first war in the history of wars between imperialist countries; it indicated that the development of capitalism had reached the imperialist stage.

Feb. 1899   Germany militarily seized the Carolina and Mariana Islands.

1899–1902   Britain used the protection of its colonists' well-being as an excuse to launch war against the South African Boers, conquering the republics of Transvaal and the Orange Free State. This was the British-Boer war. It also indicated that the development of capitalism had reached the imperialist stage. In 1910 Britain incorporated the republics of Transvaal and the Orange Free State into the new British autonomous Union of South Africa.

Jun. 1900   The allied forces of Germany, France, Russia, Japan, Italy, and Austria launched a military invasion of China, cruelly suppressing the uprising of the Chinese Boxers.

Nov. 1903   Germany invaded and occupied the Panama Straits.

Feb. 1904   The imperialist countries of Japan and Russia started the Japanese-Russian war because they wanted to repartition their spheres of influence in Northeast China. The battle took place on Chinese territory, and the Chinese people experienced misfortunes of a historical proportion. The Russo-Japanese war was another sign indicating that the development of capitalism had reached the imperialist stage.

211

Aug. 1906   The Cuban people had an uprising; American forces invaded Cuba.

Aug. 1910   While suppressing the armed resistance of the Korean people, Japan invented the so-called "treaty of Japanese-Korean integration," blatantly annexing Korea.

1911   French troops invaded and occupied Morocco.

1911–1912   Because it wanted to seize overseas markets and colonies, Italy launched a war against Turkey.

1912   American forces invaded Nicaragua.

1912–1913   After the Balkan states, such as Serbia, launched the first Balkan war against Turkey, Germany, Austria-Hungary, and Russia became separate backers of some of the Balkan countries, urging these countries to start the second Balkan war between themselves.

1914   The United States intervened militarily for the first time in the Mexican revolution.

1916–1917   The United States intervened militarily for the second time in the Mexican revolution.

1914–1918   World War I.

1918–1920   After the success of the Russian October revolution led by Lenin, imperialist countries connived with counterrevolutionaries inside Russia and launched a war against the Soviet regime, attempting to kill the first socialist country under proletarian dictatorship in the world.

May 1919   King of Afghanistan, Amanullah, declared the complete independence of Afghanistan. Britain seized this excuse to launch a war of aggression against Afghanistan.

1920   Greece declared its determination to continue war against Turkey. On March 16, the "allied" troops seized Constantinople.

Jul. 1920   The Anglo-American–backed and the Japanese-backed Chinese warlords started the war between Tsao Kun and Tuan Chi-jui. Then, using the various imperialist countries as their backers, the various Chinese warlords started the war between Tsao Kun and Chang Tso-lin, the war between Kiangsu and Chekiang, and a second war between Tsao and Chang.

Jan. 1923   French and Belgian troops militarily occupied the Ruhr district and the Rhine province of Germany.

1925   French and Spanish allied forces invaded the Rif Tribe areas in Morocco, seizing the mines of that area.

1926   Japan and seven other countries shelled the Taku Fort in order to obstruct the Chinese military defense at Tientsin.

Mar. 1927   Chinese North Expedition forces captured Nanking; British, American, and other imperialists' battleships on the Yangtze shelled Nanking, killing and wounding about 2,000.

Apr. 1929   British forces from Burma invaded Kiansingpo, Yunnan, China.

Sep. 18, 1931   The Japanese Kwantung Army, stationed in Northeast China, attacked Mukden, launching the "November 18" incident. The Japanese invasion army seized Liaoning, Kirin, and Heilungkiang provinces.

Jan. 28, 1932   The Japanese invasion army started the "January 28" incident, invading Shanghai.

1933   The Japanese invasion army occupied Niehho province.

Oct. 1935   Italy invaded Abyssinia (Ethiopia), conquering all of Abyssinia by May 1936.

1936   Germany and Italy carried out military intervention against Spain.

Jul. 7, 1937   Japanese imperialists initiated the "Marco Polo Bridge" incident, attempting to use military force to annex all of China through a large-scale war of invasion.

Aug. 13, 1937   Japanese imperialists launched the "August 13" incident; it started with a large-scale attack on Shanghai and expanded the war of invasion against China.

Mar. 1938   The Fascist leader of Germany, Hitler, ordered his troops to occupy Austria, declaring Austria was a province of Germany.

Nov. 1938   Hitler's Germany seized the Sudeten area of Czechoslovakia, and in March 1939 completely occupied Czechoslovakia.

Apr. 7, 1939   Italian Fascist Mussolini launched a surprise attack against Albania, attacking it from all sides.

1939-1945   World War II. Hitlerian Germany launched a surprise attack against Poland on September 1, 1939. On September 3, 1939, England and France declared war on Germany.

Jun. 22, 1942   Hitlerian Germany launched war against the Soviet Union contrary to their agreement, starting the war between the Soviet Union and Germany.

Dec. 8, 1941   Japan launched a surprise attack against the American naval base at Pearl Harbor, starting the Pacific war.

1945-1946   American and British imperialists supported Dutch colonialists in the latter's colonial war in Indonesia.

1946   With the United States supplying the money and advisers and with Chiang Kai-shek supplying the manpower, they launched the nationwide counterrevolutionary civil war in China. The Chinese people under the leadership of Chairman Mao conducted three years of war of liberation, achieving the great victory of the Chinese national revolution and establishing the People's Republic of China.

Dec. 1946   French troops occupied Haiphong, Vietnam, starting the war of invasion against Vietnam.

1947   American imperialists, allied with the Greek counterrevolutionaries, established the U.S.-Greek military joint command, suppressing the armed forces of the Greek people.

1948	Imperialists led by the United States supported Israel in its war of aggression against the Arab countries.
Apr. 1948	American imperialists used airborne forces to suppress the Colombian people.
Sep. 1948	The Dutch colonial army started a large-scale attack against Indonesia.
Jun. 25, 1950	American imperialists launched the war of aggression against Korea, and then used military force to seize our territory of Taiwan.
1952	Britain sent military forces to suppress the national liberation movement of Kenya, establishing colonial rule.
1954	American imperialists instigated an invasion by Guatemalan counterrevolutionary military officers from Honduras, establishing a pro-American dictatorship in Guatemala.
1955	American imperialists instigated an attack against Costa Rica by the Nicaraguan dictatorship.
Oct. 1956	Imperialist forces led by the American imperialists, conniving with the Hungarian counterrevolutionaries, started counterrevolutionary riots.
Oct.–Nov. 1956	After Egypt took back the Suez Canal, Britain, France, and Israel launched a war of invasion against Egypt.
1956–1958	American-supported Indonesian counterrevolutionaries launched a military revolt.
Jul. 1958	American imperialists invaded Lebanon.
Jul. 1958	With the support of the American imperialists, British forces invaded Jordan.
May 1959	American imperialists supported the Laotian rightists to start a counterrevolutionary civil war.
May 1959	An anti-American, antidictatorship people's armed struggle broke out in Nicaragua; American imperialists sent battleships to conduct military intervention.
Aug. 1959	India, supported by the Soviet revisionists, launched the Sino-Indian border war.
1959	American imperialists sent the Marines to conduct an armed intervention against the antidictatorship struggle of the Dominican people.
1960	Belgian colonialists, supported by the American and British imperialists, launched armed aggression against the Congo, murdering the Congolese President Lumumba.
1960	American imperialists deployed troops in the Caribbean, directly intervening against the anti-American, patriotic struggles of the Nicaraguan and Guatemalan peoples.
Feb. 5, 1960	Four thousand American Marines landed in the Dominican Republic, intervening militarily in the internal affairs of that nation.

Feb. 1960–1962   American imperialists sent mercenaries to launch two attacks in its military intervention against Guatemala.

1961   American imperialists started the "special war" in the southern part of Vietnam, attempting to destroy the military forces of the people's liberation movement of South Vietnam.

Mar. 1961   Portuguese colonialists started a large-scale suppression of the anticolonial war of the Angolan people.

Apr. 1961   American mercenaries landed in Cuba but were destroyed by the Cuban people.

Jul. 1961   British troops landed in Kuwait. French troops launched a surprise attack against the Tunisian port of Bizerte.

1962   Against the will of the Cuban people, Khrushchev carried out adventurist practices, introducing missiles into Cuba. American imperialists immediately started movements in the Caribbean, blockading Cuba.

May 1962   Using the excuse of military exercises, American troops were introduced to be stationed in Thailand, posing a threat to Laos.

1962–1970   American and British imperialists, supporting the royal feudal forces in Yemen, repeatedly carried out military attacks against the new Yemeni regime.

Jan. 1963   Portuguese colonialists launched the colonial war against the people of Guinea (Bisseau).

1963   American imperialists ordered their South Vietnamese puppets to invade repeatedly Cambodian territories.

1963   American imperialists supported several hundred overseas Haitians to invade Haiti.

Aug. 1964   American imperialists fabricated the "Gulf of Tonkin" incident, starting air raids against the Democratic Republic of Vietnam.

Sep. 1964   Portuguese colonialists initiated a large-scale suppression of the Mozambique people, starting a colonial war.

Nov. 1964   American imperialists, allied with Britain and Belgium, launched a military attack against the Stanleyville area under the control of the Congolese patriotic armed forces.

1964   American imperialists joined the United Nations "peacekeeping" forces to carry out military intervention in Cyprus.

Mar. 1965   American President Johnson ordered a major introduction of U.S. forces to Vietnam, escalating the war of invasion against Vietnam.

May 1965   American imperialists again sent the Marines to the Dominican Republic to suppress the struggle of its people against dictatorship.

Apr. 1966   The white colonial government of Rhodesia launched a suppression of the Bantu people, starting a colonial war.

Jun. 1967   American and British imperialists supported Israel's war of aggression against the United Arab Republic, Syria, and Jordan.

	American and British imperialists directly participated in the combat, carrying out air attacks against the Arab countries.
Aug. 1968	Soviet social imperialists militarily occupied Czechoslovakia.
1969	Soviet revisionists repeatedly invaded the Chinese island of Chenpao.
1969–1970	Under the instigation of the American imperialists, the Palestinian guerrillas repeatedly encountered bloody suppression in certain countries.
Mar. 18, 1970	American imperialists instigated the counterrevolutionary military coup of Lon Nol in Cambodia, attempting to topple the legitimate government of Cambodia under the leadership of Sihanouk.
Apr. 1970	Nixon sent troops to invade Cambodia, spreading the war of aggression across all of Indo-China.
Nov. 1970	American-supported Portuguese colonialists sent mercenaries to invade Guinea.
Feb. 1971	With American instigations and air force cover, South Vietnamese puppet troops launched a major invasion of Laos.
Feb. 1971	With the support and planning of the American imperialists, a group of mercenaries invaded the Yemeni Democratic People's Republic.
Nov. 1971	Soviet social imperialists supported the Indian military effort to carve up Pakistan.
Mar. 20, 1973	With the support of the Soviet social imperialists, foreign troops invaded Kuwait.
Oct. 1973	Supported by the American imperialists, Israel carried out a war of aggression against Egypt and Syria.
Jan. 1974	Supported by the American imperialists, the Saigon puppet troops invaded China's Paracel Islands.

In the seventy-six years from the American-Spanish war in 1898 until 1974, various wars and military interventions started by imperialism never ceased. This historical fact fully demonstrates one undeniable truth: imperialism is war. War is the constant companion of imperialism. History mercilessly declared the bankruptcy of the Trotskyite theories of "super imperialism" and the "peaceful coexistent world" advocated by Khrushchev and his followers.

SEMANTIC ANALYSIS: PROCEDURES AND SOURCES

Our use of verbal-association measures and analysis of refugee perceptions warrant more extensive description of the procedures and sources than has been provided in the text. Accordingly, we will describe the Associative Group Analysis procedure we have employed in some detail and discuss the limitations that are imposed by the particular "sample" with which we had to work.

The procedures for administering the Associative Group Analysis instrumentation developed by Szalay and his associates (Szalay and Maday 1973; Szalay and Brent 1967) are simple. The stimuli are printed on single sheets of paper or cards (one stimulus for each sheet). On each of these sheets, space is provided for a large number of responses. The various stimuli are randomized to eliminate order effects and are then administered in a group fashion, each individual in the group being given a test set. The respondents are allowed one minute for each stimulus to write down as many single-word associations as possible. They are instructed not to "chain associate"—that is, they should respond only to the original stimulus and not to their own responses.

This methodology has been used to examine the perceptions of such diverse cultural groups as Koreans (Szalay et al. 1973), U.S. blacks (Szalay and Bryson 1973), and Slovenians (Szalay and Pecjak 1973). Additionally, it has been subjected to a number of different tests of its validity and reliability (e.g., Szalay and Bryson 1976, 1974; Szalay et al. 1972), which indicate its substantial capacity to measure perceptions. In our application of this procedure, analysis of the reliability of A.G.A. responses for Chinese subjects has indicated reliability levels comparable to those previously obtained for U.S. populations (Kringen 1978: 238–50).

Several features of the A.G.A. procedure are well suited to our purposes. First, the technique allows subjects to pattern their own responses. It avoids forcing respondents to select possibly biased, predetermined responses. Second, unlike standard attitude measures, it allows the researcher to analyze efficiently both affective and cognitive dimensions of belief. Since cognitive dimensions of belief are central to our analysis, the advantages of a measure of this sort are obvious. Finally, since the procedure uses single words or concepts as stimuli, the problem of establishing stimulus equivalence is less complex. For the symbols analyzed here, we can be sure that the Chinese terms used are the translation equivalents of their English counterparts.

In applying the Associative Group Analysis methodology to the study of Mainland Chinese perceptions, some compromises had to be made. The most significant relates to the selection of the Mainland Chinese sample. Obviously, it is not possible in the current political world to survey people in China, not to mention Chinese decision makers, about their political perceptions. Accordingly, in 1974–1975 a group of sixty-two refugees from Mainland China were interviewed in Hong Kong. These interviews, which included administration of a set of A.G.A. stimuli, were restricted to refugees who had come to Hong Kong in the prior two-year period. For purposes of comparison, students from Hong Kong Baptist College and the Chinese University of Hong Kong were given A.G.A. instruments as well. Since the students share essentially the same language as the Mainland respondents, linguistic factors do not account for any differences between the two groups. Likewise, the Hong Kong group provides a control for any response effects due to shared cultural traits (that is, being Chinese) or to the general environment of Hong Kong. However, no effort was made to match the socioeconomic characteristics of the Hong Kong group to those of the Mainland group, on the grounds that such an effort would produce only illusory precision given the essentially unrepresentative nature of the Mainland Chinese group.

From a social science perspective, the general context for interviewing refugees in Hong Kong can scarcely be described as advantageous. A major problem is that there is no way to identify the population of refugees from which one can select a sample for interviews. Thus, the approach to finding interviewees relied on the gradual development of a refugee pool through sharing of names among researchers, referrals by interviewees, and other forms of personal contact. This procedure for obtaining interviewees (the only one possible) was deficient in that it did not allow for much control, other than a veto, over who would be interviewed. A related problem with this procedure was that it was long and time-consuming. This meant that gathering a larger number of interviewees was impossible. Further, rather than administering the A.G.A. instrumentation in a group fashion as was done in previous applications, the instrument had to be given to the refugees on an individual basis.

As indicated by the background data listed in table C-1, the Mainland refugees interviewed were overwhelmingly male, predominantly from Kwangtung, and largely in the young adult age bracket. Clearly, then, this group is not a microcosm of the population of Mainland China. On the other hand, those interviewed were not simply a group of "professional" refugees; for the majority, this was their first interview (Kringen 1978: 255).

The use of refugees as a data source raises a number of analytic problems

TABLE C - 1

BACKGROUND CHARACTERISTICS OF MAINLAND REFUGEES

Characteristic	Frequency
Sex	
Male	54
Female	8
Residential Location	
City	43
Small town	7
Village	12
Province	
Kwangtung	48
Hunan	5
Fukien	3
Hopei	3
Shanghai	1
Kweichou	1
Kwangsi	1
Year of Birth	
1956–1960	2
1951–1955	23
1946–1950	23
1941–1945	3
1936–1940	6
Prior to 1936	5
Level of Education	
Primary	6
Lower middle	26
Middle	6
Upper middle	20
College	4
Overseas Chinese	12
(mean years in China)	(15.3)

(Whyte 1974; Cohen 1967; Wong 1967; Inkeles and Bauer 1959). Generally, three criticisms of their use are made: (1) the refugee group is not a representative sample of the homeland population to which one wants to make inferences; (2) by the very fact of leaving, refugees are more likely to be hostile to the political regime than those who did not leave; and (3) refugees are likely to respond in ways that are thought to please the interviewer.

These criticisms raise significant issues about research using refugee sources. Because these problems are inherent in the data source, procedures to cope with them must necessarily deal with complex questions of analysis and inference. Nonetheless, one should not overstate the significance of these problems. The first criticism noted that refugee groups do not constitute a representative sample. Granting the accuracy of this observation, this should not be taken to mean that only scientifically selected samples can tell us anything about human behavior. The analysis of human behavior through nonrepresentative groups has been carried out by psychologists and sociologists for many years and it has not constituted an insurmountable barrier to their inquiries. The third criticism refers to the responses of refugees in interview situations. In their study of daily life in Soviet society, Inkeles and Bauer state that the situation for interviewing refugees should not be regarded as unique.

> The entire doctrine of social science interviewing and questioning is based on the explicit premise that the response which a person makes to a question may be consciously or unconsciously biased by virtue of the relationship of the person answering the question to the situation in which the question is asked. . . . All this is no more than to say that the problems of acquiring information by interviewing

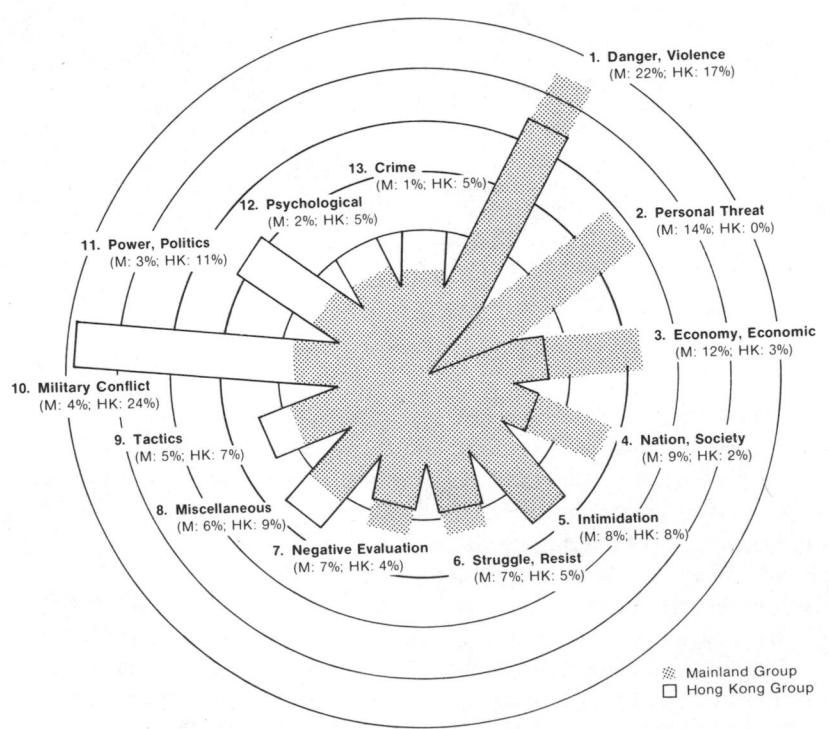

FIGURE C-1
RELATIVE FREQUENCY OF THEMATIC RESPONSES TO THE TERM "THREAT"

émigrés may be somewhat distinctive and acute, but they are continuous with the problems of all interviewing, and in fact with all problems of data gathering and evaluation [Inkeles and Bauer 1959: 42].

Thus, the problems of refugee interviewing may be regarded as formidable but not hopeless.

For our analysis here, the problems of inferring from refugee data are lessened by the fact that our principal analytic concerns relate to the cognitive, rather than the affective, dimensions of belief. We are less interested in whether or not the Mainland refugee group expresses positive affect toward the homeland regime than that they interpret political symbolism in ways compatible with the thinking advocated by the elite in the public media. To the extent that the Mainland refugee group perceives political-military symbols in

TABLE C-2
DESCRIPTION OF THEMATIC RESPONSES TO THE TERM "THREAT"*

1. **Danger, Violence** (M. 139, H.K. 106). References to danger and violence constitute the largest set of responses for the Mainland group. The most salient responses were *terrible* (M. 36, H.K. 5) and *dangerous* (M. 20); the most salient Hong Kong response was *frightening* (H.K. 30).

2. **Personal Threat** (M. 88, H.K. 0). Only the Mainland group made explicit reference to personal threat. The most frequent references were *others* (M. 25) and *friends* (M. 20).

3. **Economy, Economic** (M. 76, H.K. 19). Mention of economic types of threat was greater for the Mainland group. *Economy, economic* (M. 18, H.K. 8) and *livelihood* (M. 18, H.K. 5) were the most significant references.

4. **Nation, Society** (M. 60, H.K. 10). *Nation* (M. 19, H.K. 10) and *the people* (M. 19) were the largest responses.

5. **Intimidation** (M. 54, H.K. 51). The response of *intimidation* (M. 24, H.K. 36) was the largest one for both groups.

6. **Struggle, Resist** (M. 46, H.K. 35). In coping with threats, the injunction to *be unafraid* (M. 23) was significant for the Mainland group; the Hong Kong group emphasized efforts to *struggle* (M. 9, H.K. 14) and *resist* (H.K. 21).

7. **Negative Evaluation** (M. 45, H.K. 22). Threats were criticized not only as being *shameful* (M. 7) and *immoral* (H.K. 9), they were also criticized by the Mainland group as *ineffective* (M. 10) and a *failure* (M. 10).

9. **Tactics** (M. 33, H.K. 43). In a minor way, both groups saw threats as tactics that are used to attain goals.

10. **Military Conflict** (M. 27, H.K. 149). References to military conflict constitute the largest response component for the Hong Kong group. *War* (M. 27, H.K. 15) was the only response given by the Mainland group. The most salient Hong Kong responses were *armed force* (H.K. 38) *crisis* (H.K. 23), and *nuclear weapons* (H.K. 20).

11. **Power, Politics** (M. 21, H.K. 72). This theme is more significant in the Hong Kong responses. *Power* (H.K. 37) and *politics* (M. 21, H.K. 18) were the most frequently given responses.

12. **Psychological** (M. 11, H.K. 29). The only Mainland response was *spirit* (M. 11); the largest Hong Kong response was *psychological* (H.K. 19).

13. **Crime** (M. 5, H.K. 34). Responses making explicit reference to crime were only important for the Hong Kong group.

*Total response scores: M., 643; H.K., 628.

patterns that conform to the public rationales offered by the Chinese elite, we can have more confidence that the Mainland group's responses are not simply the views of a highly idiosyncratic interviewee population. While, naturally, this does not mean that such views mirror those of elite decision makers, it does provide some strong indication that the logics presented in public forums represent something more than post hoc rationalization.

In our discussion of the differences between Hong Kong and Mainland responses to the term "crisis," we noted that the groups differ in their relative emphasis on economic and military aspects, with the Mainland groups giving more attention to the economic (page 69). As we indicated, a similar relative difference also characterizes responses to the term "threat," as shown in Figure C-1 and Table C-2 on the preceding pages.

References

ABELSON, R. P.; ARONSON, E.; McGUIRE, N. J.; NEWCOMB, T. M.; ROSENBERG, M. J.; and TANNENBAUM, P. H.; eds. 1968. *Theories of Cognitive Consistency: A Sourcebook.* Chicago: Rand McNally.

ALKER, H. R., Jr.; and CHRISTENSEN, C. 1972. "From Causal Modelling to Artificial Intelligence: The Evolution of a U.N. Peace-Making Simulation." Pp. 177–224 in J. A. Laponce and P. Smoker, eds., *Experimentation and Simulation in Political Science.* Toronto: University of Toronto Press.

ALLISON, G. T. 1971. *Essence of Decision: Explaining the Cuban Missile Crisis.* Boston: Little, Brown.

ANDRIOLE, S. J. 1976. "Progress Report on the Development of a Crisis Early Warning Prototype System." McLean, Va.: Decisions and Designs, Incorporated. Technical Report, December.

ANDRIOLE, S. J.; and YOUNG, R. A. 1977. "Toward the Development of an Integrated Crisis Warning System." *International Studies Quarterly* 21 (March): 107–50.

AXELROD, R. 1976. *Structure of Decision: The Cognitive Maps of Political Elites.* Princeton, N.J.: Princeton University Press.

AZAR, E. E.; COHEN, S. H.; JUKAM, T. O.; and McCORMICK, J. M. 1972. "The Problem of Source Coverage in the Use of International Events Data." *International Studies Quarterly* 16 (September): 373–88.

BAILEY, F.; and HOLT, R. T. 1971. "Towards a Science of Complex Systems." Minneapolis: University of Minnesota. (mimeo)

BANKS, A. S.; and GREGG, P. M. 1965. "Grouping Political Systems: *Q* Factor Analysis of a Cross-Polity Survey." *The American Behavioral Scientist* 9 (November): 3–5.

BANKS, A. S.; and TEXTOR, R. 1963. *A Cross-Polity Survey.* Cambridge, Mass.: M.I.T. Press.

BELL, C. 1971. *The Conventions of Crisis: A Study in Diplomatic Management.* New York: Oxford University Press.

BENNETT, J. P.; and ALKER, H. R., Jr. 1977. "When National Security Policies Bred Collective Insecurity: The War of the Pacific in a World Politics Simulation." Pp. 215–99 in K. W. Deutsch, B. Fritsch, H. Jaguaribe, and A. S. Markovits, eds., *Problems of World Modelling.* Cambridge, Mass.: Ballinger.

BEN-ZVI, A. 1976. "Hindsight and Foresight: A Conceptual Framework for the Analysis of Surprise Attack." *World Politics* 28 (April): 381–95.

BLECHMAN, B. M.; and KAPLAN, S. S. 1976. "Use of the Armed Forces as a Political Instrument: An Interim Report." Presented at the annual meeting of the International Studies Association, Toronto, February 25–29.

———. 1975. "Use of Military Force Abroad by United States since 1798: An Annotated Bibliography of Unclassified Lists of Incidents Prepared by the U.S. Government." *Journal of Conflict Resolution* 19 (December): 708–12.

BOARDMAN, R. 1974. "Themes and Explanation in Sinology." Pp. 5–50 in R. Dial, ed., *Advancing and Contending Approaches to the Study of Chinese Foreign Policy.* Halifax, Nova Scotia: Dalhousie University.

BOBROW, D.; and COLLINS, A.; eds. 1975. *Representation and Understanding: Studies in Cognitive Science.* New York: Academic Press.

BOBROW, D. B. 1969a. "Ecology of International Games: Requirement for a Model of the International System." *Papers, Peace Science Society (International)* 11: 67–87.

———. 1969b. "Chinese Communist Response to Alternative U.S. Continental Defense Postures." Pp. 151–213 in D. B. Bobrow, ed., *Weapons System Decisions: Political and Psychological Perspectives on Continental Defense.* New York: Praeger.

———. 1968. "Liberation Wars, National Environment, and American Decision-Making." Pp. 311–32 in T. Tsou, ed., *China in Crisis,* vol. 2. Chicago: University of Chicago Press.

———. 1966. "The Chinese Communist Conflict System." *Orbis* 9 (Winter): 930–52.

———. 1965. "Peking's Military Calculus." Pp. 39–52 in D. B. Bobrow, ed., *Components of Defense Policy.* Chicago: Rand McNally.

BOBROW, D. B.; CHAN, S.; and KRINGEN, J. A. 1977. "Understanding How Others Treat Crises: A Multimethod Approach." *International Studies Quarterly* 21 (March): 199–223.

———. 1976. "Capturing Inaccessible Decision Processes: Some Chinese Examples." Presented at the annual North American meeting of the Peace Science Society (International), Ann Arbor, Mich., November 15–17.

BOBROW, D. B.; and KUDRLE, R. T. 1976. "Theory, Policy and Resource Cartels: The Case of OPEC." *Journal of Conflict Resolution* 20 (March): 3–56.

BONHAM, G. M.; TRUMBLE, T. L.; and SHAPIRO, M. J. 1976. "The October War: Congealed Beliefs and Historical Analogizing." Presented at the annual meeting of the International Studies Association, Toronto, February 25–29.

BOORMAN, S. A. 1972. "Deception in Chinese Strategy." Pp. 313–37 in W. Whitson, ed., *Military and Political Power in China in the 1970's.* New York: Praeger.

———. 1969. *The Protracted Game: A Wei-ch'i Interpretation of Maoist Revolutionary Strategy.* New York: Oxford University Press.

BOYD, G. 1972. "China." Pp. 2–31 in W. Wilcox, L. E. Rose, and G. Boyd, eds., *Asia and the International System.* Cambridge, Mass.: Winthrop.

BRANDON, H. 1973. "Skybolt." Pp. 402–18 in M. H. Halperin and A. Kanter, eds., *Readings in American Foreign Policy: A Bureaucratic Perspective.* Boston: Little, Brown.

BRECHER, M. 1977. "Toward a Theory of International Crisis Behavior: A Preliminary Report." *International Studies Quarterly* 21 (March): 34–74.

____. 1974. "Inputs and Decisions for War and Peace: The Israel Experience." *International Studies Quarterly* 18 (June): 131–77.

____. 1972. *The Foreign Policy System of Israel.* London: Oxford University Press.

BURCHETT, W. 1976. "China's Foreign Policy." *Guardian* (May 5): 14, 19.

BURROWES, R. 1974. "Mirror, Mirror, on the Wall . . . : A Comparison of Event Data Sources." Pp. 383–406 in J. N. Rosenau, ed., *Comparing Foreign Policies: Theories, Findings, and Methods.* Beverly Hills, Calif.: Sage.

CAMPBELL, D. T.; and FISKE, D. W. 1959. "Convergent and Discriminant Validation by the Multitrait–Multimethod Matrix." *Psychological Bulletin* 56: 81–105.

CAMPBELL, D. T.; and ROSS, H. L. 1968. "The Connecticut Crackdown on Speeding: Time Series Data in Quasi-Experimental Analysis." *Law and Society Review* 3 (August): 33–53.

CAMPBELL, D. T.; and STANLEY, J. C. 1966. *Experimental and Quasi-Experimental Designs for Research.* Chicago: Rand McNally.

CAPORASO, J. A.; and PELOWSKJ, A. 1971. "Economic and Political Integration in Europe: A Time-Series Quasi-Experimental Analysis." *American Political Science Review* 65 (June): 418–33.

CAPORASO, J. A.; and ROOS, L. L.; eds. 1973. *Quasi-Experimental Approaches: Testing Theory and Evaluating Policy.* Evanston, Ill.: Northwestern University Press.

Central Party School Writing Team. 1974. *Imperialism Is the Highest Stage of Capitalism: Notes and Annotation.* Peking: People's Publishing House.

CHALFONT, A. 1972. "Reluctant Giant." *Guardian Weekly* (October 7): 5.

CHANS, 1978a. "Chinese Conflict Calculus and Behavior: assessment from a Perspective of Conflict Management." *World Politics* 30 (April): 391–410.

____. 1978b. "Temporal Delineation of International Conflicts: Poisson Results from the Vietnam War, 1963–1965." *International Studies Quarterly* 22 (June): 237–65.

CHAN, S.; KRINGEN, J. A.; and BOBROW, D. B. 1976. "Chinese Views on Crisis Diagnosis and Management: Insights from Documentary Analysis." College Park, Md.: University of Maryland, Crisis Warning and Management report. (mimeo)

CHANG, C. 1973. "Imperialism Is the Eve of the Social Revolution of the Proletariat." *Peking Review* 39 (September 28): 6–10.

CHEN, C. S., ed. 1969. *Rural People's Communes in Lien-chiang: Documents Concerning Communes in Lien-chiang County, Fukien Province, 1962–1963.* Stanford, Calif.: Hoover Institution.

CHENG, J. C., ed. 1966. *The Politics of the Chinese Red Army: A Translation of the Bulletin of Activities of the People's Liberation Army.* Stanford, Calif.: Hoover Institution.

CHIANG, H. 1973. "Great Benefits Derive from a Good Analysis." *Peking Review* 50 (December 14): 12–15.

CHOU, E. L. 1973. "Report to the Tenth National Congress of the Communist Party of China." *Peking Review* 35–36 (September 7): 17–25.

CHOUCRI, N.; and NORTH, R. C. 1975. *Nations in Conflict: Domestic Growth and International Violence.* San Francisco: W. H. Freeman.

___. 1972. "Dynamics of International Conflicts: Some Policy Implications of Population, Resources, and Technology." Pp. 80–122 in R. Tanter and R. H. Ullman, eds., *Theory and Policy in International Relations*. Princeton, N.J.: Princeton University Press.

CLAUDE, I. L. 1962. *Power and International Relations*. New York: Random House.

CLEVELAND, H. 1976. *China Diary*. Washington, D.C.: Georgetown University.

COHEN, J. A. 1967. "Interviewing Chinese Refugees: Indispensable Aid to Legal Research on China." *Journal of Legal Education* 20: 33–62.

COHEN, M. D.; MARCH, J. G.; and OLSEN, J. P. 1972. "A Garbage Can Model of Organizational Choice." *Administrative Science Quarterly* 17: 1–25.

COSER, L. A. 1956. *The Functions of Social Conflict*. New York: Free Press.

CYERT, R. M.; and MARCH, J. G. 1963. *A Behavioral Theory of the Firm*. Englewood Cliffs, N.J.: Prentice-Hall.

DAVIS, W. W.; DUNCAN, G. T.; and SIVERSON, R. M. 1976. "Stochastic Models of the Distribution of Dyadic Warfare in Time." Pittsburgh: Carnegie-Mellon University. (mimeo)

DE RIVERA, J. 1968. *The Psychological Dimension of Foreign Policy*. Columbus, Ohio: Merrill.

DEUTSCH, K. W. 1966. *The Nerves of Government: Models of Political Communication and Control*. New York: Free Press.

DEWEERD, H. A. 1962. "The Strategic Surprise in the Korean War." *Orbis* 6 (Fall): 435–52.

DIAL, R. 1973. *Studies on Chinese External Affairs: An Instructional Bibliography of Commonwealth and American Literature*. Halifax, Nova Scotia: Dalhousie University.

DILLON, L. D.; BURTON, B.; and SODERLUND, W. C. 1977. "Who Was the Principal Enemy?: Shifts in Official Chinese Perceptions of the Two Superpowers, 1968–1969." *Asian Survey* 17 (May): 456–73.

DORAN, C. F.; PENDLEY, R. E.; and ANTUNES, G. E. 1973. "A Test of Cross-National Event Reliability: Global versus Regional Data Sources." *International Studies Quarterly* 17 (June): 175–203.

DUNCAN, G. T.; and SIVERSON, R. M. 1975. "Markov Chain Models for Conflict Analysis: Results from Sino-Indian Relations, 1959–1964." *International Studies Quarterly* 19 (September): 344–76.

EBON, M., ed. 1975. *Five Chinese Communist Plays*. New York: John Day.

EL GUINDI, F. 1972. "The Nature of Belief Systems." Ph.D. dissertation, University of Texas, Austin.

EL GUINDI, F.; and SELBY, H. A. 1976. "Dialectics in Zapotec Thinking." Pp. 181–96 in K. H. Basso and H. A. Selby, eds., *Meaning in Anthropology*. Albuquerque: University of New Mexico Press.

ELLSBERG, D. 1971. "The Quagmire Myth and the Stalemate Machine." *Public Policy* 19 (Spring): 217–74.

ENTESSAR, N. 1978. "The People's Republic of China and Iran: An Overview of Their Relationship." *Asia Quarterly* 1: 79–88.

FAN, K., ed. 1972. *Mao Tse-tung and Lin Piao: Post-Revolutionary Writings.* Garden City, N.Y.: Anchor Books.

FIELD, J. O. 1972. "The Sino-Indian Border Conflict: An Exploratory Analysis of Action and Perception." Pp. 31–59 in J. H. Sigler, J. O. Field, and M. L. Adelman, *Applications of Events Data Analysis: Cases, Issues, and Programs in International Interaction.* Sage International Studies Series, vol. 1, no. 02–002. Beverly Hills, Calif.: Sage.

FINLAY, D. J.; HOLSTI, O. R.; and FAGEN, R. R. 1967. *Enemies in Politics.* Chicago: Rand McNally.

FORRESTER, J. W. 1971. *World Dynamics.* Cambridge, Mass.: Wright-Allen.

FU, C. Y. 1973. "Imperialists Shift Burden of Economic Crises on to Developing Countries." *Peking Review* 16 (May 4): 15–16.

GEORGE, A. L. 1969. "The 'Operational Code': A Neglected Approach to the Study of Political Leaders and Decision-Making." *International Studies Quarterly* 13 (June): 190–222.

____. 1959. *Propaganda Analysis.* Evanston, Ill.: Row-Peterson.

GEORGE, A. L.; HALL, D. K.; and SIMONS, W. E. 1971. *The Limits of Coercive Diplomacy.* Boston: Little, Brown.

GEORGE, A. L.; and SMOKE, R. 1974. *Deterrence in American Foreign Policy: Theory and Practice.* New York: Columbia University Press.

GOTTLIEB, T. M. 1977. "Chinese Foreign Policy Factionalism and the Origins of the Strategic Triangle." Santa Monica, Calif.: RAND Corporation. R–1902–NA, November.

GRIFFITH, S. B., trans. 1963. *Sun Tzu: The Art of War.* London: Oxford University Press.

GRIFFITH, W. E. 1967a. *Communist Esoteric Communications: Explication de Texte.* Cambridge, Mass.: Center for International Studies, Massachusetts Institute of Technology.

____. 1967b. *Sino-Soviet Relations, 1964–1965.* Cambridge, Mass.: M.I.T. Press.

____. 1964. *The Sino-Soviet Rift.* Cambridge, Mass.: M.I.T. Press.

GUETZKOW, H.; ALGER, C.; BRODY, R.; NOEL, R.; and SNYDER, R. 1963. *Simulation in International Relations.* Englewood Cliffs, N.J.: Prentice-Hall.

HALPER, T. 1971. *Foreign Policy Crises: Appearance and Reality in Decision-Making.* Columbus, Ohio: Merrill.

HALPERIN, M. H.; and KANTER, A.; eds. 1973. *Readings in American Foreign Policy: A Bureaucratic Perspective.* Boston: Little, Brown.

HANDEL, M. I. 1977. "The Yom Kippur War and the Inevitability of Surprise." *International Studies Quarterly* 21 (September): 461–502.

HARDING, H. 1976. "Linkages between Chinese Domestic and Foreign Policy." Presented at the Workshop on Chinese Foreign Policy, Ann Arbor, Mich., August 12–14.

HASTORF, A. H.; SCHNEIDER, D. J.; and POLEFKA, J. 1970. *Person Perception.* Reading, Mass.: Addison-Wesley.

HAZLEWOOD, L.; HAYES, J. J.; and BROWNELL, J. R., Jr. 1977. "Planning for Problems in Crisis Management: An Analysis of Post-1945 Behavior in the U.S. Department of Defense." *International Studies Quarterly* 21 (March): 75–106.

HERMANN, C. F. 1972. "Threat, Time, and Surprise: A Simulation of International Crisis." Pp. 187–211 in C. F. Hermann, ed., *International Crises: Insights from Behavioral Research.* New York: Free Press.

——. 1969. "International Crisis as a Situational Variable." Pp. 409–21 in J. N. Rosenau, ed., *International Politics and Foreign Policy: A Reader in Research and Theory.* New York: Free Press.

——. 1963. "Some Consequences of Crisis Which Limit the Viability of Organizations." *Administrative Science Quarterly* 8: 61–82.

HERMANN, C. F.; EAST, M. A.; HERMANN, M. G.; SALMORE, B. G.; and SALMORE, S. A. 1973. *CREON: A Foreign Events Data Set.* Sage International Studies Series, vol. 3, no. 02-024. Beverly Hills, Calif.: Sage.

HINIKER, P. J. 1977. *Revolutionary Ideology and Chinese Reality.* Beverly Hills, Calif.: Sage.

——. 1969. "Chinese Reactions to Forced Compliance: Dissonance Reduction or National Character." *Journal of Social Psychology* 77: 157–76.

HOFFMANN, S. A. 1972. "Anticipation, Disaster, and Victory: India 1962–71." *Asian Survey* 12 (November): 960–79.

HOGGARD, G. 1974. "Differential Source Coverage in Foreign Policy Analysis." Pp. 353–81 in J. N. Rosenau, ed., *Comparing Foreign Policies: Theories, Findings and Methods.* New York: John Wiley.

HOLSTI, O. R. 1977. "The 'Operational Code' as an Approach to the Analysis of Belief Systems: Final Report to the National Science Foundation, Grant No. SOC75-15368." Durham, N.C.: Duke University. (mimeo)

——. 1972. "Time, Alternatives, and Communications: The 1914 and Cuban Missile Crises." Pp. 58–80 in C. F. Hermann, ed., *International Crises: Insights from Behavioral Research.* New York: Free Press.

——. 1969. "The Belief System and National Images: A Case Study." Pp. 543–50 in J. N. Rosenau, ed., *International Politics and Foreign Policy: A Reader in Research and Theory.* New York: Free Press.

——. 1967. "Cognitive Dynamics and Images of the Enemy: Dulles and Russia." Pp. 25–96 in D. J. Finlay, O. R. Holsti, and R. R. Fagen, *Enemies in Politics.* Chicago: Rand McNally.

HOLSTI, O. R.; BRODY, R. A.; and NORTH, R. C. 1969. "Measuring Affect and Action in International Reaction Models: Empirical Materials from the 1962 Cuban Crisis." Pp. 679–96 in J. N. Rosenau, ed., *International Politics and Foreign Policy: A Reader in Research and Theory.* New York: Free Press.

HOLSTI, O. R.; and GEORGE, A. L. 1975. "The Effects of Stress on the Performance of Foreign Policy-Makers." Pp. 255–319 in C. P. Cotter, ed., *Political Science Annual: Individual Decision Making.* Indianapolis: Bobbs-Merrill.

HOLSTI, O. R.; NORTH, R. C.; and BRODY, R. A. 1968. "Perception and Action in the 1914 Crisis." Pp. 123–58 in J. D. Singer, ed., *Quantitative International Politics.* New York: Free Press.

HOPMANN, P. T. 1967. "International Conflict and Cohesion in the Communist System." *International Studies Quarterly* 11 (September): 212–36.

HOPPLE, G. W.; and ROSSA, P. J. 1978. "International Crisis Analysis: An Assessment of Theory and Research." Presented at the annual meeting of the Midwest Political Science Association, Chicago, April 20–22.

HORELICK, A. L.; JOHNSON, A. R.; and STEINBRUNER, J. D. 1975. *The Study of Soviet Foreign Policy: Decision-Theory-Related Approaches.* Beverly Hills, Calif.: Sage.

HUA, T. H. 1972. "Know Some Geography." *Red Flag* 11 (November): 74–78.

HUNG, H. 1973. "Distinguish between Two Fundamentally Different Types of Compromises." *Peking Review* 52 (December 28): 11–12.

HUNTINGTON, S. P. 1973. "After Containment: The Functions of the Military Establishment." *The Annals of the American Academy of Political and Social Science* 4 (March): 1–16.

INKELES, A.; and BAUER, R. 1959. *The Soviet Citizen: Daily Life in a Totalitarian Society.* Cambridge, Mass.: Harvard University Press.

JANIS, I. L. 1972. *Victims of Groupthink.* Boston: Houghton Mifflin.

JERVIS, R. 1976. *Perception and Misperception in International Politics.* Princeton, N.J.: Princeton University Press.

———. 1969. "Hypotheses on Misperception." Pp. 239–54 in J. N. Rosenau, ed., *International Politics and Foreign Policy: A Reader in Research and Theory.* New York: Free Press.

KAPLAN, M. A. 1957. *Systems and Process in International Politics.* New York: John Wiley.

KATZ, P. 1972. *Psyop Automated Management Information System (PAMIS)/ Foreign Media Analysis File.* Kensington, Md.: American Institutes for Research.

KATZ, P.; LENT, M. M.; and NOVOTNY, E. J. 1973. *Survey of the Chinese News Media Content in 1972: A Quantitative Analysis.* Kensington, Md.: American Institutes for Research.

KE, N. 1975. "The Present Economic Crisis of the Capitalist World." *Red Flag* 2 (February): 96–102.

KENDE, I. 1971. "Twenty-five Years of Local Wars." *Journal of Peace Research* 8: 5–22.

KILPATRICK, F. P. 1969. "Problems of Perception in Extreme Situations." Pp. 168–73 in R. R. Evans, ed., *Readings on Collective Behavior.* Chicago: Rand McNally.

KLEIN, D. W. 1968. "The State Council and the Cultural Revolution." Pp. 351–72 in J. W. Lewis, ed., *Party Leadership and Revolutionary Power in China.* London: Cambridge University Press.

———. 1962. "The 'Next Generation' of Chinese Communist Leaders." *China Quarterly* 12 (October–December): 57–74.

KRINGEN, J. A. 1978. "Political Mobilization and Chinese Belief Systems." Ph.D. dissertation, University of Minnesota, Minneapolis.

LAMBERT, G. 1974. "The Utility of Elite Aggregate Data Analysis in the Explanation of Chinese Foreign Policy." Pp. 397–412 in R. Dial, ed., *Advancing and Contending Approaches to the Study of Chinese Foreign Policy.* Halifax, Nova Scotia: Dalhousie University.

LASSWELL, H. D.; LEITES, and associates. 1949. *Language of Politics.* New York: George Stewart.

LEITES, N. 1953. *A Study of Bolshevism.* New York: Free Press.

LENTNER, H. H. 1972. "The Concept of Crisis as Viewed by the U.S. Department of State." Pp. 112–35 in C. F. Hermann, ed., *International Crises: Insights from Behavioral Research.* New York: Free Press.

LEWIS, J. W. 1964. "China's Secret Military Papers: 'Continuities' and 'Revelations.' " *China Quarterly* 18 (April–June): 68–78.

LI, R. P. Y.; and THOMPSON, W. R. 1975. "The 'Coup Contagion' Hypothesis." *Journal of Conflict Resolution* 19 (March): 63–88.

LIAO, K. S. 1976. "Linkage Politics in China: Internal Mobilization and Articulated External Hostility in the Cultural Revolution, 1967–1969." *World Politics* 28 (July): 590–610.

LIAO, K. S.; and WHITING, A. S. 1973. "Chinese Press Perceptions of Threat: The U.S. and India." *China Quarterly* 53 (January–March): 80–97.

LIN, P. 1969. "Report to the Ninth National Congress of the Chinese Communist Party." *Red Flag* 5 (May): 7–33.

LIU, A. P. L. 1974. "Control of Public Information and Its Effects on China's Foreign Affairs." *Asian Survey* 14 (October): 936–51.

MAO, TSE-TUNG. 1969. *Long Live the Thought of Mao Tse-tung.* Unauthorized compilation of previously unpublished speeches. No publisher named.

MAXWELL, N. 1970. *India's China War.* New York: Pantheon.

MAY, E. R. 1973. *"Lessons" of the Past.* New York: Oxford University Press.

McCLELLAND, C. A. 1977. "The Anticipation of International Crisis: Prospects for Theory and Research." *International Studies Quarterly* 21 (March): 15–38.

____. 1974. "Threat Situations: A Search for a Controlled Definition." Los Angeles: International Relations Research Institute, University of Southern California. (mimeo)

____. 1972. "The Beginning, Duration, and Abatement of International Crises: Comparisons in Two Conflict Arenas." Pp. 83–105 in C. F. Hermann, ed., *International Crises: Insights from Behavioral Research.* New York: Free Press.

____. 1969. "Action Structures and Communication in Two International Crises: Quemoy and Berlin." Pp. 473–82 in J. N. Rosenau, ed., *International Politics and Foreign Policy: A Reader in Research and Theory.* New York: Free Press.

____. 1961. "The Acute International Crisis." *World Politics* 14 (January): 182-204.

McCLELLAND, C. A.; and HOGGARD, G. 1969. "Conflict Patterns in the Interactions among Nations." Pp. 711–24 in J. N. Rosenau, ed., *International Politics and Foreign Policy: A Reader in Research and Theory.* New York: Free Press.

McCLELLAND, C. A.; and YOUNG, R. 1970. "The Flow of International Events, July/December, 1969." Los Angeles: University of Southern California. (mimeo)

McCORMICK, J. 1975. "Evaluating Models of Crisis Behavior: Some Evidence from the Middle East." *International Studies Quarterly* 19 (March): 17–45.

MEAD, M.; and METRAUX, R.; eds. 1953. *The Study of Culture at a Distance.* Chicago: University of Chicago Press.

MIDLARSKY, M. 1970. "Mathematical Models of Instability and a Theory of Diffusion." *International Studies Quarterly* 14 (March): 60–85.

MILBURN, T. 1972. "The Management of Crisis." Pp. 259–80 in C. F. Hermann, ed., *International Crises: Insights from Behavioral Research*. New York: Free Press.

MORGENTHAU, H. J. 1948. *Politics among Nations*. New York: Knopf.

NEUSTADT, R. 1970. *Alliance Politics*. New York: John Wiley.

——. (1960). *Presidential Power*. New York: Columbia University Press.

NEWCOMB, T. M. 1953. "An Approach to the Study of Communicative Acts." *Psychology Review* 60: 393–404.

NICHOLSON, M. 1972. "Uncertainty and Crisis Behavior: An Illustration of Conflict and Peace Research." Pp. 237–65 in C. F. Carter and J. Ford, eds., *Uncertainty and Expectation in Economics*. Oxford: Blackwell's.

OLSEN, J. P. 1972. "Public Policy-Making and Theories of Organizational Choice." *Scandinavian Political Studies* 7: 45–62.

ONATE, A. D. 1976. "A Case Study of Chinese Foreign Policy in the Post–Cultural Revolution Period: The Four-Point Program, 1969–1972." Presented at the Workshop on Chinese Foreign Policy, Ann Arbor, Mich., August 12–14.

——. 1974. "The Conflict Interactions of the People's Republic of China, 1950–1970." *Journal of Conflict Resolution* 18 (December): 578–94.

ORGANSKI, A. F. K. 1958. *World Politics*. New York: Knopf.

PAIGE, G. 1968. *The Korean Decision: June 24–30, 1950*. New York: Free Press.

People's Publishing House Editorial Staff. 1974. *Marx, Engels, Lenin, and Stalin: On Economic Crises*. Peking: People's Publishing House.

——. 1972. *International Knowledge, 3*. Peking: People's Publishing House.

PHILLIPS, W. R.; and MOORE, J. A. 1975. "U.S. Policy Positions and Actions in Crises." Presented at the annual North American meeting of the Peace Science Society (International), Cambridge, Mass., November 10–12.

Political Education Section of the Shanghai Teachers' College. 1975. *The Economic Crises of Capitalism: Questions and Answers*. Shanghai: People's Publishing House.

POOL, I. DE S.; and KESSLER, A. 1969. "The Kaiser, the Tsar, and the Computer: Information Processing in a Crisis." Pp. 664–78 in J. N. Rosenau, ed., *International Politics and Foreign Policy: A Reader in Research and Theory*. New York: Free Press.

PUTNAM, R. D. 1967. "Toward Explaining Military Intervention in Latin American Politics." *World Politics* 20 (October): 83–110.

PYE, L. W. 1968. *The Spirit of Chinese Politics*. Cambridge, Mass.: M.I.T. Press.

——. 1967. *The Authority Crisis in Chinese Politics*. Chicago: University of Chicago Press.

RA'ANAN, U. 1968. "Peking's Foreign Policy 'Debate,' 1965–1966." Pp. 23–72 in T. Tsou, ed., *China in Crisis*, vol. 2. Chicago: University of Chicago Press.

RHEE, S. W. 1973. "China's Co-operation, Conflict, and Interaction Behaviour: Viewed from Rummel's Field Theoretic Prespective." Pp. 111–96 in R. Dial, ed., *Advancing and Contending Approaches to the Study of Chinese Foreign Policy*. Halifax, Nova Scotia: Dalhousie University.

ROBINSON, J. A. 1972. "Crisis: An Appraisal of Concepts and Theories." Pp. 20–35 in C. F. Hermann, ed., *International Crises: Insights from Behavioral Research*. New York: Free Press.

——. 1962. "The Concept of Crisis in Decision Making." *Series Studies in Social and Economic Sciences* 11. Washington, D.C.: National Institute of Social and Behavioral Science.

ROBINSON, T. W. 1972. "The Sino-Soviet Border Dispute: Background, Development, and the March 1969 Clashes." *American Political Science Review* 66 (December): 1175–1202.

ROSS, L. 1977. "The Intuitive Psychologist and His Shortcomings: Distortions in the Attribution Process." Pp. 1974–221 in L. Berkowitz, ed., *Advances in Experimental Social Psychology*, vol. 10. New York: Academic Press.

RUMMEL, R. J. 1971a. "Dimensions of Conflict Behavior within Nations, 1946–59." Pp. 39–48 in J. V. Gillespie and B. A. Nesvold, eds., *Macro-Quantitative Analysis: Conflict, Development and Democratization*. Beverly Hills, Calif.: Sage.

——. 1971b. "Dimensions of Conflict Behavior within and between Nations." Pp. 49–84 in J. V. Gillespie and B. A. Nesvold, eds., *Macro-Quantitative Analysis: Conflict, Development and Democratization*. Beverly Hills, Calif.: Sage.

——. 1969a. "Some Dimensions in the Foreign Behavior of Nations." Pp. 600–621 in J. N. Rosenau, ed., *International Politics and Foreign Policy: A Reader in Research and Theory*. New York: Free Press.

——. 1969b. "Indicators of Cross-National and International Patterns." *American Political Science Review* 63 (March): 127–49.

——. 1965. "A Social Field Theory of Foreign Conflict." *Papers, Peace Research Society (International)* 4: 131–59.

RUSSETT, B. M. 1969. "Refining Deterrence Theory: The Japanese Attack on Pearl Harbor." Pp. 127–35 in D. G. Pruitt and R. C. Snyder, eds., *Theory and Research on the Causes of War*. Englewood Cliffs, N. J.: Prentice-Hall.

SATHRE, E. F. 1978. "Communication and Conflict: Japanese Foreign Policy Leading to the Pacific War." Ph.D. dissertation, University of Minnesota, Minneapolis.

SCHANK, R. C.; and COLBY, K. M.; eds. 1973. *Computer Models of Thought and Language*. San Francisco: W. H. Freeman.

SCHELLING, T. C. 1960. *The Strategy of Conflict*. Cambridge, Mass.: Harvard University Press.

SCHILLING, W. R. 1961. "The H-Bomb Decision." *Political Science Quarterly* 16 (March): 24–46.

SCHRAM, S. R., ed. 1975. *Chairman Mao Talks to the People: Talks and Letters 1956–1971*. New York: Pantheon.

——. 1967. *Quotations from Chairman Mao Tse-tung*. New York: Bantam.

SCHWARZ, H. 1966. "The Ts'an K'ao Hsiao Hsi: How Well Informed Are Chinese Officials about the Outside World?" *China Quarterly* 27 (July–September): 54–83.

SCOTT, G. L. 1973. "Treaties of the People's Republic of China: A Quantitative Analysis." *Asian Survey* 13 (May): 496–512.

SEARING, D. D. 1969. "The Comparative Study of Elite Socialization." *Comparative Political Studies* 1 (January): 471–500.

SHIH, C. 1972a. "Understanding the History of National Liberation Movements." *Red Flag* 11 (November): 68–73.

——. 1972b. "Some History about Imperialism." *Red Flag* 6 (June): 33–40.

——. 1972c. "More Talks on Learning World History." *Red Flag* 5 (May): 18–24.

——. 1972d. "Learning Some World History." *Red Flag* 4 (April): 16–21.

SIGLER, J. H. 1972a. "Cooperation and Conflict in United States–Soviet–Chinese Relations, 1966–71: A Quantitative Analysis." *Papers, Peace Science Society (International)* 19: 107–128.

——. 1972b. "Reliability Problems in the Measurement of International Events in the Elite Press." Pp. 9–29 in J. H. Sigler, J. O. Field, and M. L. Adelman, *Applications of Events Data Analysis: Cases, Issues, and Programs in International Interaction.* Sage International Studies Series, vol. 1, no. 02–002, Beverly Hills, Calif.: Sage.

SIMMONDS, J. D. 1970. *China's World: The Foreign Policy of a Developing State.* Canberra: Australian National University Press.

SIMON, H. A. 1969. *The Sciences of the Artificial.* Cambridge, Mass.: M.I.T. Press.

SINGER, J. D.; and SMALL, M. 1972. *The Wages of War, 1816–1965: A Statistical Handbook.* New York: John Wiley.

SMITH, R. F. 1969. "On the Structure of Foreign News: A Comparison of the *New York Times* and the Indian White Papers." *Journal of Peace Research* 6: 23–36.

SMOKER, P. 1969. "A Time Series Analysis of Sino-Indian Relations." *Journal of Conflict Research* 13 (June): 172–91.

——. 1964. "Sino-Indian Relations: A Study of Trade, Communication and Defense." *Journal of Peace Research* 1: 65–76.

SNOW, E. 1971. *The Long Revolution.* New York: Random House.

SNYDER, R. C.; BRUCK, H. W.; and SAPIN, B. 1962. *Foreign Policy Decision-Making: An Approach to the Study of International Politics.* New York: Free Press.

SOLOMON, R. 1971. *Mao's Revolution and the Chinese Political Culture.* Berkeley, Calif.: University of California Press.

STEEL, R. 1973. "The Kennedys and the Missile Crisis." Pp. 202–10 in M. H. Halperin and A. Kanter, eds., *Readings in American Foreign Policy: A Bureaucratic Perspective.* Boston: Little, Brown.

STEINBRUNER, J. 1974. *The Cybernetic Theory of Decision.* Princeton, N. J.: Princeton University Press.

Study Team. 1974. *Study to Realize "The Critique of the Gotha Programme."* Shanghai: People's Publishing House.

SUNG, G. C. S. 1975. "A Bibliographical Approach to Chinese Political Analysis." Santa Monica, Calif.: RAND Corporation. R–1665–ARPA, October.

SZALAY, L. B.; and BRENT, J. E. 1967. The Analysis of Cultural Meanings through Free Verbal Associations." *Journal of Social Psychology* 72: 161–87.

SZALAY, L. B.; and BRYSON, J. A. 1976. "Comparative Analysis of Words and Pictures through Associations." *Psychological Reports* 38: 275–96.

_____. 1974. "Psychological Meaning: Comparative Analyses and Theoretical Implications." *Journal of Personality and Social Psychology* 30: 860–70.

_____. 1973. "Measurement of Psychocultural Distance: A Comparison of American Blacks and Whites." *Journal of Personality and Social Psychology* 26: 166–77.

SZALAY, L. B.; LYSNE, D. A.; and BRYSON, J. A. 1972. "Designing and Testing Cogent Communications." *Journal of Cross-Cultural Psychology* 3 (September): 247–58.

SZALAY, L. B.; and MADAY, B. C. 1973. "Verbal Associations in the Analysis of Subjective Culture." *Current Anthropology* 14: 33–50.

SZALAY, L. B.; MOON, W. T.; and BRYSON, J. 1973. *Communication Lexicon on Three South Korean Audiences: Family, Education, and International Relations Domains.* Kensington, Md.: American Institutes for Research.

_____. 1971. *Communication Lexicon on Three South Korean Audiences: Social, National, and Motivational Domains.* Kensington, Md.: American Institutes for Research.

SZALAY, L. B.; and PECJAK, V. 1973. "A Comparative Analysis of U.S. and Slovenian Social, Political Frames of Reference." Presented at the Ninth International Congress of Anthropological and Ethnological Sciences, Chicago, August –September.

TANTER, R. 1978. "International Crisis Behavior: An Appraisal of the Scholarly Product." Ann Arbor, Mich.: University of Michigan. (mimeo)

_____. 1974. *Modelling and Managing International Conflicts: The Berlin Crises.* Beverly Hills, Calif.: Sage.

_____. 1966. "Dimensions of Conflict Behavior within and between Nations, 1958–60." *Journal of Conflict Resolution* 10 (March): 41–64.

TAYLOR, J. 1974. *China and Southeast Asia: Peking's Relations with Revolutionary Governments.* New York: Praeger.

TERHUNE, K. W. 1970. "From National Character to National Behavior: A Reformulation." *Journal of Conflict Resolution* 14 (June): 203–63.

THOMSON, J. C. 1973. "How Could Vietnam Happen? An Autopsy." Pp. 98–110 in M. H. Halperin and A. Kanter, eds., *Readings in American Foreign Policy: A Bureaucratic Perspective.* Boston: Little, Brown.

THORSON, S. J. 1974. "National Political Adaptation." Pp. 71–114 in J. N. Rosenau, ed., *Comparing Foreign Policy: Theories, Findings, and Methods.* New York: John Wiley.

Tientsin Writing Group 1975. *Talks on Dialectical Materialism.* Peking: People's Publishing House.

TIEWES, F. C. 1967. *Provincial Personnel in Mainland China, 1964–1966.* New York: Columbia University Press.

TRETIAK, D. 1971. "Is China Preparing to 'Turn Out'?: Changes in Chinese Levels of Attention to the International Environment." *Asian Survey* 6 (March): 219–37.

_____. 1969. "Changes in Chinese Attention to Southeast Asia, 1967–1969: Their Relevance for the Future of the Area." *Current Scene* 7 (November): 1–17.

_____. 1966. "Challenge and Control." *Far Eastern Economic Review* (October 17): 216–21.

TUCHMAN, B. 1962. *The Guns of August.* New York: Dell Books.

TVERSKY, A.; and KAHNEMAN, D. 1975. "Judgment under Uncertainty: Heuristics and Biases." Pp. 66–80 in R. Zeckhauser, A. C. Harberger, R. H. Haveman, L. E. Lynn, W. A. Niskanen, and A. Williams, eds., *Benefit-Cost and Policy Analysis.* Chicago: Aldine.

TZEI, T. P. 1975. *The Great Victory of Chairman Mao's Military Line.* Peking: People's Publishing House.

VAN NESS, P. 1970. *Revolution and China's Foreign Policy: Peking's Support for Wars of National Liberation.* Berkeley, Calif.: University of California Press.

WALKER, S. G. 1977. "The Interface between Beliefs and Behavior: Henry Kissinger's Operational Code and the Vietnam War." *Journal of Conflict Resolution* 21 (March): 129–68.

WASSERMAN, B. 1960. "The Failure of Intelligence Prediction." *Political Studies* 8 (June): 156–69.

WHALEY, B. 1973. *Codeword Barbarossa.* Cambridge, Mass.: M.I.T. Press.

WHITE, R. K. 1966. " 'Socialism' and 'Capitalism': An International Misunderstanding." *Foreign Affairs* 44 (January): 216–28.

WHITING, A. S. 1975a. *The Chinese Calculus of Deterrence: India and Indo-China.* Ann Arbor, Mich.: University of Michigan Press.

——. 1975b. "New Light on Mao; Quemoy 1958: Mao's Miscalculations." *China Quarterly* 62 (June): 263–70.

——. 1960. *China Crosses the Yalu: The Decision to Enter the Korean War.* New York: Macmillan.

WHITSON, W. W. 1969. "The Field Army in Chinese Communist Military Politics." *China Quarterly* 37 (January–March): 1–30.

WHYTE, M. K. 1974. *Small Groups and Political Rituals in China.* Berkeley, Calif.: University of California Press.

WILKENFELD, J. 1969. "Some Further Findings Regarding the Domestic and Foreign Conflict Behavior of Nations." *Journal of Peace Research* 2: 147–56.

WILLIAMS, P. 1976. *Crisis Management: Confrontation and Diplomacy in the Nuclear Age.* New York: John Wiley.

WOHLSTETTER, R. 1962. *Pearl Harbor: Warning and Decision.* Stanford, Calif.: Stanford University Press.

WONG, P. 1967. "The Social Psychology of Refugees in an Alien Milieu." *International Migration* 5: 195–211.

Worker-Peasant-Soldier Team of the Central Party School for Studying Philosophy. 1971a. *Thoroughly Study Marxist Theory of Knowledge.* Peking: People's Publishing House.

——. 1971b. *Study to Use Dialectical Materialism.* Peking: People's Publishing House.

Writing Team. 1974. *Imperialism Is the Highest Stage of Capitalism: A Layman's Explanation.* Shanghai: People's Publishing House.

YAHUDA, M. 1972. "Kremlinology and the Chinese Strategic Debate, 1965–1966." *China Quarterly* 49 (January–March): 32–75.

YEH, C. Y. 1975. "Chairman Yeh Chien-ying's Speech on the Occasion of the Meeting of the Capital's People to Celebrate the Cambodian People's Liberation of

Pnom-Penh." Pp. 14–18 in *Current International Situation.* Hong Kong: Ta Chien Publishing Company.

YOUNG, O. R. 1975. "Responses to Uncertainty under Conditions of Crisis." Pp. 150–56 in C. F. Hermann, ed., *Research Tasks for International Crisis Avoidance and Management.* Columbus: Ohio State University. Final Report, October.

——. 1968. *The Politics of Force.* Princeton, N.J.: Princeton University Press.

ZAGORIA, D. S. 1967. *Vietnam Triangle: Moscow, Peking, Hanoi.* New York: Pegasus.

——. 1962. *The Sino-Soviet Conflict, 1956–1961.* Princeton, N.J.: Princeton University Press.

Index